Foundations in Accountancy/ACCA

Applied knowledge

Financial Accounting (FFA/FA)

Workbook

For exams from 1st September 2021 to 31st August 2022

BPP
LEARNING
MEDIA

First edition 2021

ISBN 9781 5097 3763 5

ISBN (for internal use only) 9781 5097 3762 8

e-ISBN 9781 5097 3713 0

British Library Cataloguing-in-Publication Data

A catalogue record for this book is available from the British Library.

Published by

BPP Learning Media Ltd

BPP House, Aldine Place

142–144 Uxbridge Road

London W12 8AA

learningmedia.bpp.com

Printed in the United Kingdom

> Your learning materials, published by BPP Learning Media Ltd, are printed on paper sourced from sustainable, managed forests.

Contains public sector information licensed under the Open Government Licence v3.0.

We are grateful to the Association of Chartered Certified Accountants for permission to reproduce past examination questions and extracts from the syllabus. The suggested solutions in the practice answer bank have been prepared by BPP Learning Media Ltd, except where otherwise stated.

BPP Learning Media is grateful to the IASB for permission to reproduce extracts from the International Financial Reporting Standards including all International Accounting Standards, SIC and IFRIC Interpretations (the Standards). The Standards together with their accompanying documents are issued by:

The International Accounting Standards Board (IASB) 30 Cannon Street, London, EC4M 6XH, United Kingdom. Email: info@ifrs.org Web: www.ifrs.org

Disclaimer: The IASB, the International Financial Reporting Standards (IFRS) Foundation, the authors and the publishers do not accept responsibility for any loss caused by acting or refraining from acting in reliance on the material in this publication, whether such loss is caused by negligence or otherwise to the maximum extent permitted by law.

Contents

Helping you to pass

BPP Learning Media – ACCA Approved Content Provider

As an ACCA Approved Content Provider, BPP Learning Media gives you the opportunity to use study materials reviewed by the ACCA examining team. By incorporating the examining team's comments and suggestions regarding the depth and breadth of syllabus coverage, the BPP Learning Media Workbook provides excellent, ACCA-approved support for your studies.

These materials are reviewed by the ACCA examining team. The objective of the review is to ensure that the material properly covers the syllabus and study guide outcomes, used by the examining team in setting the exams, in the appropriate breadth and depth. The review does not ensure that every eventuality, combination or application of examinable topics is addressed by the ACCA Approved Content. Nor does the review comprise a detailed technical check of the content as the Approved Content Provider has its own quality assurance processes in place in this respect.

BPP Learning Media do everything possible to ensure the material is accurate and up to date when sending to print. In the event that any errors are found after the print date, they are uploaded to the following website: www.bpp.com/learningmedia/Errata.

The PER alert

Before you can qualify as an ACCA member, you not only have to pass all your exams but also fulfil a three-year practical experience requirement (PER). To help you to recognise areas of the syllabus that you might be able to apply in the workplace to achieve different performance objectives, we have introduced the 'PER alert' feature (see the next section). You will find this feature throughout the Workbook to remind you that what you are learning to pass your Foundations in Accountancy and ACCA exams is equally useful to the fulfilment of the PER requirement. Your achievement of the PER should be recorded in your online My Experience record.

Chapter features

Studying can be a daunting prospect, particularly when you have lots of other commitments. This Workbook is full of useful features, explained in the key below, designed to help you get the most out of your studies and maximise your chances of exam success.

Key to icons

Key term

Central concepts are highlighted and clearly defined in the Key terms feature. Key terms are also listed in bold in the Index, for quick and easy reference.

Formula to learn

This boxed feature will highlight important formula which you need to learn for your exam.

PER alert

This feature identifies when something you are reading will also be useful for your PER requirement (see 'The PER alert' section above for more details).

Real world examples

These will give real examples to help demonstrate the concepts you are reading about.

Illustration

Illustrations walk through how to apply key knowledge and techniques step by step.

Activity

Activities give you essential practice of techniques covered in the chapter.

Essential reading

Links to the Essential reading are given throughout the chapter. The Essential reading is included in the free eBook, accessed via the Exam Success Site (see inside cover for details on how to access this).

At the end of each chapter you will find a Knowledge diagnostic, which is a summary of the main learning points from the chapter to allow you to check you have understood the key concepts. You will also find a Further study guidance which contains suggestions for ways in which you can continue your learning and enhance your understanding. This can include: recommendations for question practice from the Further question practice and solutions, to test your understanding of the topics in the Chapter; suggestions for further reading which can be done, such as technical articles; and ideas for your own research.

BPP
LEARNING
MEDIA

Introduction to the Essential reading

The electronic version of the Workbook contains additional content, selected to enhance your studies. Consisting of revision materials and further explanations of complex areas (including illustrations and activities), it is designed to aid your understanding of key topics which are covered in the main printed chapters of the Workbook. The Essential reading section of the eBook also includes further illustrations of complex areas.

A summary of the content of the Essential reading is given below.

Chapter		Summary of Essential reading content
1	Introduction to accounting	• Advantages and disadvantages of the three business types – sole trader, partnership and limited liability company • Legal responsibilities of directors
2	The regulatory framework	• A detailed list of the current IFRS and IASs
3	The qualitative characteristics of financial information	• There is no essential reading for this chapter.
4	Sources, records and books of prime entry	• There is no essential reading for this chapter.
5	Ledger accounts and double entry	• Why do we need ledger accounts? • Accounting for cash and credit sales
6	From trial balance to financial statements	• A full example from ledger accounts to financial statements
7	Inventory	• Cost of inventories
8	Tangible non-current assets	• Revaluations
9	Intangible non-current assets	• There is no essential reading for this chapter.
10	Accruals and prepayments	• There is no essential reading for this chapter.
11	Provisions and contingencies	• There is no essential reading for this chapter.
12	Irrecoverable debts and allowances	• There is no essential reading for this chapter.
13	Sales tax	• How to record sales tax in the day books
14	Control accounts	• There is no essential reading for this chapter.
15	Bank reconciliations	• There is no essential reading for this chapter.
16	Correction of errors	• Essential reading provides more detail on the types of errors that can be found in accounting and the use of journal entries.
17	Incomplete records	• The essential reading goes into more detail about the cash book and how it is used in incomplete records. • It also covers the impact of accruals and prepayments on incomplete records.
18	Preparation of financial	• Additional question practice in this area

Chapter		Summary of Essential reading content
	statements for sole traders	
19	Introduction to company accounting	• More detail of the regulation surrounding limited companies • Expands on the information given in this chapter on the various types of shares and reserves
20	Preparation of financial statements for companies	• More detail of the terminology used in this chapter and also includes extra practice questions
21	Events after the reporting period	• There is no essential reading for this chapter.
22	Statement of cash flows	• There is no essential reading for this chapter.
23	Introduction to consolidated financial statements	• There is no essential reading for this chapter.
24	The consolidated statement of financial position	• There is no essential reading for this chapter.
25	The consolidated statement of profit or loss	• There is no essential reading for this chapter.
26	Interpretation of financial statements	• There is no essential reading for this chapter.

Introduction to Financial Accounting (FFA/FA)

Overall aim of the syllabus

FFA/FA aims to develop your knowledge and understanding of the underlying principles, concepts and regulations relating to financial accounting. You will need to demonstrate technical proficiency in the use of double-entry techniques, including the preparation of basic financial statements for incorporated and unincorporated entities, as well as simple consolidated financial statements for groups. You also need to be able to conduct a basic interpretation of financial statements. If you plan to progress through the ACCA qualification, the skills you learn at FFA/FA will be built on in Financial Reporting (FR) and Strategic Business Reporting (SBR).

Brought forward knowledge

There is no brought forward knowledge required for this exam.

The syllabus

The broad syllabus headings are:

A	The context and purpose of financial reporting
B	The qualitative characteristics of financial information
C	The use of double-entry systems
D	Recording transactions and events
E	Preparing a trial balance
F	Preparing basic financial statements
G	Preparing simple consolidated financial statements
H	Interpretation of financial statements

Main capabilities

On successful completion of this exam, you should be able to:

A	Explain the context and purpose of financial reporting.
B	Define the qualitative characteristics of financial information.
C	Demonstrate the use of double-entry and accounting systems.
D	Record transactions and events.
E	Prepare a trial balance (including identifying and correcting errors).
F	Prepare basic financial statements for incorporated and unincorporated entities.
G	Prepare simple consolidated financial statements.
H	Interpretation of financial statements.

Links with other exams

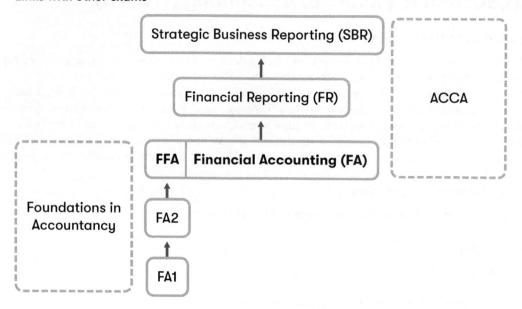

The diagram shows where direct (solid line arrows) and indirect (dashed line arrows) links exist between this exam and other exams preceding or following it.

Achieving ACCA's Study Guide Learning Outcomes

This BPP Workbook covers all the Financial Accounting (FA/FFA) syllabus learning outcomes. The tables below show in which chapter(s) each area of the syllabus is covered.

A	The context and purpose of financial reporting	
A1	The scope and purpose of financial statements for external reporting	Chapter 1
A2	Users' and stakeholders' needs	Chapters 1, 2
A3	The main elements of financial reports	Chapters 1, 3
A4	The regulatory framework (legislation and regulation, reasons and limitations, relevance of accounting standards)	Chapters 2, 3
A5	Duties and responsibilities of those charged with governance	Chapter 1

B	The qualitative characteristics of financial information	
B1	The qualitative characteristics of financial information	Chapter 3

C	The use of double-entry and accounting systems	
C1	Double-entry book-keeping principles including the maintenance of accounting records and sources of accounting information	Chapters 4, 5

| C2 | Ledger accounts, books of prime entry, and journals | **Chapters 4, 5** |

H	Interpretations of financial statements	
H1	Importance and purpose of analysis of financial statements	Chapter 26
H2	Ratios	Chapter 26
H3	Analysis of financial statements	Chapter 26

The complete syllabus and study guide can be found by visiting the exam resource finder on the ACCA website: www.accaglobal.com/gb/en.html.

The exam

Computer-based exams

Computer-based examinations (CBEs) are available for all of the Foundations in Accountancy exams. The CBE exams for the first seven modules can be taken at any time; these are referred to as 'exams on demand'. The Option exams can be sat in June and December of each year; these are referred to as 'exams on sitting'. For more information on CBE exams and to access Specimen exams in the CBE software, please visit the ACCA website.

How do CBEs work?

- Questions are displayed on a monitor.
- Candidates enter their answer directly onto the computer.
- Candidates have two hours to complete the examination.
- Candidates sitting exams on demand are provided with a Provisional Result Notification showing their results before leaving the examination room.
- The CBE Licensed Centre uploads the results to the ACCA (as proof of the candidate's performance) within 72 hours.
- Candidates sitting the Option exams will receive their results approximately five weeks after the exam sitting once they have been expert marked.
- Candidates can check their exam status on the ACCA website by logging into myACCA.

Benefits

- **Flexibility** – the first seven modules, exams on demand can be sat at any time.
- **Resits** for the first seven modules can also be taken at any time and there is no restriction on the number of times a candidate can sit a CBE.
- **Instant feedback** for the exams on demand as the computer displays the results at the end of the CBE.

For more information on computer-based exams, visit the ACCA website.

www.accaglobal.com/gb/en/student/exam-entry-and-administration/computer-based-exams.html

Essential skills areas to be successful in Financial Accounting (FFA/FA)

We think there are three areas you should develop in order to achieve exam success in FFA/FA:

(a) Knowledge application

(b) Specific Financial Accounting skills

(c) Exam success skills

These are shown in the diagram below.

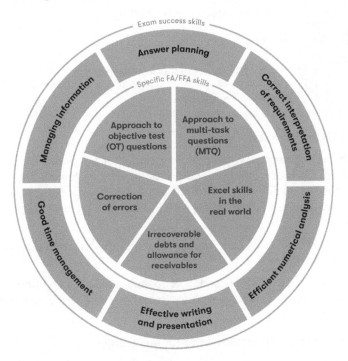

Specific FFA/FA skills

These are the skills specific to FFA/FA that we think you need to develop in order to pass the exam.

In this Workbook, there are five **Skills Checkpoints** which define each skill and show how it is applied in answering a question. A brief summary of each skill is given below.

Skill 1: Approach to objective test (OT) questions

The FFA exam contains two sections. Section A consists of 35 objective test (OT) questions worth 2 marks each and Section B contains 2 multi-task questions worth 15 marks each. The multi-task questions are made up of OT questions and therefore being able to answer OT questions effectively is extremely important.

This skills checkpoint will focus on Section A questions, explaining the best way to tackle these questions and illustrating the technique through worked examples.

BPP recommends a step-by-step technique for approaching objective test questions:

Step 1	Read the requirement first!
Step 2	Apply your technical knowledge to the data in the question.
Step 3	Answer the questions you know first – flag the ones you don't know and come back to them later.
Step 4	Answer all questions – there is no penalty for an incorrect answer

Skill 2: Approach to multi-task questions (MTQs)

MTQs in Section B might ask you to prepare financial statements for a single entity or for a group of companies. There may also be some element of ratio calculation/interpretation. You may not always be required to prepare the full financial statement and may instead be asked to complete a partial statement. In this situation there will be additional elements to the question.

In this skills checkpoint, we will focus on the specific skills required in a multi-task question. We take you through the technique you should adopt and illustrate that through the use of questions.

BPP recommends a step-by-step technique for approaching multi-task questions:

Step 1	Read the requirements of all tasks
Step 2	Recall any relevant technical theory.
Step 3	Answer the questions you know first.
Step 4	Answer all questions.

Skill 3: Excel skills in the real world

As you move through your ACCA examinations and your accountancy career you will need good spreadsheet skills. It is crucial that you have a good working knowledge of spreadsheets and that you are able to use them quickly and effectively. Many people do not use Excel to its full potential, for example they type in totals rather than asking Excel to sum it for them. This often leads to errors.

This is a practical skill aimed at your working life rather than being directly related to a skill that you need to pass this exam.

Whilst this section is not exam focussed, spreadsheets will be a key part of your accountancy career. Future employers will always look for good core spreadsheet skills when selecting a candidate for a role.

Skill 4: Irrecoverable debts and allowance for receivables

The 2018/2019 examiners' report commented that the topic of 'irrecoverable debts and allowance for receivables' continues to be an area of the syllabus where performance is mixed with many candidates not providing the correct response. There is often a lot of detail in these questions and they need to be read very carefully.

In this skills checkpoint we will recap some of the key areas and identify where students typically struggle with this topic and how to get to grips with it.

Skills Checkpoint 4 covers this technique in detail through application to an exam-standard question.

Skill 5: Correction of errors

The correction of errors area of the examination often causes difficulties for candidates as they are required to think around the subject rather than just rote learning.

A step-by-step technique for attempting these questions is outlined in the checkpoint along with a reminder of the key areas of this topic.

Questions are used to highlight the problems students face and how to address them. It is similar to the structure we have seen for our other skills.

Exam success skills

Passing the FFA exam requires more than applying syllabus knowledge and demonstrating the specific FFA skills; it also requires the development of excellent exam techniques through question practice.

We consider the following six skills to be vital for exam success. The Skills Checkpoints show how each of these skills can be applied in the exam.

1 Exam success skill 1

Managing information

You will not have to deal with large amounts of information in each individual question in FFA. Some of the questions in the exam will present you with a short scenario, particularly in the Section B questions. The skill is how you handle this information while working under time pressure.

You must take an active approach to reading each scenario. Focus on the requirement first, underlining/ highlighting key instructions, including words like 'NOT'. Then think about any technical knowledge that is relevant before reading the scenario for the question. Doing this means that your mind will be focussed as you read the scenario, which means you will take in the information better.

2 Exam success skill 2

Correct interpretation of the requirements

It is important to note the requirement carefully. Look out for the number of options you have to choose, as not all questions require only one option. Also, beware of challenges, such as the information being presented in one particular order in the scenario, but being presented in a different order in the options.

3 Exam success skill 3

Answer planning: Priorities, structure and logic

This skill is not so relevant for the Applied Knowledge exams.

4 Exam success skill 4

Efficient numerical analysis

An important tip in numerical questions is not to look at the options until you have completed the calculation as you think it should be done. The reason for this is that the 'wrong answers' are chosen carefully to look very realistic, and you may be tempted to choose one of these if you don't do the calculation first.

5 Exam success skill 5

Effective writing and presentation

This skill is not relevant for FA/FFA as all the questions are objective test and multi-task questions so you will not have to write.

6 Exam success skill 6

Good time management

The exam is two hours long. You should therefore spend 1.2 minutes per mark. It is best to work through Section A first, which should take you 84 minutes, before spending the remaining 36 minutes on Section B.

Don't get stuck on difficult questions – if a particular question does appear difficult, move on, and come back to it after you have answered all the easier questions.

Don't time yourself for each question, but do check every half hour that you have answered 25 marks worth of questions.

Two minutes before the end of your time for Section A, go back and answer all outstanding questions, even if you have to guess. There is no harm in guessing as there is no negative marking in ACCA exams, so the worst that can happen is you don't gain two marks for the question.

If you find that this approach doesn't work for you, don't worry – you can develop your own technique.

Keep an eye on the clock

Aim to attempt all requirements, but be ready to be ruthless and move on if your answer is not going as planned. The challenge for many is sticking to planned timings. Be aware this is difficult to achieve in the early stages of your studies and be ready to let this skill develop over time.

Question practice

Question practice is a core part of learning new topic areas. When you practice questions, you should focus on improving the Exam success skills – personal to your needs – by obtaining feedback or through a process of self-assessment.

Introduction to accounting

Learning objectives

On completion of this chapter, you should be able to:

	Syllabus reference no.
Define financial reporting – recording, analysing and summarising financial data.	A1(a)
Identify and define types of business entity – sole trader, partnership, limited liability company.	A1(b)
Recognise the legal differences between a sole trader, partnership and a limited liability company.	A1(c)
Identify the advantages and disadvantages of operating as a limited liability company, sole trader or partnership.	A1(d)
Understand the nature, principles and scope of financial reporting.	A1(e)
Identify the users of financial statements and state and differentiate between their information needs.	A2(a)
Understand and identify the purpose of each of the main financial statements.	A3(a)
Define and identify assets, liabilities, equity, revenue and expenses.	A3(b)
Explain what is meant by governance specifically in the context of the preparation of financial statements.	A5(a)
Describe the duties and responsibilities of directors and other parties covering the preparation of the financial statements.	A5(b)

Exam context

This chapter introduces the subject of accounting. Questions on this area will most likely focus on the different characteristics of the three types of business entity: sole trader, partnership and limited liability company, the users of financial statements and the definitions of assets, liability, income, expense and capital.

Chapter overview

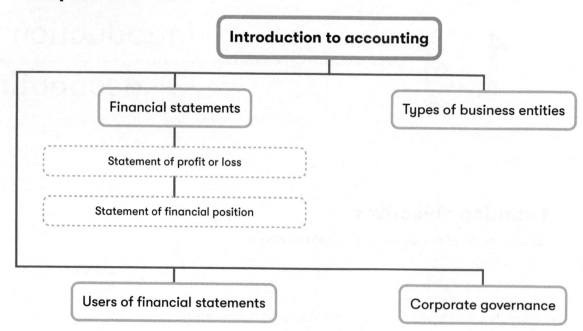

Introduction to accounting

Financial statements

Statement of profit or loss

Statement of financial position

Types of business entities

Users of financial statements

Corporate governance

1 Nature, principles and scope of financial reporting

You may have a broad understanding of what accounting and financial reporting is all about, but your job may be in just one area or type of accounting. It is important to understand the breadth of work which an accountant undertakes.

Financial reporting: Financial reporting is a way of recording, analysing and summarising transactions of a business.

The transactions are recorded and analysed in the books of prime entry. The totals are then posted to the ledger accounts and finally the transactions are summarised in the financial statements.

1.1 Financial accounting

Financial accounting is mainly a method of reporting the financial performance and financial position of a business. It is not primarily concerned with providing information towards the more efficient running of the business. Although financial accounts are of interest to management, their principal function is to satisfy the information needs of persons not involved in running the business. They provide historical information.

1.2 Management accounting

The information needs of management go far beyond those of other account users. Managers have the responsibility of planning and controlling the resources of the business. Therefore, they need much more detailed information. They also need to plan for the future (eg budgets, which predict future revenue and expenditure).

Management (or cost) accounting: Management (or cost) accounting is a management information system which analyses data to provide information as a basis for managerial action. The concern of a management accountant is to present accounting information in the form most helpful to management.

It is important that you understand the distinction between management accounting and financial accounting.

2 Financial statements

The principal financial statements of a business are the statement of profit or loss and the statement of financial position.

2.1 Statement of profit or loss

Statement of profit or loss: A statement of profit or loss is a record of income generated and expenditure incurred over a given period. The statement shows whether the business has had more revenue (sales) than expenditure (profit) or vice versa (loss).

Revenue: Revenue is the income generated by the operations of a business for a period.

Expenses: Expenses are the costs of running the business for the same period.

The IASB's *Conceptual Framework for Financial Reporting 2018* defines income and expenses as follows:

Income: "Income is increases in assets or decreases in liabilities that result in increases in equity, other than those relating to contributions from holders of equity claims" (*Conceptual Framework for Financial Reporting 2018*, para. 4.68).

> **Expenses:** "Expenses are decreases in assets or increases in liabilities that result in decreases in equity, other than those relating to distributions to holders of equity claims" (*Conceptual Framework for Financial Reporting 2018*, para. 4.69).

2.1.1 Form of the statement of profit or loss

The statement of profit or loss which forms part of the published annual financial statements of a limited liability company will usually be for the period of a year, commencing from the date of the previous year's statements. On the other hand, management might want to keep a closer eye on a company's profitability by making up quarterly or monthly statements.

2.1.2 Statement of profit or loss – sole trader

		$	$
Sales			200,000
Less:	Cost of sales		
	Opening inventories	40,000	
	Purchases	110,000	
	Carriage inwards	20,000	
		170,000	
	Closing inventories	(50,000)	
			(120,000)
Gross profit			80,000
Sundry income			5,000
Discounts receivable			3,000
			88,000
Less:	Expenses		
	Rent	11,000	
	Carriage outwards	4,000	
	Telephone	1,000	
	Electricity	2,000	
	Wages and salaries	9,000	
	Depreciation	7,000	
	Bad and doubtful debts	3,000	
	Motor expenses	5,000	
	Insurance	1,000	
			(43,000)
Profit for the year			45,000

Key features of statement of profit or loss:

* This is headed up with the period for which the income and expenses are being included.
* The top part is called the trading account as it records just the trading activities (buying and selling) of the business: Sales less Cost of sales = Gross profit.
* Sundry income includes items like bank account interest received.
* Do not include nil value captions.

2.2 Statement of financial position

Statement of financial position: The statement of financial position is simply a list of all the assets owned and all the liabilities owed by a business as at a particular date.

It is a snapshot of the financial position of the business at a particular moment. Monetary amounts are attributed to each of the assets and liabilities.

Activity 1: Idea generation

List out everything you own and owe.

Solution

2.2.1 Assets

An asset is something valuable which a business owns or can use. The International Accounting Standards Board (IASB) defines an asset in the *Conceptual Framework for Financial Reporting 2018*, as follows:

Asset: "An asset is a present economic resource controlled by the entity as a result of past events. An economic resource is a right that has the potential to produce economic benefits." (*Conceptual Framework for Financial Reporting 2018*, paras. 4.3 and 4.4)

Examples of assets are factories, office buildings, warehouses, delivery vans, lorries, plant and machinery, computer equipment, office furniture, cash and goods held in store awaiting sale to customers.

Some assets are held and used in operations for a long time. An office building is occupied by staff for years. Similarly, a machine has a productive life of many years before it wears out.

Other assets are held for only a short time. The owner of a newsagent shop, for example, has to sell their daily newspapers on the same day that they get them. The more quickly a business can sell the goods it has in store, the more profit it is likely to make; provided, of course, that the goods are sold at a higher price than what it cost the business to acquire them.

2.2.2 Liabilities

A liability is something which is owed to somebody else. 'Liabilities' is the accounting term for the debts of a business. The IASB's *Conceptual Framework for Financial Reporting 2018* defines a liability as follows:

> **Liability:** "A liability is a present obligation of the entity to transfer economic resource as a result of past events. An obligation is a duty of responsibility that the entity has no practical ability to avoid." (*Conceptual Framework for Financial Reporting 2018*, paras. 4.26 and 4.29)

Examples of liabilities are amounts owed to a supplier for goods bought on credit, amounts owed to a bank (or other lender), a bank overdraft and amounts owed to tax authorities (eg in respect of sales tax).

Some liabilities are due to be repaid fairly quickly (eg suppliers). Other liabilities may take some years to repay (eg a bank loan).

Activity 2: Assets

Which of the following is an asset according to the definition in the *Conceptual Framework*?

○ Bank overdraft

○ Factory buildings

○ Payables

○ Amounts owed to tax authorities

Activity 3: Liabilities

Which of the following is an example of a liability?

○ Inventory

○ Receivables

○ Plant and machinery

○ Loan

2.2.3 Capital or equity

The amounts invested in a business by the owner are amounts that the business owes to the owner. This is a special kind of liability, called capital. In a limited liability company, capital usually takes the form of shares. Share capital is also known as equity. The IASB's *Conceptual Framework for Financial Reporting 2018* defines equity as follows:

> **Equity:** "Equity is the residual interest in the assets of the entity after deducting all its liabilities" (*Conceptual Framework for Financial Reporting 2018*, para. 4.63).

2.2.4 Statement of financial position – sole trader

	$	$
Assets		
Non-current assets		
Land and buildings		100,000
Office equipment		50,000

	$	$
Motor vehicles		30,000
Furniture and fixtures		20,000
		200,000
Current assets		
Inventories		50,000
Trade receivables	30,000	
Less: allowance for receivables	(2,000)	
		28,000
Prepayments		5,000
Cash in hand and at bank		7,000
		90,000
Total assets		290,000
Capital and liabilities		
Capital		170,000
Profit		45,000
Less: drawings		(25,000)
		190,000
Non-current liabilities		
Bank loans		40,000
Current liabilities		
Bank overdraft		16,000
Trade payables		40,000
Accruals		4,000
		60,000
Total capital and liabilities		290,000

Key features of statement of financial position:

- The heading is always, **as at,** a certain date.
- **Non-current assets** – assets held and used in the business over the long term (ie more than one year).
- **Current assets** – not non-current assets! Conventionally listed in increasing order of liquidity (ie closeness of assets to cash).
- Capital – what the business owes the proprietor/owner. In this case, the sole trader owns all of the business, ie its total net worth: Capital = Assets – Liabilities = Net Assets.
- Do not include a caption (item heading) if there is not a value for it.

PER alert

One of the competences you require to fulfil Performance Objective 5 (PO5) Leadership and management of the PER is the ability to manage time and tasks effectively to meet business needs and professional commitments, and be capable of working under pressure. In the course of you FFA/FA studies, you will be demonstrating this competence.

2.2.5 Relationship between the statement of financial position and the statement of profit or loss

Statement of financial position shows the worth of business at a point in time.

Statement of profit or loss shows the trading activities over a period of time (financial performance).

The accounting period is the period for which the statement of profit or loss was prepared. This is usually a year.

Therefore, there will be a statement of financial position at the beginning of the year (prior year end) and at the end of the accounting period.

The statement of profit or loss is for the intervening period.

Statement of profit or loss for the year ended 31.12.X7

Statement of financial position as at 31.12.X6		Statement of financial position as at 31.12.X7

3 Users of financial information

Financial information has to be useful to a wide range of users.

Activity 4: Users of financial information

What information would these users of financial information be interested in?

- Investors
- Employees
- Lenders
- Suppliers
- Customers
- Government and their agencies
- Public

Solution

Activity 5: Managers

Which of the following sources of information would be most useful for managers to use when making decisions for the year ahead?

O   Financial statements for the last financial year

O   Tax records for the past five years

O   Budgets for the coming financial year

O   Bank statements for the past year

Exam focus point

The needs of users can be examined easily. For example, you could be given a list of types of information and asked which user group would be most interested in this information.

4 Accounting records

In order to be able to produce a statement of profit or loss and a statement of financial position, a business needs to keep a record of all its transactions.

This process is called **bookkeeping**.

Accounting records should be complete, accurate and valid if the information produced is to be useful for the users of financial information.

The mechanics of bookkeeping and the accounting records a business should keep will be covered in Chapters 4, 5 and 6.

5 Types of business entities

5.1 Three main types of businesses

Businesses fall into three main types:

*   **Sole trader** – A sole trader is a business owned and run by one individual, perhaps employing one or two assistants and controlling their work. The individual's business and personal affairs are, for legal and tax purposes, identical.

*   **Partnership** – These are arrangements between individuals to carry on business in common with a view to profit. A partnership, however, involves obligations to others, and so a partnership is usually governed by a partnership agreement. Unless it is a limited liability partnership (LLP), partners will be fully liable for debts and liabilities, for example if the partnership is sued.

- **Limited liability company** – Limited liability status means that the business's debts and the personal debts of the business's owners (shareholders) are legally separate. The shareholders cannot be sued for the debts of the business unless they have given some personal guarantee.

The **sole trader** is the simplest of these forms.

In law, sole traders and partnerships are not separate entities from their owners. However, a limited liability company is **legally a separate entity** from its owners. Contracts can therefore be issued in the company's name.

For **accounting purposes**, all three entities are treated as separate from their owners. This is called the **business entity concept**.

5.1.1 Limited liability companies

Limited liability companies are formed under specific legislation (eg in the UK, the Companies Act 2006). A limited liability company is legally a separate entity from its owners, and can confer various rights and duties.

There is a clear distinction between shareholders and directors of limited companies.

(a) Shareholders are the owners, but have limited rights as shareholders over the day-to-day running of the company. They provide capital and receive a return (dividend).

(b) The board of directors are appointed to run the company on behalf of shareholders. In practice, they have a great deal of autonomy. Directors are often shareholders.

The reporting requirements for limited liability companies are much more stringent than for sole traders or partnerships. In the UK, there is a legal requirement for a company to:

- Be registered at Companies House;
- Complete a Memorandum of Association and Articles of Association to be deposited with the Registrar of Companies;
- Have at least one director (two for a public limited company (PLC)) who may also be a shareholder;
- Prepare financial accounts for submission to Companies House;
- Have its financial accounts audited (larger companies only); and
- Distribute the financial accounts to all shareholders.

Essential reading

Advantages and disadvantages of business types

There are numerous advantages and disadvantages of the three business types. See Chapter 1 of the Essential reading for more detail.

The Essential reading is available as an Appendix of the digital edition of the Workbook.

Activity 6: True or false

Mark the following statements as true or false.

Shareholders receive annual accounts, prepared in accordance with legal and professional requirements.	
The accounts of limited liability companies are sometimes filed with the Registrar of Companies.	
Employees always receive the company's accounts and an employee report.	
The tax authorities receive as much supplementary detail as they need to assess the tax payable on profits.	
Banks frequently require more information than is supplied in the published	

accounts when considering applications for loans and overdraft facilities.	☐

6 The concept of business entity (separate entity)

A business is considered to be a separate entity from its owner and so the personal transactions of the owner should never be mixed with the business transactions.

When considering a limited liability company, this distinction is laid down in law – the company has a separate legal identity.

In preparing accounts, any type of business is treated as being a separate entity from its owner(s).

7 Governance

KEY TERM

> **Governance:** Those charged with governance of a company are responsible for the preparation of the financial statements.

Corporate governance is the system by which companies and other entities are directed and controlled. Good corporate governance is important because the owners of a company and the people who manage the company are not always the same, which can lead to conflicts of interest.

The board of directors of a company are usually the top management and are those who are charged with governance of that company. The responsibilities and duties of directors are usually laid down in law and are wide ranging.

7.1 Legal responsibilities of directors

Directors have a duty of care to show reasonable competence and may have to indemnify the company against loss caused by their negligence. Directors are also said to be in a fiduciary position in relation to the company, which means that they must act honestly in what they consider to be the best interest of the company and in good faith.

In the UK, the Companies Act 2006 sets out seven statutory duties of directors. Directors should:

- "Act within their powers;
- Promote the success of the company;
- Exercise independent judgement;
- Exercise reasonable skill, care and diligence;
- Avoid conflicts of interest;
- Not accept benefits from third parties; and
- Declare interest in a proposed transaction or arrangement."

(Companies Act 2006, Sections 171–177)

An overriding theme of the Companies Act 2006 is the principle that the purpose of the legal framework surrounding companies should be to help companies do business. A director's main aim should be to create wealth for the shareholders.

In essence, this principle means that the law should encourage long-termism and regard for all stakeholders by directors and that stakeholder interests should be pursued in an enlightened and inclusive way.

When exercising, this duty directors should consider:

- The consequences of decisions in the long term
- The interests of their employees

- The need to develop good relationships with customers and suppliers
- The impact of the company on the local community and the environment
- The desirability of maintaining high standards of business conduct and a good reputation
- The need to act fairly as between all members of the company

This list identifies areas of particular importance and modern-day expectations of responsible business behaviour, for example the interests of the company's employees and the impact of the company's operations on the community and the environment.

7.2 Responsibility for the financial statements

Directors are responsible for the **preparation of the financial statements** of the company. Specifically, directors are responsible for:

- The preparation of the financial statements of the company in accordance with the applicable financial reporting framework (eg IFRSs)
- The internal controls necessary to enable the preparation of financial statements that are free from material misstatement, whether due to error or fraud
- The prevention and detection of fraud

It is the directors' responsibility to ensure that the entity complies with the **relevant laws and regulations**.

Directors should **explain** their **responsibility for preparing accounts** in the financial statements. They should also report that the business is a **going concern**, with supporting assumptions and qualifications as necessary.

Directors should present a **balanced and understandable assessment** of **the company's position and prospects** in the annual accounts and other reports, such as interim reports and reports to regulators. The directors should also explain the basis on which the company generates or preserves value and the strategy **for delivering the company's longer-term objectives**.

Companies over a certain size limit are subjected to an **annual audit** of their financial statements. An audit is an independent examination of the accounts to ensure that they comply with legal requirements and accounting standards. Note that the auditors are not responsible for preparing the financial statements. The findings of an audit are reported to the **shareholders** of the company. An audit gives the shareholders assurance that the accounts, which are the responsibility of the directors, fairly present the financial performance and position of the company. An audit therefore goes some way in helping the shareholders assess how well management have carried out their responsibility for stewardship of the company's assets.

Exam focus point

The ACCA examining team reported that questions on governance had been particularly poorly answered in the past. Make sure you read this section carefully and be prepared to answer questions on it in the exam.

Chapter summary

Introduction to accounting

Financial statements

Statement of profit or loss
- A statement of profit or loss is a record of revenue (income) generated and expenditure incurred over a given period.
- Revenue is the income generated by the operations of a business for a period.
- Expenses are the costs of running the business for the same period.

Statement of financial position
- The statement of financial position is simply a list of all the assets owned and all the liabilities owed by a business as at a particular date.
- An asset is a present economic resource controlled by the entity as a result of past events. An economic resource is a right that has the potential to produce economic benefits.
- A liability is a present obligation of the entity to transfer economic resource as a result of past events. An obligation is a duty of responsibility that the entity has no practical ability to avoid.
- Equity is the residual interest in the assets of the entity after deducting all its liabilities.

Types of business entities
- Sole trader
  - A sole tradership is a business owned and run by one individual.
- Partnership
  - These are arrangements between individuals to carry on business in common with a view to profit.
- Limited liability company
  - Limited liability status means that the business's debts and the personal debts of the business's owners (shareholders) are legally separate.

Users of financial statements
- Management
- Government
- Public
- Lenders
- Analysts and advisers
- Third parties
- Employees
- Shareholders

Corporate governance
- Corporate governance is the system by which companies and other entities are directed and controlled.

Knowledge diagnostic

1. Financial reporting

Financial reporting is a way of recording, analysing and summarising financial data.

2. Types of business entities

There are three types of business entities – sole trader, partnership and limited liability company.

3. What is the separate entity concept?

The 'separate entity' concept is that a business is considered to be a separate entity from its owner so the personal transactions of the owner should never be mixed with the business transactions.

4. The statement of financial position

The statement of financial position is simply a list of all the assets owned and all the liabilities owed by a business as at a particular date.

It is a snapshot of the financial position of the business at a particular moment. Monetary amounts are attributed to each of the assets and liabilities.

5. An asset

An asset is a present economic resource controlled by the entity as a result of past events. An economic resource is a right that has the potential to produce economic benefits.

6. A liability

A liability is a present obligation of the entity to transfer economic resource as a result of past events. An obligation is a duty of responsibility that the entity has no practical ability to avoid.

7. Capital or equity

Equity is the residual interest in the assets of the entity after deducting all its liabilities.

8. The statement of profit or loss

A statement of profit or loss is a record of income generated and expenditure incurred over a given period. The statement shows whether the business has had more revenue than expenditure (a profit) or vice versa (loss).

9. Income

Income is increases in assets or decreases in liabilities that result in increases in equity, other than those relating to contributions from holders of equity claims.

10. Expenses

Expenses are decreases in assets or increases in liabilities that result in decreases in equity, other than those relating to distributions to holders of equity claims.

11. Corporate governance

Corporate governance is the system by which companies and other entities are directed and controlled. Good corporate governance is important because the owners of a company and the people who manage the company are not always the same, which can lead to conflicts of interest.

Further study guidance

Question practice

Now try the following from the Further question practice bank (available in the digital edition of the Workbook):

Questions 1 to 5

Activity answers

Activity 1: Idea generation

Examples:

Own: house, car, cash

Owe: loan, credit card, mortgage

Activity 2: Assets

The correct answer is: Factory buildings

Factory buildings is the only one which the business owns rather than owes.

Activity 3: Liabilities

The correct answer is: Loan

The other options are assets (owned) rather than liabilities (owed).

Activity 4: Users of financial information

Investors

- Profitability
- Future prospects
- Likely risk and return
- Chance of capital growth
- Ability to pay dividends

Employees

- Profitability
- Long-term growth
- Security of their job
- Likelihood of bonus
- Number of employees
- Ability to pay retirement benefits

Lenders

- Whether return on finance will continue to be met
- Other providers and security of their debt
- Likelihood of repayment of capital amount

Suppliers

- Likelihood of payment on time
- Likelihood of payment at all
- Whether they should continue to supply
- Customers
- Ability of entity to continue supplying
- Profitability as a measure of value for money of goods bought

Government and their agencies

- Statistics
- Size of company
- Growth rates

- Average payment periods
- Foreign trade
- Profits made
- Corporate income tax liability
- Sales tax liability

Public

- Contribution to local economy
- Information about trends in the prosperity of the entity
- Range of products and services provided

Activity 5: Managers

The correct answer is: Budgets for the coming financial year

Managers need to look forward and make plans to keep the business profitable. Therefore, the most useful information for them would be the budgets for the coming financial year.

The other sources of information – financial statements, bank statements and tax records – are all historic. While these may help managers to plan and make their budgets, these are of less use for future decision making.

Activity 6: True or false

Shareholders receive annual accounts, prepared in accordance with legal and professional requirements.	True
The accounts of limited liability companies are sometimes filed with the Registrar of Companies.	False
Employees always receive the company's accounts and an employee report.	False
The tax authorities receive as much supplementary detail as they need to assess the tax payable on profits.	False
Banks frequently require more information than is supplied in the published accounts when considering applications for loans and overdraft facilities.	True

Shareholders receive annual accounts, prepared in accordance with legal and professional requirements and in addition, companies listed on the stock exchange have to comply with the regulations in the stock exchange's listing rules.

The accounts of limited liability companies must always be filed with the Registrar of Companies and be available for public inspection. In addition, the company itself will often distribute these accounts on request to potential shareholders, the bank and financial analysts. These accounts are all that is usually available to suppliers and customers.

Employees will not necessarily receive company accounts (unless they are shareholders, for example) but many companies do distribute the accounts to employees as a matter of policy. Some companies produce employee reports which summarise and expand on matters which are covered in the annual accounts and are of particular interest to them.

The tax authorities receive a copy of the financial statements in iXBRL format, the tax return and a copy of the tax calculation.

Banks may require cash flow and profit forecasts and budgets prepared to show management's estimates of future activity in the business.

The regulatory framework

Learning objectives

On competition of this chapter, you should be able to:

	Syllabus reference no.
Understand the role of the regulatory system including the roles of the IFRS Foundation (IFRSF), the International Accounting Standards Board (IASB®), the IFRS Advisory Council (IFRS AC) and the IFRS Interpretations Committee (IFRIC®).	A4(a)
Understand the role of International Financial Reporting Standards.	A4(b)

Exam context

Questions on this chapter are likely to be knowledge based and focus on the role of each of the bodies within the regulatory framework.

Chapter overview

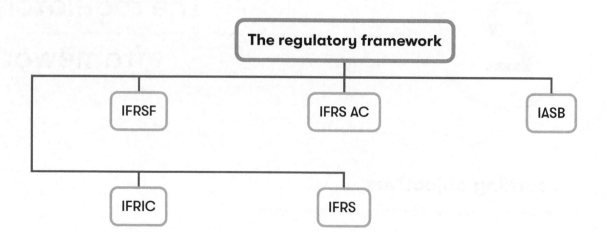

1 Introduction

The purpose of this section is to give a **general picture** of some of the factors which have shaped financial accounting. We will concentrate on the accounts of limited liability companies, as these are the accounts most closely regulated by statute or otherwise.

Financial statements are produced by an entity's managers in order to show its owners how the entity has performed over a period of time.

Company financial statements particularly need to show a true and fair view.

This means a system of regulation is necessary to ensure that financial statements are produced to a high standard and are comparable across different companies.

2 The Regulatory System

2.1 National/local legislation

In most countries, limited liability companies are required by law to prepare and publish accounts annually. The form and content of the accounts is regulated primarily by national legislation.

2.2 Accounting concepts and individual judgement

Many figures in financial statements are derived from the **application of judgement** in applying fundamental accounting assumptions and conventions. This can lead to subjectivity.

Working from the same data, different groups of people could produce very different financial statements. If the exercise of judgement is completely unfettered, there will be no comparability between the accounts of different organisations. This will be all the more significant in cases where deliberate manipulation occurs, in order to present accounts in the most favourable light.

2.3 Accounting standards

In an attempt to deal with some of the subjectivity, and to achieve comparability between different organisations, **accounting standards** were developed. These are developed at both a national level (in most countries) and an international level. The FFA/FA syllabus is concerned with **International Financial Reporting Standards** (IFRSs).

2.4 International Financial Reporting Standards Foundation (IFRSF)

The IFRS Foundation is a not-for-profit, public interest organisation established to develop a single set of high-quality, understandable, enforceable and globally accepted accounting standards—IFRSs—and to promote and facilitate adoption of the standards.

Its Trustees **appoint members** to the IASB, IFRIC and IFRS AC. They also **oversee** the regulatory system and **raise the finance** necessary to support it.

It has **no** involvement in the standard setting process.

The objectives of the IFRS Foundation, taken from its document *IFRS Foundation Constitution, 2018* are:

(a) To develop in the public interest a single set of high quality, understandable, enforceable and globally accepted financial reporting standards based upon clearly articulated principles. These standards should require high quality, transparent and comparable information in financial statements and other financial reporting to help investors, other participants in the world's capital markets and other users of financial information make economic decisions.

(b) To promote the use and rigorous application of those standards.

(c) In fulfilling the objectives associated with (a) and (b), to take account of, as appropriate, the needs of a range of sizes and types of entities in diverse economic settings.

(d) To promote and facilitate adoption of the IFRSs, being the standards and IFRIC® interpretations issued by the board, through the convergence of national accounting standards and IFRSs.

The IFRSF comprises of 22 trustees from diverse geographical and professional backgrounds.

2.5 International Accounting Standards Board (IASB)

The International Accounting Standards Board (IASB) is an independent, privately funded body whose principal aim is to **develop** a single set of high-quality **accounting standards**: International Financial Reporting Standards (IFRSs).

It also liaises with national accounting standard setters (for example, the UK's ASB) to achieve convergence in accounting standards around the world.

Prior to 2003, standards were issued as International Accounting Standards (IASs). In 2003, IFRS 1 was issued and all new standards are now designated as IFRSs. Therefore, the term IFRSs encompass both IFRSs and IASs still in force (eg IAS 7 *Statement of Cash Flows*).

The members of the IASB come from several countries and have a variety of backgrounds, with a mix of auditors, preparers of financial statements, users of financial statements and academics.

The IASB operates under the oversight of the **IFRS Foundation**.

2.6 IFRS Interpretations Committee (IFRIC)

The IFRS Interpretations Committee (IFRIC) comprises 14 voting members, appointed by the trustees of the IFRS Foundation.

The IFRIC issues **guidance** on both how to apply existing IFRSs in company financial statements and how to account for new financial reporting issues where no IFRSs exists. The members provide the best available technical expertise and diversity of international business and market experience relating to the application of IFRSs and it reports to the IASB.

The IFRIC has two main responsibilities:

- To review, on a timely basis, newly identified financial reporting issues not specifically addressed in International Financial Reporting Standards; and
- To clarify issues where unsatisfactory or conflicting interpretations have developed, or seem likely to develop in the absence of authoritative guidance, with a view to reaching a consensus on the appropriate treatment.

2.7 International Financial Reporting Standards Advisory Council (IFRS AC)

The IFRS Advisory Council (IFRS AC) (formerly called the Standards Advisory Council or SAC) is essentially a forum used by the IASB to consult with the outside world. It consults with national standard setters, academics, user groups and a host of other interested parties to advise the IASB on a range of issues, from the IASB's work programme for developing new IFRSs to giving practical advice on the implementation of particular standards.

The IFRS AC meets the IASB at least three times a year and puts forward the views of its members on current standard-setting projects and advises the IASB on its agenda and timetable for developing IFRSs.

Essential reading

There are currently 28 IASs and 16 IFRSs. A full list can be found in Chapter 2 of the Essential reading (you do not have to learn these).

The Essential reading is available as an Appendix of the digital edition of the Workbook.

2.8 Scope and application of IFRSs

Scope

Any limitation of the applicability of a specific IFRS is made clear within that standard. IFRSs are **not intended to be applied to immaterial items, nor are they retrospective**. Each individual standard lays out its scope at the beginning of the standard.

Application

Within each individual country local regulations govern, to a greater or lesser degree, the issue of financial statements. These local regulations include accounting standards issued by the national regulatory bodies and/or professional accountancy bodies in the country concerned.

Standard setting process

The IASB prepares IFRSs in accordance with **due process**. You do not need to know this for your exam, but the following diagram may be of interest.

The procedure can be summarised as follows.

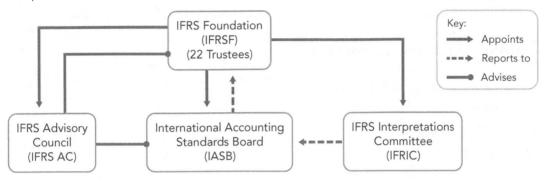

3 The role of IFRSs

IFRSs provide guidance as to how transactions and events should be:

- Recognised – when and where recorded?
- Measured – what amount?
- Presented – what heading?
- Disclosed – what information should be shown in the notes to the accounts?

in a set of financial statements.

For example: IAS 2 *Inventory* states at what amount a company should value its inventory and also requires that the financial statements breakdown the inventory figure between its components such as raw materials, work in progress and finished goods.

If a company follows the relevant accounting standards, its financial statements should show a true and fair view.

Activity 1: The role of the IFRSF

What is the role of the International Financial Reporting Standards Foundation?

- ○ To appoint the members of the IASB
- ○ To advise the IASB on new accounting standards they should consider issuing
- ○ To give guidance to businesses regarding how to apply accounting standards in their financial statements
- ○ To issue International Financial Reporting Standards

Activity 2: Convergence

Which of the following bodies is involved in trying to achieve convergence of global accounting standards?

- ○ The IASB
- ○ The IFRIC
- ○ The IFRSF
- ○ The IFRS AC

Activity 3: Accounting standards

Accounting standards are issued by:

- ○ The IASB
- ○ The IFRS Foundation
- ○ The IAASB
- ○ The IFRIC

Activity 4: The role of the IFRIC

Which of the following best describes the role of the International Financial Reporting Standards Interpretations Committee?

- ○ Issues International Financial Reporting Standards
- ○ Provides advice on the development of standards
- ○ Interprets International Financial Reporting Standards
- ○ Investigates listed companies to ensure they comply with International Financial Reporting Standards

Activity 5: True or false

Are the following statements in relation to IFRSs true or false?

They must be applied to achieve fair presentation in financial statements.	
They are primarily designed for non-for-profit entities.	
They are designed to apply to general purpose financial statements.	
They set out recognition, measurement, presentation and disclosure requirements for transactions and events.	

Chapter summary

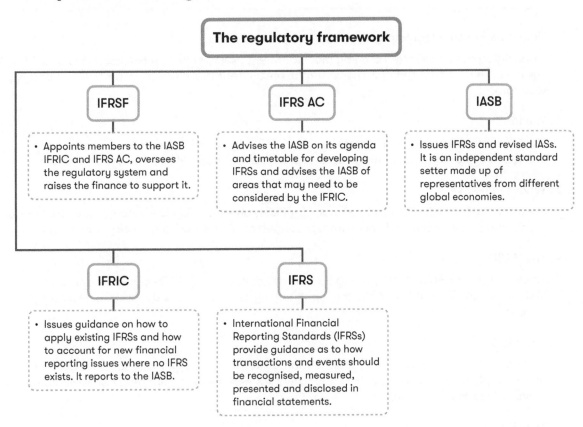

Knowledge diagnostic

1. Why do we need a regulatory system?

Financial statements are relied on by many different user groups to make economic decisions. A system of regulation is therefore necessary to ensure that the information produced is of a high standard.

2. The IASB

The International Accounting Standards Board (IASB) issues IFRSs and revised IASs. It is an independent standard setter made up of representatives from different global economies.

3. What are IFRSs?

International Financial Reporting Standards (IFRSs) provide guidance as to how transactions and events should be recognised, measured, presented and disclosed in financial statements.

4. The IFRSF

The International Financial Reporting Standards Foundation (IFRSF) appoints members to the IASB, IFRIC and IFRS AC, oversees the regulatory system and raises the finance necessary to support it.

5. The IFRIC

The International Financial Reporting Standards Interpretations Committee issues guidance on how to apply existing IFRSs and how to account for new financial reporting issues where no IFRS exists. It reports to the IASB.

6. The IFRS AC

The International Financial Reporting Standards Advisory Council advises the IASB on its agenda and timetable for developing IFRSs and advises the IASB of areas that may need to be considered by the IFRIC.

Further study guidance

Question practice

Now try the following from the Further question practice bank (available in the digital edition of the Workbook):

Questions 6 to 10

Activity answers

Activity 1: The role of the IFRSF

The correct answer is: To appoint the members of the IASB

Activity 2: Convergence

The correct answer is: The IASB

Activity 3: Accounting standards

The correct answer is: The IASB

Activity 4: The role of the IFRIC

The correct answer is: Interprets International Financial Reporting Standards

Activity 5: True or false

They must be applied to achieve fair presentation in financial statements.	True
They are primarily designed for non-for-profit entities.	False
They are designed to apply to general purpose financial statements.	True
They set out recognition, measurement, presentation and disclosure requirements for transactions and events.	True

The qualitative characteristics of financial information

Learning objectives

On competition of this chapter, you should be able to:

	Syllabus reference no.
Understand and identify the purpose of each of the main financial statements.	A3(a)
Define and identify assets, liabilities, equity, revenue and expenses.	A3(b)
Define, understand and apply qualitative characteristics: i) Relevance ii) Faithful representation iii) Comparability iv) Verifiability v) Timeliness vi) Understandability	B1(a)
Define, understand and apply accounting concepts: i) Materiality ii) Substance over form iii) Going concern iv) Business entity concept v) Accruals vi) Prudence vii) Consistency	B1(b)

Exam context

Questions on this chapter are likely to test your understanding of the qualitative characteristics of information. For example, you may be required to identify the factors that make information relevant. You are also required to have a good understanding of what constitutes an asset, liability, income and expense.

Chapter overview

The qualitative characteristics of financial information

The structure of the Conceptual Framework

Qualitative characteristics of financial information

Elements of the financial statements

1 Introduction

Financial statements should show a true and fair view of, or present fairly, the entity's activities. They are produced to provide information to the entity's owners and, for this information to be useful, it must possess certain characteristics.

Our next step is to look at some of the more important concepts which are taken for granted in preparing accounts. In this chapter, we shall single out the important assumptions and concepts for discussion.

2 The IASB's *Conceptual Framework*

The IASB's *Conceptual Framework* is the basis on which IFRSs are formulated but it is **not** an accounting standard. It is a set of principles which underpin the foundations of financial reporting.

Whenever a new accounting standard is issued, it will be based on the principles of the *Conceptual Framework*. Furthermore, its principles should be applied to account for any item where no accounting standard exists.

2.1 Structure of the Conceptual Framework

The *Conceptual Framework* is divided into eight chapters:

Chapter 1	*The objective of general purpose financial reporting**
Chapter 2	*Qualitative characteristics of useful financial information**
Chapter 3	*Financial statements and the reporting entity**
Chapter 4	*The elements of the financial statements**
Chapter 5	*Recognition and derecognition*
Chapter 6	*Measurement*
Chapter 7	*Presentation and disclosure*
Chapter 8	*Concepts of capital and capital maintenance*

(*Conceptual Framework for Financial Reporting 2018*)

* Only these chapters are examinable at this level.

2.2 Going concern

The *Conceptual Framework* sets out one important assumption for financial statements, the **going concern concept**.

> **Going concern:** "The financial statements are normally prepared on the assumption that an entity is a **going concern** and will continue in operation for the foreseeable future. Hence, it is assumed that the entity has neither the intention nor the need to enter into liquidation or to cease trading. If such an intention or need exists, the financial statements may have to be prepared on a different basis. If so, the financial statements describe the basis used."
> (*Conceptual Framework for Financial Reporting 2018*, para. 3.9)

This concept assumes that, when preparing a normal set of accounts, the business will **continue to operate** in approximately the same manner for the foreseeable future (at least the next 12 months). In particular, the entity will not go into liquidation or scale down its operations in a material way.

The main significance of the going concern concept is that the assets **should not be valued at their 'break-up' value** (the amount they would sell for if they were sold off piecemeal and the business were broken up).

Illustration 1: Going concern

A retailer commences business on 1 January and buys inventory of 20 washing machines, each costing $100. During the year, the retailer sells 17 machines at $150 each.

Required

(a) How should the remaining machines be valued at 31 December if the retailer is forced to close down its business at the end of the year and the remaining machines will realise only $60 each in a forced sale?

(b) How should the remaining machines be valued at 31 December if they intend to continue their business into the next year?

Solution

(a) If the business is to be closed down, the remaining three machines must be valued at the amount they will realise in a forced sale, ie 3 × $60 = $180.

(b) If the business is regarded as a going concern, the inventory unsold at 31 December will be carried forward into the following year, when the cost of the three machines will be matched against the eventual sale proceeds in computing that year's profits. The three machines will therefore be valued at cost, 3 × $100 = $300.

If the going concern assumption is not followed, that fact must be disclosed, together with the following information:

(a) The basis on which the financial statements have been prepared; and

(b) The reasons why the entity is not considered to be a going concern.

2.3 Accruals basis

> **Accruals basis:** The effects of transactions and other events are recognised when they occur (and not as cash or its equivalent is received or paid) and they are recorded in the accounting records and reported in the financial statements of the periods to which they relate.

The accruals basis is not an underlying assumption but para. 1.17 of the *Conceptual Framework for Financial Reporting 2018* makes it clear that financial statements should be prepared on an accruals basis.

Entities should prepare their financial statements on the basis that transactions are recorded in them, not as the cash is paid or received, but as the revenues or expenses are **earned or incurred** in the accounting period to which they relate.

According to the accruals assumption, in computing profit, revenue earned must be **matched against** the expenditure incurred in earning it. This is also known as the **matching convention**.

Real world example: Accruals

Emma purchases 20 T-shirts in her first month of trading (May) at a cost of $5 each. She then sells all of them for $10 each. Emma has therefore made a profit of $100, by matching the revenue ($200) earned against the cost ($100) of acquiring them.

All of Emma's sales and purchases are on credit and no cash has been received or paid.

If, however, Emma only sells 18 T-shirts, it is incorrect to charge her statement of profit or loss with the cost of 20 T-shirts, as she still has two T-shirts in inventory. Therefore, only the purchase cost of 18 T-shirts (18 × $5 = $90) should be matched with her sales revenue (18 × $10 = $180), leaving her with a profit of $90.

Her statement of financial position will look like this.

	$
Assets	
Inventory (at cost, ie 2 × $5)	10
Accounts receivable (18 × $10)	180
	190
Capital and liabilities	
Proprietor's capital (profit for the period)	90
Accounts payable (20 × $5)	100
	190

However, if Emma had decided to give up selling T-shirts, then the going concern assumption no longer applies and the value of the two T-shirts in the statement of financial position is break-up valuation not cost.

Similarly, if the two unsold T-shirts are unlikely to be sold at more than their cost of $5 each (say, because of damage or a fall in demand) then they should be recorded on the statement of financial position at their **net realisable value** (ie the likely eventual sales price less any expenses incurred to make them saleable) rather than cost. This shows the application of the **prudence concept**.

In this example, the concepts of going concern and accruals are linked. Since the business is assumed to be a going concern, it is possible to carry forward the cost of the unsold T-shirts as a charge against profits of the next period.

Exam focus point

The ACCA examining team commented that questions on the *Conceptual Framework* have been particularly well answered in past exams.

3 Qualitative characteristics of financial information

The *Conceptual Framework* states that qualitative characteristics are the attributes that make the information provided in financial statements useful to users.

The two fundamental qualitative characteristics are **relevance and faithful representation**.

Enhancing qualitative characteristics are **comparability, verifiability, timeliness** and **understandability**.

3.1 The fundamental qualitative characteristics

Relevance	Faithful representation
• Capable of making a difference to decisions made by users	Three characteristics:
• Predictive value, confirmatory value or both	• Complete
	• Neutral
	• Free from error

3.1.1 Relevance

KEY TERM

Relevance: "Relevant financial information is capable of making a difference in the decisions made by users. Financial information is capable of making a difference in decisions if it has

predictive value, confirmatory value or both." (*Conceptual Framework for Financial Reporting 2018*, paras. 2.6–7)

The predictive and confirmatory roles of information are interrelated. Information on financial position and performance is often used to predict future position and performance and other things of interest to the user, eg likely dividend, wage rises. The **manner of showing information** will enhance the ability to make predictions, eg by highlighting unusual items.

The relevance of information is affected by its nature and **materiality**.

3.1.2 Materiality

> **Materiality:** "Information is material if omitting it or misstating it could influence decisions that the primary users of general-purpose financial reports make on the basis of those reports which provide financial information about a specific reporting entity" (*Conceptual Framework for Financial Reporting 2018*, para. 2.11).

An error which is too trivial to affect anyone's understanding of the accounts is referred to as **immaterial**. In preparing accounts, it is important to assess what is material and what is not, so that time and money are not wasted in the pursuit of excessive detail.

Real world example: Materiality

In assessing whether or not an item is material, it is not only the value of the item which needs to be considered. The **context** is also important.

(a) If a statement of financial position shows non-current assets of $2 million and inventories of $30,000, an error of $20,000 in the depreciation calculations might not be regarded as material. However, an error of $20,000 in the inventory valuation would be material. In other words, the total of which the error forms part must be considered.

(b) If a business has a bank loan of $50,000 and a $55,000 balance on bank deposit account, it will be a material misstatement if these two amounts are netted off on the statement of financial position as 'cash at bank $5,000'. In other words, incorrect presentation may amount to material misstatement even if there is no monetary error.

3.1.3 Faithful representation

> **Faithful representation:** "Financial reports represent **economic phenomena** in words and numbers. To be useful, financial information must not only represent relevant phenomena but must **faithfully represent** the substance of the phenomena that it purports to represent." (*Conceptual Framework for Financial Reporting 2018*, para. 2.12)

To be a faithful representation, information must be **complete, neutral** and **free from error**.

A **complete** depiction includes all information necessary for a user to understand the phenomenon being depicted, including all necessary descriptions and explanations.

A **neutral** depiction is without bias in the selection or presentation of financial information. A neutral depiction is not slanted, weighted, emphasised, de-emphasised or otherwise manipulated to increase the probability that financial information will be received favourably or unfavourably by users.

Neutrality is supported by the exercise of prudence.

Prudence is the exercise of caution when making judgements under conditions of uncertainty. The exercise of prudence means that assets and income are not overstated and liabilities and expenses are not understated.

Free from error means there are no errors or omissions in the description of the phenomenon and the process used to produce the reported information has been selected and applied with no errors in the process. In this context, free from error does not mean perfectly accurate in all respects.

(Conceptual Framework for Financial Reporting 2018, paras. 2.12–2.18)

3.1.4 Substance over form

This is a characteristic of **faithful representation.**

3.2 Enhancing qualitative characteristics

Comparability

- For same entity over different periods
- Between different entities

Verifiability

- Different observers could reach consensus
- Can be direct (eg counting cash) or indirect (eg checking inputs and recalculating outputs)

Timeliness

- Available to decision makers in time to influence their decisions

Understandability

- Classify, characterise and present information clearly and concisely
- Assume users have reasonable knowledge

KEY TERM

Comparability: "Comparability is the qualitative characteristic that enables users to identify and understand similarities in, and differences among, items" (*Conceptual Framework for Financial Reporting 2018*, para. 2.25).

"Information about a reporting entity is more useful if it can be compared with similar information about other entities and with similar information about the same entity for another period or date" (*Conceptual Framework for Financial Reporting 2018*, para. 2.24).

Verifiability: "Verifiability helps assure users that information faithfully represents the economic phenomena it purports to represent. It means that different knowledgeable and independent observers could reach consensus, although not necessarily complete agreement, that a particular depiction is a faithful representation." (*Conceptual Framework for Financial Reporting 2018*, para. 2.30)

Timeliness: "Timeliness means having information available to decision makers in time to be capable of influencing their decisions. Generally, the older information is the less useful it is." (*Conceptual Framework for Financial Reporting 2018*, para. 2.33)

Understandability: "Classifying, characterising and presenting information clearly and concisely makes it understandable" (*Conceptual Framework for Financial Reporting 2018*, para. 2.34).

3.2.1 Comparability

To be useful, information should be comparable, not only to different accounting periods but also to other companies.

The disclosure of accounting policies is important as it enables users of financial statements to make valid comparisons of similar items in the accounts of different entities.

3.2.2 Verifiability

Information that can be independently verified is generally more useful for decision making than information that cannot.

3.2.3 Timeliness

Information may become less useful if there is a delay in reporting it. There is a **balance between timeliness and the provision of reliable information**.

If information is reported on a timely basis when not all aspects of the transaction are known, it may not be complete or free from error.

Conversely, if every detail of a transaction is known, it may be too late to publish the information because it has become irrelevant. The overriding consideration is how best to satisfy the economic decision-making needs of the users.

3.2.4 Understandability

Financial reports are prepared for users who have a **reasonable knowledge of business and economic activities** and who review and analyse the information diligently. Some phenomena are inherently complex and cannot be made easy to understand. Excluding information on those phenomena might make the information easier to understand but, without it, those reports would be incomplete and therefore misleading. As such, matters should not be left out of financial statements simply due to their difficulty, as even well-informed and diligent users may sometimes need the aid of an adviser to understand information about complex economic phenomena.

Activity 1: Faithful representation

The IASB's *Conceptual Framework for Financial Reporting* identifies characteristics which make financial information faithfully represent what it purports to represent.

Required

Which of the following are examples of those characteristics?

O   Neutrality and accruals

O   Neutrality and free from error

O   Accruals and free from error

O   Accruals and going concern

There are other accounting concepts which are useful in the preparation of financial statements.

3.3 Consistency

To maintain consistency, the presentation and classification of items in the financial statements should **stay the same from one period to the next**, except as follows:

(a)   Where there is a significant change in the **nature of the operation** or a review of the financial statements indicates a **more appropriate presentation.**

(b)   Where a change in presentation is **required by an IFRS.**

3.4 Business entity concept

Financial statements always treat the business as a **separate entity.**

It is crucial that you understand that the convention adopted in preparing accounts (the **business entity concept**) is **always** to treat a business as a separate entity from its owner(s). This means the transactions of the owner should never be mixed with the business's transactions. This applies whether or not the business is recognised in law as a separate legal entity.

Activity 2: Consistency

Which of the following statements **best** describes the consistency concept?

○ Only material items are disclosed.

○ The way an item is presented always remains the same.

○ Presentation and classification of items should remain the same unless a change is required by an IFRS.

Activity 3: Accounting concepts

Making an allowance for receivables is an example of which concept?

○ Accruals

○ Going concern

○ Materiality

○ Fair presentation

Exam focus point

The syllabus shows that you must understand and be able to apply both qualitative characteristics and accounting concepts. Do not neglect this section.

4 The elements of the financial statements

The five elements of financial statements and their definitions are listed as follows:

Asset: An asset is a **present economic resource controlled** by the entity as a result of **past events.** An economic resource is a **right** that has the **potential to produce economic benefits.**

Liability: A liability is a **present obligation** of the entity to **transfer an economic resource** as a result of **past events.**

Equity: Equity is the **residual interest** in the assets of an entity after deducting all its liabilities, so:

EQUITY = NET ASSETS = ASSETS − LIABILITIES = SHARE CAPITAL + RESERVES

Income: Income is **increases in assets,** or **decreases in liabilities,** that result in increases in equity, **other than** those relating to **contributions from holders of equity** claims. The definition of income encompasses both **revenue** (which arises in the course of ordinary activities of the entity) and **gains** (other items meeting the definition of income).

Expenses: Expenses are **decreases in assets, or increases in liabilities,** that result in decreases in equity, **other than** those relating to **distributions to holders of equity** claims.

Chapter summary

The qualitative characteristics of financial information

The structure of the Conceptual Framework

- A set of principles which underpin the foundations of financial accounting.
- **Going concern**
  - The financial statements are normally prepared on the assumption that an entity is a going concern and will continue in operation for the foreseeable future.
- **Accruals**
  - Transactions are accounted for in the period to which they relate rather than when they are received or paid.

Qualitative characteristics of financial information
- **Relevance**
- Nature
- Materiality
- **Faithful representation**
- Complete
- Neutral
- Free from bias
- Prudence
- **Comparability**
- **Verifiability**
- **Timeliness**
- **Understandability**

Elements of the financial statements
- Asset
- Liability
- Income
- Expense
- Capital

Knowledge diagnostic

1. IASB's *Conceptual Framework*

The IASB's *Conceptual Framework* is the basis on which IFRSs are formulated.

2. Going concern

Going concern is the main **assumption** in financial statements and assumes that the business will continue in existence for the foreseeable future.

3. Qualitative characteristics

The *Conceptual Framework* states that qualitative characteristic are attributes that make the information provided in financial statements useful to users.

4. Fundamental qualitative characteristics

The two fundamental qualitative characteristics are **relevance and faithful representation.**

5. Enhancing qualitative characteristics

Enhancing qualitative characteristics are **comparability, verifiability, timeliness** and **understandability.**

Further study guidance

Question practice

Now try the following from the Further question practice bank (available in the digital edition of the Workbook):

Questions 8 to 10

Activity answers

Activity 1: Faithful representation

The correct answer is: Neutrality and free from error

For information to be faithfully represented, it must be complete, neutral and free from error.

Activity 2: Consistency

The correct answer is: Presentation and classification of items should remain the same unless a change is required by an IFRS

Activity 3: Accounting concepts

The correct answer is: Fair presentation

It is an example of fair presentation, as it shows the likely recoverability of receivables.

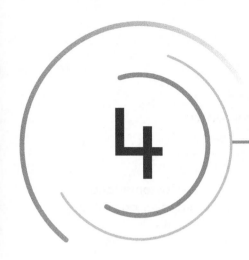

4

Sources, records and books of prime entry

Learning objectives

On completion of this chapter, you should be able to:

	Syllabus reference no.
Identify and explain the function of the main data sources in an accounting system.	C1(a)
Outline the contents and purpose of different types of business documentation, including: quotation, sales order, purchase order, goods received note, goods despatched note, invoice, statement, credit note, debit note, remittance advice, receipt.	C1(b)
Identify the main types of business transactions, for example, sales, purchases, payments and receipts.	C1(f)
Identify the main types of ledger account and books of prime entry, and understand their nature and function.	C2(a)
Understand and record sales and purchase returns	D1(b)
Record cash transactions in ledger accounts.	D2(a)
Understand the need for a record of petty cash transactions.	D2(b)

Exam context

You should be aware of the principal contents of each book of prime entry and the purpose of the memorandum ledgers.

Chapter overview

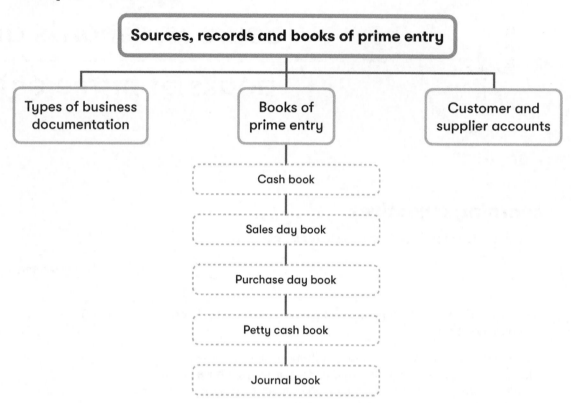

1 From business transaction to financial statements

A business will enter into a number and variety of transactions during an accounting period.

All of these transactions must be summarised in the business's financial statements (ie the statement of financial position and statement of profit or loss). This is achieved by having accounting records to record each stage of the process.

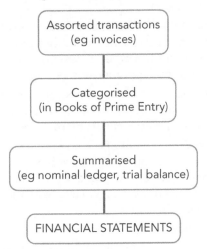

2 Types of business documentation

Each transaction is recorded on the relevant business document. Typically, there are six stages to a sale or purchase, although there could be more, and at each stage a document is generated.

Stage	Process	Sale: Name of document	Purchase: Name of document
1	Quotation is requested for goods/services (goods or service, price, terms and conditions)	Quotation	Quotation
2	Order is placed	Sales order	Purchase order
3	Goods are despatched and signed for on receipt	Goods despatched note (confirmation that goods sent out to customer)	Goods received note (confirmation that goods received from supplier)
4	Payment requested	Sales invoice	Purchase invoice
5	Goods may be returned to vendor	Credit note (negative invoice)	Debit note (request to supplier for credit note)
6	Payment	Receipt (confirmation that receipt received)	Remittance advice note (detailing which invoices are being paid and which credit notes offset)

The list below details all the documents that could be used to record the business transactions in the 'books of account' of the business:

- **Quotation.** A document sent to a customer by a company stating the fixed price that would be charged to produce or deliver goods or services. Quotations tend to be used when businesses do not have a standard listing of prices for products, for example when the time, materials and skills required for each job vary according to the customer's needs. Quotations can't be changed once they have been accepted by the customer.

- **Purchase order**. A document of the company that details goods or services which the company wishes to purchase from another company. Two copies of a purchase order are often made, one is sent to the company from which the goods or services will be purchased, and the other is kept internally so the company can keep track of its orders. Purchase orders are often sequentially numbered.

- **Sales order**. A document of the company that details an order placed by a customer for goods or services. The customer may have sent a purchase order to the company from which the company will then generate a sales order. Sales orders are usually sequentially numbered so that the company can keep track of orders placed by customers.

- **Goods received note**. A document of the company that lists the goods that a business has received from a supplier. A goods received note is usually prepared by the business's own warehouse or goods receiving area. There is more detail on this below.

- **Goods despatched note**. A document of the company that lists the goods that the company has sent out to a customer. The company will keep a record of goods despatched notes in case of any queries by customers about the goods sent. The customer will compare the goods despatched note to what they receive to make sure all the items listed have been delivered and are the right specification.

- **Invoice**. This is discussed below.

- **Statement**. A document sent out by a supplier to a customer listing the transactions on the customer's account, including all invoices and credit notes issued and all payments received from the customer. The statement is useful, as it allows the customer to reconcile the amount that they believe they owe the supplier to the amount the supplier believes they are owed. Any differences can then be queried.

- **Credit note**. A document sent by a supplier to a customer in respect of goods returned, a correction to an invoice previously sent out or overpayments made by the customer. It is a 'negative' invoice.

- **Debit note**. A document sent by a customer to a supplier in respect of goods returned or an overpayment made. It is a formal request for the supplier to issue a credit note.

- **Remittance advice**. A document sent to a supplier with a payment, detailing which invoices are being paid and which credit notes offset. A remittance advice allows the supplier to update the customer's records to show which invoices have been paid and which are still outstanding. It also confirms the amount being paid, so that any discrepancies can be easily identified and investigated.

- **Receipt**. A document confirming confirmation that a payment has been received. This is usually in respect of cash sales, eg a till receipt from a cash register.

2.1 Invoices

An invoice relates to a sales order or a purchase order.

(a) When a business sells goods or services on credit to a customer, it sends out an invoice. The details on the invoice should match the details on the sales order. The invoice is a request for the customer to pay what they owe.

(b) When a business buys goods or services on credit, it receives an invoice from the supplier. The details on the invoice should match the details on the purchase order.

The invoice is primarily a demand for payment, but it is used for other purposes as well, as we shall see. Most accounting software packages can generate invoices.

2.1.1 What does an invoice show?

Invoices should be numbered, so that the business can keep track of all the invoices it sends out. Information usually shown on an invoice includes the following:

(a) Name and address of the seller and the purchaser

(b) Date of the sale

(c) Description of what is being sold

(d) Quantity and unit price of what has been sold (eg 20 pairs of shoes at $25 a pair)

(e) Details of trade discount, if any (eg 10% reduction in cost if buying over 100 pairs of shoes)

(f) Total amount of the invoice including details of any of sales tax if applicable

(g) Sometimes, the date by which payment is due, and other terms of sale

(h) Details of any cash, or settlement discount (eg 5% reduction of invoiced amount if paid within ten days), and the discounted amount

2.1.2 Uses of invoices

Invoices may be used for different purposes.

- Copy to customer as a request for payment
- Copy to accounts department to match to eventual payment
- Copy to warehouse to generate a despatch of goods, as evidenced by a goods despatched note
- Copy matched to sales order and kept in sales department as a record of sales

2.2 Goods received note

Goods received notes (GRNs) record a receipt of goods, most commonly in a warehouse. They may be used in addition to suppliers' advice notes.

Note. Although referred to as 'goods' received notes, GRNs can be used as a record that a service has been carried out. This is especially the case in electronic purchase order systems where a fundamental step in the purchase order process is for the accounts department to match a GRN to a purchase order for goods and services received, before paying a supplier's invoice. This is a key control to ensure that invoices are not paid if the goods or services have not been received (although there are exceptions to this, as some suppliers may require payment in advance).

Even where GRNs are not routinely used, the details of a consignment from a supplier which arrives without an advice note must always be recorded.

GRNs are also key documents in estimating a company's figure for accrued purchases (accruals) that needs to go into the financial statements. This is because they are evidence of liabilities to pay for goods or services received, that have not yet been invoiced by the suppliers. The figure goes into the accruals account or, sometimes, more specifically a 'GRNI' account (Good Received Not Invoiced) which forms part of the overall accruals figure.

2.3 The credit note

Illustration 1: The credit note

Crockery Supplies sent out an invoice for 20 dinner plates, but the accounts assistant accidentally typed in a total of $162.10, instead of $62.10. The homeware shop has been overcharged by $100.

Required

What is Crockery Supplies to do?

Solution

The answer is that Crockery Supplies sends out a credit note to the customer for $100. A credit note is sometimes printed in red to distinguish it from an invoice. Otherwise, it will be made out in much the same way as an invoice, but with less detail and 'Credit Note Number' instead of 'Invoice Number'.

Activity 1: Documentation

Fill in the blanks in the following sentence.

Crockery Supplies sends out a/an [   ] to a credit customer in order to correct an

error where a customer has been overcharged on a/an [   ].

3 Books of prime entry

In the course of business, source documents are created. The details on these source documents need to be summarised as, otherwise, the business might forget to ask for some money, or forget to pay some, or even accidentally pay something twice. It needs to keep records of source documents – of transactions – so that it knows what is going on. Such records are made **in books of prime entry**.

> **Books of prime entry:** Books of prime entry are books in which we first record transactions.

The main books of prime entry are:

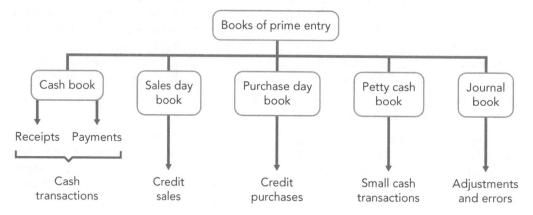

Note. Some businesses have two extra books of prime entry:

- Sales returns day book – for returns of goods from credit customers; and
- Purchase returns day book – for returns of goods to credit suppliers.

It is worth bearing in mind that, for convenience, this chapter describes books of prime entry as if they are actual books written by hand. However, books of prime entry are often not books at all, but rather files stored on a computer or within accounting software. The principles remain the same whether they are manual or computerised.

> ### Exam focus point
>
> The ACCA examining team commented that this topic has been particularly well answered in past exams.

4 Sales and purchase day books

Invoices and credit notes are recorded in day books.

4.1 Sales day book

> **Sales day book:** The **sales day book** is the book of prime entry for CREDIT sales.

BPP LEARNING MEDIA

The sales day book is used to keep a list of all invoices sent out to customers each day. An extract from a sales day book might look like this:

Date	Invoice number	Customer	$
3.1.X7	212	J Spalding	200
5.1.X7	213	G McGregor	400
8.1.X7	214	J Spalding	400
14.1.X7	215	G McGregor	300
		TOTAL	**1,300**

Most businesses 'analyse' their sales. For example, this business sells boots and shoes. The sales to J Spalding were entirely boots and the sales to G McGregor were entirely shoes.

As such, the sales day book might look like this:

Date	Invoice number	Customer	TOTAL	Boot sales	Shoe sales
			$	$	$
3.1.X7	212	J Spalding	200	200	
5.1.X7	213	G McGregor	400		400
8.1.X7	214	J Spalding	400	400	
14.1.X7	215	G McGregor	300		300
		TOTAL	**1,300**	**600**	**700**

The analysis gives the managers of the business useful information which helps them to decide how best to run the business.

Most accounting software allows you to raise sales invoices, and automatically generate sales day book reports of the invoices raised.

4.2 Purchase day book

> **Purchase day book:** The **purchase day book** is the book of prime entry for CREDIT purchases.

The purchase day book is used to keep a list of all the invoices received from suppliers. An extract from the purchase day book might look like this:

Date	Supplier invoice number	Supplier	$
3.1.X7	17986	Cook & Co	200
5.1.X7	20018	W Butler	400
8.1.X7	5001	Fair Co	200
		TOTAL	**800**

The purchase day book records other people's invoices, which have all sorts of different numbers. For ease of reference, the business may assign its own sequential internal invoice number to each purchase invoice.

Like the sales day book, the purchase day book can be analysed further into categories of purchases.

Most accounting software allows you to enter details of the purchase invoices onto the system, and automatically generate purchases day book reports of the invoices entered.

Date	Sequential invoice number	Supplier		Electricity	Purchases of inventory	Telephone
			$	$	$	$
3.1.X7	200	Cook & Co	200	200		
5.1.X7	201	W Butler	400		400	
8.1.X7	202	Fair Co	200			200
		TOTAL	**800**	**200**	**400**	**200**

4.3 Sales returns book and purchase returns book

> **Sales returns day book:** The **sales returns day book** is the book of prime entry for credit notes raised.
>
> **Purchase returns day book:** The **purchase returns day book** is the book of prime entry for credit notes received from suppliers.

When customers return goods to the business, a credit note is raised. All credit notes are recorded in the sales returns day book. Likewise, when a business returns goods to a supplier, they are issued with a credit note that will be recorded in the purchase returns day book.

A sales returns day book would look like this:

Date	Customer and goods	$
11.1.X7	J Spalding boots	200

A purchase returns book would look exactly the same except it would use the term supplier instead of customer.

5 Cash book

> **Cash book:** The cash book is the book of prime entry for cash receipts and payments to and from the bank.

5.1 The cash book

The cash book is also a day book, used to keep a record of money received and money paid out by the business. The cash book deals with money paid into and out of the business bank account. This could be money received on the business premises in notes, coins and cheques, subsequently paid into the bank. There are also receipts and payments made by bank transfer, standing order, direct debit and bank interest and charges, directly by the bank. The cash book can be a manual, physical book or a computer file.

Some cash, in notes and coins, is usually kept on the business premises in order to make occasional payments for odd items of expense. This cash is usually accounted for separately in a petty cash book.

5.2 The cash book (receipts)

Date	Narrative	Total	Capital	Sales	Receivables
		$	$	$	$
2.1.X7	F Bloggs	4,000	4,000		
5.1.X7	J Spalding	200			200

Date	Narrative	Total	Capital	Sales	Receivables
		$	$	$	$
6.1.X7	J Smith	500		500	
		4,700	**4,000**	**500**	**200**
		TOTAL CASH RECEIVED	REASON WHY THE CASH HAS BEEN RECEIVED	REASON WHY THE CASH HAS BEEN RECEIVED	REASON WHY THE CASH HAS BEEN RECEIVED

5.3 The cash book (payments)

Date	Narrative	Total	Purchases	Payables	Electricity	Telephone
		$	$	$	$	$
2.1.X7	Manley & Co	350		350		
5.1.X7	Telephone	50				50
508.1.X7	Digby Co	1,000	1,000			
		1,400	**1,000**	**350**	**0**	**50**
		TOTAL CASH PAID	REASON WHY CASH HAS BEEN PAID	REASON WHY CASH HAS BEEN PAID	REASON WHY CASH HAS BEEN PAID	REASON WHY CASH HAS BEEN PAID

Illustration 2: Cash Book

At the beginning of 1 September, Robin Plenty had $900 in the bank.

During 1 September 20X7, Robin Plenty had the following receipts and payments.

(1) Cash sale: receipt of $80

(2) Payment from credit customer Hay $380

(3) Payment from credit customer Been $720

(4) Payment from credit customer Seed $140

(5) Cheque received from Len Dinger $1,800 to provide a short-term loan

(6) Second cash sale: receipt of $150

(7) Cash received for sale of machine $200

(8) Payment to supplier Kew $120

(9) Payment to supplier Hare $310

(10) Payment of telephone bill $400

(11) Payment of gas bill $280

(12) $100 in cash withdrawn from bank for petty cash

(13) Payment of $1,500 to Hess for new plant and machinery

If you look through these transactions, you will see that seven of them are receipts and six of them are payments.

Required

Prepare the cash book for 1 September 20X7.

Solution

The receipts part of the cash book for 1 September would look like this:

Cash book (receipts)

Date	Narrative	Total
		$
1 Sep 20X7	Balance b/d *	900
	Cash sale	80
	Accounts receivable: Hay	380
	Accounts receivable: Been	720
	Accounts receivable: Seed	140
	Loan: Len Dinger	1,800
	Cash sale	150
	Sale of non-current asset	200
		4,370

* 'b/d' = brought down (ie brought forward) is the balance at the start of the day

Notes.

1   There is a space on the right-hand side of the cash book so that the receipts can be analysed under various headings – for example, 'cash from receivables', 'cash sales' and 'other receipts'.

2   The cash received in the day amounted to $3,470. Added to the $900 at the start of the day, this comes to $4,370. This is not the amount to be carried forward to the next day, because first we have to subtract all the payments made during 1 September.

The payments part of the cash book for 1 September would look like this.

Cash book (payments)

Date	Narrative	Total
		$
1 Sep 20X7	Accounts payable: Kew	120
	Accounts payable: Hare	310
	Telephone	400
	Gas bill	280
	Petty cash	100
	Machinery purchase	1,500
	Balance c/d (balancing figure)	1,660
		4,370

As you can see, this is very similar to the receipts part of the cash book. The only points to note are as follows:

(1)   The analysis on the right would be under headings like 'payments to payables', 'payments into petty cash', 'wages' and 'other payments'.

(2) Payments during 1 September totalled $2,710. We know that the total of receipts was $4,370. That means that there is a balance of $4,370 – $2,710 = $1,660 to be 'carried down' to the start of the next day. As you can see, this 'balance carried down' is noted at the end of the payments column, so that the receipts and payments totals show the same figure of $4,370 at the end of 1 September.

With analysis columns completed, the cash book given in the examples above might look as follows:

Cash book (receipts)

Date	Narrative	Total	Accounts receivable	Cash sales	Other
		$	$	$	$
1 Sep 20X7	Balance b/d	900			
	Cash sale	80		80	
	Accounts receivable: Hay	380	380		
	Accounts receivable: Been	720	720		
	Accounts receivable: Seed	140	140		
	Loan: Len Dinger	1,800			1,800
	Cash sale	150		150	
	Sale of non-current asset	200	____	____	200
		4,370	1,240	230	2,000

Cash book (payments)

Date	Narrative	Total	Accounts payable	Petty cash	Wages	Other
		$	$	$	$	$
1 Sep 20X7	Accounts payable: Kew	120	120			
	Accounts payable: Hare	310	310			
	Telephone	400				400
	Gas bill	280				280
	Petty cash	100		100		
	Machinery purchase	1,500				1,500
	Balance c/d	1,660	____	____	–	____
		4,370	430	100	–	2,180

5.4 Bank statements

A business will receive regular bank statements and/or have accounting software that automatically connects to their bank account. These should be used to check that the amount shown by the business in the cash book agrees with the amount shown on the bank statement, and that no cash has 'gone missing'. We will cover bank reconciliations later on in this Workbook.

6 Petty cash

> **Petty cash:** A petty cash book is a cash book for small payments.

6.1 What is petty cash?

Most businesses keep a small amount of cash on the premises to make occasional small payments in cash, eg staff refreshments, postage stamps, to pay the office cleaner, taxi fares, etc. This is often called the cash float or petty cash account. The cash float can also be the resting place for occasional small receipts, eg cash paid by a visitor for a coffee.

Although the amounts are small, petty cash transactions still need to be recorded, otherwise the cash float could be abused for personal expenses or even stolen.

6.2 The petty cash book

There are usually more payments than receipts in a petty cash book. The main receipt is usually money from the business bank account that is withdrawn and put into petty cash to create a float or an amount paid monthly to top the balance back up to the amount of the original float.

A typical layout is as follows (receipts on the left and payments on the right):

Receipts	Date	Narrative	Total	Milk	Postage	Travel	Other
$			$	$	$	$	$
250	1.9.X7	Balance b/d					
		Milk bill	25	25			
		Postage stamps	9		9		
		Taxi fare	10			10	
		Flowers for staff birthday	15				
		Balance c/d	191				
			250	25	9	10	15

6.3 The imprest system

Under what is called 'the imprest system', the amount of money in petty cash is kept at an agreed sum or 'float' (say, $250). This is called the imprest amount. Expense items are recorded on vouchers as they occur, so that at any time:

Cash still held in the petty cash tin + vouchers for payments = the imprest amount.

Using the example above, this would be:

$191 + $(25 + 9 + 10 + 15) = $250

Activity 2: The imprest system

JGW Ltd operates an imprest system for petty cash. During the month, the following petty cash transactions took place:

$30 stationery

$10 taxi ride

$5 tea and coffee purchases.

The amount remaining in petty cash at the end of the month was $105.

Required

What is the imprest amount?

Solution

Exam focus point

You will not get numerical questions on the imprest system in your exam. However, you do need to be aware of how the imprest system works, so make sure you work through the above example carefully.

Activity 3: Books of prime entry

State which books of prime entry the following transactions would be entered into.

A   Your business pays A Brown (a supplier) $450.00.

B   You send D Smith (a customer) an invoice for $650.

C   Your accounts manager asks you for $12 urgently in order to buy some envelopes.

D   You receive an invoice from A Brown for $300.

E   You pay D Smith $500.

F   F Jones (a customer) returns goods to the value of $250.

G   You return goods to J Green to the value of $504.

H   F Jones pays you $500.

Solution

7 Journal book

Certain transactions do not 'fit' in the main books of prime entry, for example:

*   Period end adjustments
*   Correction of errors

The journal book is used to record these sundry transactions.

Activity 4: Accounting systems

Which of the following statements about the accounting system is correct?

O   The cash book only records small cash payments.

O   The sales day book shows amounts owed by individual customers and the purchase day book shows amounts owed to individual suppliers.

O   Transactions are categorised in the books of prime entry, summarised in the nominal ledger and extracted from the trial balance to produce financial statements.

O   Entities do not need accounting systems to prepare their annual financial statements.

8 Memorandum ledgers

8.1 Sales (receivables) ledger

Memorandum ledgers are used to record how much is owed by a particular customer or to a particular supplier at a point in time.

We have seen that the sales day book records sales and the cash book receipts records money from our customers (receivables) but this does not show us how much is owed by a particular customer. For this, we have our **sales (receivables) ledger**.

Sales ledger Mr Jones

Date	Narrative	Sales	Cash	Balance owing
		$	$	$
3.1.X7	Invoice 1032	200		200
5.1.X7	Cash received		200	0
8.1.X7	Invoice 1101	400		400

The final column keeps a running balance of the total owed by this specific customer. So, we can see that on 8 January X7, Mr Jones owed the business $400.

The **purchase (payables) ledger** works in exactly the same way except that the balance will be how much the business owes to that specific supplier.

Chapter summary

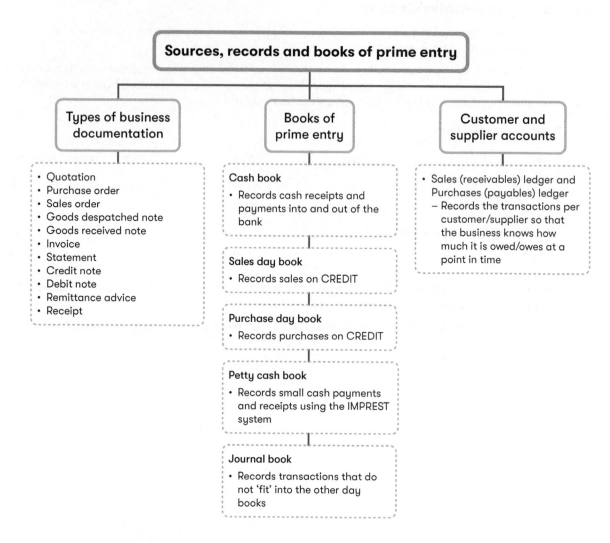

Sources, records and books of prime entry

Types of business documentation

- Quotation
- Purchase order
- Sales order
- Goods despatched note
- Goods received note
- Invoice
- Statement
- Credit note
- Debit note
- Remittance advice
- Receipt

Books of prime entry

Cash book
- Records cash receipts and payments into and out of the bank

Sales day book
- Records sales on CREDIT

Purchase day book
- Records purchases on CREDIT

Petty cash book
- Records small cash payments and receipts using the IMPREST system

Journal book
- Records transactions that do not 'fit' into the other day books

Customer and supplier accounts

- Sales (receivables) ledger and Purchases (payables) ledger
  - Records the transactions per customer/supplier so that the business knows how much it is owed/owes at a point in time

Knowledge diagnostic

1. Books of prime entry

Books of prime entry are the books in which we first record transactions. The main books of prime entry are:

- Sales day book
- Purchase day book
- Sales returns day book
- Purchase returns day book
- Journal
- Cash book
- Petty cash book

2. Source documents

These documents are the source of all information recorded by a business in the books of prime entry. Examples of source documents are:

- Invoice
- Receipt
- Credit/debit note
- Goods received/despatched notes
- Purchase/sales order
- Statement
- Remittance advice

3. Sales and purchase day book

The sales and purchase day books record all sales and purchases on credit.

4. Cash book

The cash book records cash received and cash paid out of the business bank account.

5. Sales and purchase returns day book

When goods are returned by customers or to suppliers, the credit notes received/issued are recorded in the sales returns or purchase returns day book.

6. Petty cash book

The petty cash book records small payments from a cash float. The float is replenished on a timely basis to restore the balance to the imprest amount.

7. The imprest system

The imprest system is a system of petty cash where the amount of money in petty cash is kept at an agreed amount (the imprest amount).

8. Memorandum ledger

There are two memorandum ledgers: the sales (receivables) ledger and the purchase (payables) ledger. The sales (receivables) ledger shows how much the business is owed by each individual customer at a point in time and the payables ledger shows how much it owes to each individual supplier at any point in time.

Further study guidance

Question practice

Now try the following from the Further question practice bank (available in the digital edition of the Workbook):

Questions 11 to 15

Activity answers

Activity 1: Documentation

Crockery Supplies sends out a/an ⌐credit note¬ to a credit customer in order to correct an error where a customer has been overcharged on a/an ⌐invoice¬ .

Activity 2: The imprest system

$150

The imprest amount is the balance of petty cash at the start of the month (often referred to as the 'float').

Using the equation we saw earlier, we know that:

Cash still held in petty cash + vouchers for payments = the imprest amount.

Therefore,

$105 + ($30 + $10 + $5) = $150

Activity 3: Books of prime entry

A	Cash book
B	Sales day book
C	Petty cash book
D	Purchases day book
E	Cash book
F	Sales returns day book
G	Purchase returns day book
H	Cash book

Activity 4: Accounting systems

The correct answer is: Transactions are categorised in the books of prime entry, summarised in the nominal ledger and extracted from the trial balance to produce financial statements.

Statement one is incorrect as the petty cash book records small cash payments.

Statement two is incorrect as the receivables ledger (not the sales day book) shows how much individual customers owe and the payables ledger (not the purchase day book) shows how much is owed to individual suppliers. Statement four is incorrect as accounting systems are necessary to record, categorise and summarise transactions for the preparation of financial statements.

5

Ledger accounts and double entry

Learning objectives

On completion of this chapter, you should be able to:

	Syllabus reference no.
Understand how the accounting system contributes to providing useful accounting information and complies with organisational policies and deadlines.	C1(e)
Identify the main types of business transactions, for example, sales, purchases, payments and receipts.	C1(f)
Understand and apply the concept of double-entry accounting and the duality concept.	C1(c)
Understand and illustrate the uses of journals and the posting of journal entries into ledger accounts.	C2(b)
Identify correct journals from given narrative.	C2(c)
Illustrate how to balance and close a ledger account.	C2(d)
Record sale and purchase transactions in ledger accounts.	D1(a)
Record cash transactions in ledger accounts.	D2(a)

Exam context

Your understanding of double entry will be crucial to passing the exam. For example, a question may ask you to derive the statement of profit or loss expense for electricity where amounts need to be accrued at the year end. You will only get this right if you understand the double entry for recording expenses and accruals. An objective test question could also describe a transaction and ask you to identify the correct double entry to record this. Part of the accounts preparation multi-task question could ask you to select which accounts to debit and credit and to calculate the required amount for the journal entry.

Chapter overview

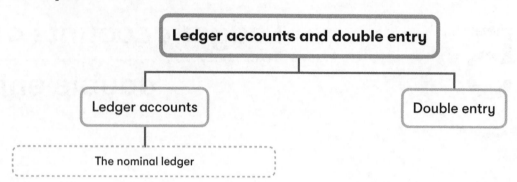

1 Introduction

This chapter is designed to enable you to explain the principles of double entry and apply these principles to the preparation of accounting records within the nominal/general ledger.

In the previous chapter, we saw how transactions were categorised in books of prime entry. The next step is to summarise the information in a format nearer to that of the final financial statements.

1.1 Ledger accounts

Ledger accounts **summarise** all the individual transactions listed in the books of prime entry.

A business is continually making transactions, eg buying and selling. It does not prepare a statement of profit or loss and a statement of financial position on completion of every individual transaction. To do so would be a time consuming and cumbersome administrative task.

However, a business should keep a record of the transactions that it makes, the assets it acquires and liabilities it incurs. These should be recorded in chronological order and dated so that transactions can be related to a period of time. When the time comes to prepare a statement of profit or loss and a statement of financial position, the relevant information can be taken from those records.

In the previous chapter, we saw how transactions were **categorised in books of prime entry**. The next step is to **summarise** the information in a format nearer to that of the final financial statements.

Essential reading

See Chapter 5 of the Essential reading for more information on why we need ledger accounts.

The Essential reading is available as an Appendix of the digital edition of the Workbook.

1.2 From business transactions to financial statements

We saw this diagram in the previous chapter but it is here again to remind you of the process involved in taking original transactions through to the financial statements. In this chapter, we are looking at how transactions are summarised into the ledger accounts.

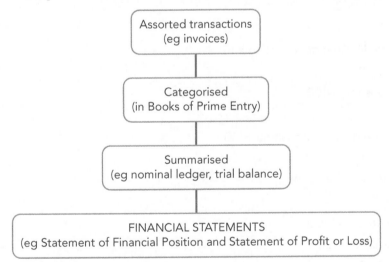

1.3 The nominal ledger

The principal accounts are contained in a ledger called the **general** or **nominal ledger**.

> **Nominal ledger:** The **nominal ledger** is an accounting record which summarises the financial affairs of a business.

Each item in the statement of financial position or statement of profit or loss will have an 'account' (which might be a page in a book or a record on a computer).

Examples of accounts in the nominal ledger include the following:

- Plant and machinery at cost (non-current asset)
- Motor vehicles at cost (non-current asset)
- Plant and machinery, accumulated depreciation (liability)
- Motor vehicles, accumulated depreciation (liability)
- Proprietor's capital (liability)
- Inventories – raw materials (current asset)
- Inventories – finished goods (current asset)
- Total trade accounts receivable (current asset)
- Total trade accounts payable (current liability)
- Wages and salaries (expense item)
- Rent and local taxes (expense item)
- Advertising expenses (expense item)
- Bank charges (expense item)
- Motor expenses (expense item)
- Telephone expenses (expense item)
- Sales (revenue item)
- Total cash or bank overdraft (current asset or liability)

When it comes to drawing up the financial statements, the revenue and expense accounts will help to form the statement of profit or loss, while the asset and liability accounts go into the statement of financial position.

1.4 The dual effect

The double entry bookkeeping method stems from the fact that every transaction affects two things, for example:

A sole trader pays $6,000 in the business bank account:

>Cash increase by $6,000

>Capital increases by $6,000

A sole trader purchases on credit some goods for sale for $400:

>Purchases increase by $400

>Trade payables increase by $400

A sole trader sells some of those goods for cash for $150:

>Cash increases by $150

>Sales increase by $150

A sole trader pays his rent with cash $100:

>Rent expenses increase by $100

>Cash decreases by $100

2 Double entry bookkeeping (T-accounts)

> **Double entry bookkeeping:** Double entry bookkeeping is the method by which a business records financial transactions. An account is maintained for every asset, liability, income and

expense. The basic rule, which must always be observed, is that every financial transaction gives rise to two accounting entries, one a debit and the other a credit. Which account is debited and which is credited depends on the nature of the transaction.

For the rest of this chapter, we will assume that a manual system is being used, in order to illustrate fully the working of the ledger accounts. Remember that a computerised system performs the same functions, although the actual ledger accounts will be stored as computer files and so may be hidden away within the system.

There are two sides to a ledger account with an account heading on top, and so they are often referred to as T-accounts.

(a) On top of the account is its name.

(b) There is a left-hand side – the debit side.

(c) There is a right-hand side – the credit side.

NAME OF ACCOUNT

Debit side	$	Credit side	$

We make two entries from each total extracted from the books of prime entry into two ledger accounts, and call one a Debit (Dr), and the other one a Credit (Cr).

TOTAL DEBITS = TOTAL CREDITS

2.1 General rules

A **DEBIT** entry represents:

- An increase in an asset;
- A decrease in a liability; or
- An item of expense.

A **CREDIT** entry represents:

- An increase in a liability;
- A decrease in an asset; or
- An item of income.

This can be remembered as follows (DEAD CLIC):

Debits	Credits
(increase)	(decrease)
Expenses	**L**iabilities
Assets	**I**ncome
Drawings	**C**apital
(and credits will decrease these)	(and debits will decrease these)

In terms of T-accounts:

ASSET				LIABILITY				CAPITAL			
DEBIT	$	CREDIT	$	DEBIT	$	CREDIT	$	DEBIT	$	CREDIT	$
Increase		Decrease		Decrease		Increase		Decrease		Increase	

For income and expenses, think about profit. Profit retained in the business increases capital. Income increases profit and expenses decrease profit.

INCOME				EXPENSE			
DEBIT	$	CREDIT	$	DEBIT	$	CREDIT	$
Decrease		Increase		Increase		Decrease	

Exam focus point

The ACCA examining team commented that the processing of ledger accounts has been particularly well answered in the past.

Activity 1: Dual effect

What is the double entry for each of the following? Explain each entry in terms of the general rules above.

Note. When we refer to cash, we are referring to money going in and out of the bank account.

Solution

Transaction	Debit	Credit
Sales for cash		
Sales on credit		
Purchase on credit		
Purchase for cash		
Pay electricity bill		
Receive cash from a credit customer		
Pay cash to a credit supplier		
Borrow money from the bank		

Once we have worked out the double entry, it is time to post the transactions to the T-accounts.

Key points

- Each asset, liability, income and expense will have its own T-account;
- The left side is the Debit and the right side is the Credit;
- Each T-account will include a narrative that tells the user of the information where the opposite double entry is eg for a cash sale, the narrative in the cash account will be sales.

Activity 2: Douglas

Douglas has the following transactions during January:

(1) Introduced $5,000 cash as capital

(2) Purchased goods on credit from Richard, worth $2,000

(3) Paid rent for one month, $500

(4) Paid electricity for one month, $200

(5) Purchased car for cash, $1,000

(6) Sold half of the goods on credit to Tish for $1,750

(7) Drew $300 for his own expenses

(8) Sold goods for cash, $2,100

Required

Post transactions 1 to 8 to the relevant ledger accounts.

Solution

Essential reading

See Chapter 5 of the Essential reading for more detail on double entries for cash and credit transactions.

The Essential reading is available as an Appendix of the digital edition of the Workbook.

3 Cash sales vs credit sales

Sales to customers could be in cash or on credit, ie the customer pays after 30 days.

The double entry for a cash sale is:

Dr Cash at bank

Cr Sales

The double entry for a sale on credit is:

Dr Receivables

Cr Sales

With a credit sale, an additional entry needs to be made when the customer pays.

Dr Cash at bank

Cr Receivables

If you look at the last two double entries and remove the receivables entries, you are left with Dr Cash at bank and Cr Sales. So, a sale on credit is exactly the same as a cash sale except it has to go via the receivables account until the cash is paid.

4 Balancing off the ledger accounts (T-accounts)

So far, we have summarised the information in books of prime entry, recorded double entry and posted the transactions to the ledger accounts (T-accounts). The next step is to 'balance off' each ledger account.

Activity 3: Balancing off

Information has been posted to the cash account below.

Required

Balance off the cash account to determine the amount of cash held.

STEPS

(1) Add the debit and credit sides separately.

(2) Fill in the **higher** of the two totals on both sides.

(3) Balance the two sides by 'filling the gap' with the number required to make both sides balance. This is called the balance carried down (c/d).

(4) Complete the double entry by putting the balance brought down (b/d) on the opposite side below the total. This will be the starting figure for the next set of transactions.

(5) If we are at the year/period end, the statement of profit or loss account balances do not get carried into the next year/period and, therefore, we will simply write 'to statement of profit or loss' instead of balance c/d.

Solution

CASH

	$		$
Sales	500	Purchases	300
Sales	500	Telephone	50

Activity 4: Ledger entries

Ron Knuckle set up a business selling keep-fit equipment, trading under the name of Buy Your Biceps Shop. He put $7,000 of his own money into a business bank account (transaction A) and, in his first period of trading to 31 March 20X7, the following transactions occurred:

Transaction		$
B	Paid rent of shop for the period	3,500
C	Purchased equipment (inventories) on credit	5,000
D	Took out a bank loan	1,000
E	Purchased shop fittings (for cash)	2,000
F	Sales of equipment – cash	10,000
G	Sales of equipment on credit	2,500
H	Payments to suppliers	5,000
I	Payments received from customers	2,500
J	Paid interest on the loan	100
K	Other expenses (all paid in cash)	1,900
L	Drawings	1,500

Required

Post transactions A to L to the ledger accounts and balance off the ledger accounts.

You will need the following ledger accounts:

- Cash at bank
- Capital
- Bank loan
- Purchases
- Trade payables
- Non-current assets
- Sales
- Trade receivables
- Bank loan interest
- Other expenses
- Drawings

Solution

5 The journal

Journal: The journal keeps a record of unusual movement between accounts. It is used to record any double entries made which do not arise from the other books of prime entry, ie non-routine transactions. For example, journal entries are made when errors are discovered and need to be corrected

The journal is a book of prime entry and is used for those transactions that do not fit into the other books of prime entry, eg an error that needs to be corrected, or a purchase of a non-current asset.

Throughout this chapter, every time you have written a two-sided entry for a transaction, you have been writing a journal. For example, for the purchase of a non-current asset, you have been writing Dr Non-current asset Cr Cash at bank.

Whatever type of transaction is being recorded, the **format of a journal entry** is:

Date

Account to be debited $X

Account to be credited $X

(Narrative to explain the transaction.)

A **narrative explanation** must accompany each journal entry. It is required for audit and control, to indicate the purpose and authority of every transaction which is not first recorded in a book of prime entry. Some larger organisations require that the above information is entered on a manual journal form (sometimes called a journal voucher form) and authorised by an appropriate member of staff, such as the financial controller. The form is usually attached to documentation to support the reason for the journal.

Exam focus point

An examination question might ask you to 'journalise' transactions which would not in practice be recorded in the journal at all. If you are asked to do this, you should simply record the debit and credit entries for every transaction.

Activity 5: Assets and liabilities

Fill in the blanks:

A _____ entry will increase a liability and decrease an asset, whereas a

_____ entry will decrease a liability and increase an asset.

Chapter summary

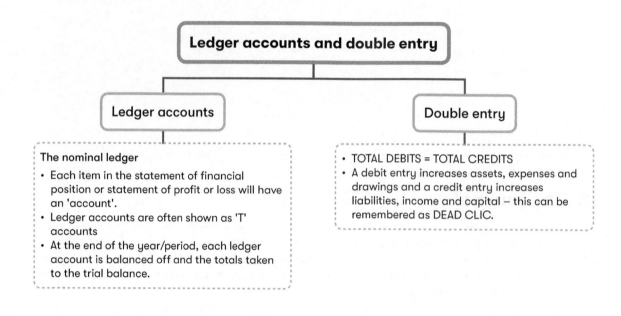

Ledger accounts and double entry

Ledger accounts

The nominal ledger
- Each item in the statement of financial position or statement of profit or loss will have an 'account'.
- Ledger accounts are often shown as 'T' accounts
- At the end of the year/period, each ledger account is balanced off and the totals taken to the trial balance.

Double entry

- TOTAL DEBITS = TOTAL CREDITS
- A debit entry increases assets, expenses and drawings and a credit entry increases liabilities, income and capital – this can be remembered as DEAD CLIC.

Knowledge diagnostic

1. The nominal ledger

Every item in the statement of profit or loss and the statement of financial position will have an account in the nominal ledger.

2. Ledger accounts

Ledger accounts are often shown as T-accounts.

3. Balancing off

At the end of the accounting period, each ledger account needs to be balanced off. The statement of profit or loss accounts go straight to the statement of profit or loss to enable the calculation of the profit or loss for the year. The statement of financial position account balances get carried into the new year.

4. Double entry

Total debits = Total credits

5. DEAD CLIC

A debit entry increases assets, expenses and drawings. A credit entry increases liabilities, income and capital.

Further study guidance

Question practice

Now try the following from the Further question practice bank (available in the digital edition of the Workbook):

Questions 17 to 19

Activity answers

Activity 1: Dual effect

Transaction	Debit	Credit
Sales for cash	Cash at bank (increase asset)	Sales (increase income)
Sales on credit	Receivables (increase asset)	Sales (increase income)
Purchase on credit	Purchases (increase expense)	Payables (increase liability)
Purchase for cash	Purchases (increase expense)	Cash at bank (decrease asset)
Pay electricity bill	Electricity (increase expense)	Cash at bank (decrease cash)
Receive cash from a credit customer	Cash at bank (increase asset)	Receivables (decrease asset)
Pay cash to a credit supplier	Payables (decrease liability)	Cash at bank (decrease asset)
Borrow money from the bank	Cash at bank (increase asset)	Loan (increase liability)

How did you get on? Students coming to the subject for the first time often have difficulty in knowing where to begin. A good starting point is the cash account, ie the nominal ledger account in which receipts and payments of cash are recorded. The rule to remember about the cash account is as follows:

- A **cash payment** is a **credit** entry in the cash at bank account. Here, the **asset is decreasing**. Cash may be paid out, for example, to pay an expense (such as tax) or to purchase an asset (such as a machine). The matching debit entry is therefore made in the appropriate expense or asset account.

- A **cash receipt** is **a debit** entry in the cash at bank account. Here, **the asset is increasing**. Cash might be received, for example, by a retailer who makes a cash sale. The credit entry would then be made in the sales account.

- This can be confusing as it is the opposite to what you see on a bank statement. This is because you are now looking at the situation from the business's perspective. When we get a bank statement, it is from the bank's perspective.

Activity 2: Douglas

CASH AT BANK

	$		$
Capital	5,000	Rent	500
Sales	2,100	Electricity	200
		Car	1,000
		Drawings	300

CAPITAL

	$		$
		Cash at bank	5,000

TRADE PAYABLES

	$		$
		Purchases	2,000

PURCHASES

	$		$
Trade payables	2,000		

RENT

	$		$
Cash at bank	500		

ELECTRICITY

	$		$
Cash at bank	200		

CAR (ASSET ACCOUNT)

	$		$
Cash at bank	1,000		

DRAWINGS

	$		$
Cash at bank	300		

TRADE RECEIVABLES

	$		$
Sales	1,750		

SALES

	$		$
		Trade receivables	1,750
		Sales	2,100

Activity 3: Balancing off

CASH

	$		$
Sales	500	Purchases	300
Sales	500	Telephone	50
		Balance c/d	650
	1,000		**1,000**
Balance b/d	650		

Activity 4: Ledger entries

CASH AT BANK

	$		$
Capital introduced by Ron (A)	7,000	Rent (B)	3,500
Bank loan (D)	1,000	Shop fittings (E)	2,000
Sales (F)	10,000	Trade payables (H)	5,000
Trade receivables (I)	2,500	Bank loan interest (J)	100
		Other expenses (K)	1,900
		Drawings	1,500
		Balance c/d	**6,500**
	20,500		**20,500**
Balance b/d	**6,500**		

CAPITAL

	$		$
Balance c/d	7,000	Cash at bank (A)	7,000
	7,000		**7,000**
		Balance b/d	7,000

BANK LOAN

	$		$
Balance c/d	1,000	Cash at bank (D)	1,000
	1,000		**1,000**
		Balance b/d	1,000

PURCHASES

	$		$
Trade payables (C)	5,000	To statement of profit or loss	5,000

		$			$
		5,000			**5,000**

Note. Purchases are a statement of profit or loss account and, as such, do not get carried into the next year like a statement of financial position account. Therefore, at the end of the period/year, we simply write 'to statement of profit or loss'. If however, we are balancing off the accounts at the end of the month, we would carry the balance into the next month: 'balance c/d' and 'balance b/d'.

TRADE PAYABLES

	$		$
Cash at bank (H)	5,000	Purchases	5,000

Note. There is no balance c/d on this account as both sides balance. Payables will be zero on the trial balance.

RENT

	$		$
Cash at bank (B)	3,500	To statement of profit or loss	3,500
	3,500		**3,500**

NON-CURRENT ASSETS (SHOP FITTINGS)

	$		$
Cash at bank (E)	2,000	Balance c/d	2,000
	2,000		**2,000**
Balance b/d	2,000		

SALES

	$		$
		Cash at bank (F)	10,000
To statement of profit or loss	12,500	Trade receivables (G)	2,500
	12,500		**12,500**

TRADE RECEIVABLES

	$		$
Sales (G)	2,500	Cash at bank (I)	2,500

BANK LOAN INTEREST

	$		$
Cash at bank (J)	100	To statement of profit and loss	100

OTHER EXPENSES

	$		$
Cash at bank (K)	1,900	To statement of profit and loss	1,900

	$		$
Cash at bank (L)	1,500	To capital account	1,500

All of these ledger account balances will now be taken to the trial balance and then onto the financial statements. We shall see this in the next chapter.

Activity 5: Assets and liabilities

A [credit] entry will increase a liability and decrease an asset, whereas a [debit] entry will decrease a liability and increase an asset.

For these kind of questions, always think back to DEAD CLIC.

Skills checkpoint 1

Approach to objective test (OT) questions

Overview

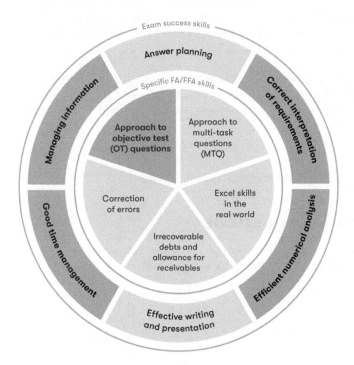

Introduction

The exam contains two sections. Section A consists of 35 objective test (OT) questions worth 2 marks each and Section B contains 2 multi-task questions worth 15 marks each. The multi-task questions are made up of OT questions and therefore being able to answer OT questions effectively, is extremely important.

This skills checkpoint will focus on Section A questions. Skills Checkpoint 2 covers the multi-task questions.

OT questions

OT questions in Section A are single, short questions that are auto marked and worth 2 marks each. You must answer the whole question correctly to earn the 2 marks. There are no partial marks. The OT questions in Section A aim for a broad coverage of the syllabus, and so all areas of the syllabus need to be carefully studied. You need to work through as many practice OT questions as possible, reviewing carefully to see how correct answers are derived.

The following types of OT questions commonly appear in the FA/FFA exam:

Question type	Explanation
Multiple choice question (MCQ)	You need to choose one correct answer from four given response options. Eg Q1 of the specimen exam
Multiple response options (MRO)	These are a type of multiple choice question where you need to select more than one answer from a number of given options. The question will specify how many answers need to be selected. It is important to read the requirement carefully. Eg Q5 of the specimen exam
Number entry (NE)	This question type requires you to type a numerical answer into a box. The unit of measurement (eg $ or $000) will sit outside the box and if there are specific rounding requirements, these will be stated in the question. Eg Q4 of the specimen exam
Multiple response matching (MRM)	This question type requires you to select a response for a number of statements, normally to identify whether the statements are true or false. You must provide a response for each statement. Eg Q9 of the specimen exam

The OT skills required for Section A are also needed for Section B questions.

Approach to answering OT questions

A step-by-step technique for approaching OT questions is outlined below. Each step will be explained in more detail when we consider the different question types below.

> **STEP 1: Read the requirement first!**
> The requirement will be stated in bold text in the exam. Identify what you are being asked to do, any technical knowledge required and **what type of OT question** you are dealing with. Look for key words in the requirement such as "Which **TWO** of the following," or "Which of the following is **NOT**".

> **STEP 2: Answer the questions you know first.**
> If you're having difficulty answering a question, move on and come back to tackle it once you've answered all the questions you know.
> It is often quicker to answer discursive style OT questions first, leaving more time for calculations.

> **STEP 3: Answer all questions.**
> There is no penalty for an incorrect answer in ACCA exams; there is nothing to be gained by leaving an OT question unanswered. If you are stuck on a question, as a last resort, it is worth selecting the option you consider most likely to be correct and moving on. Flag the question, so if you have time after you have answered the rest of the questions, you can revisit it.

> **STEP 4: Apply your technical knowledge to the data presented in the question.**
> Work through calculations taking your time and read through each answer option with care. OT questions are designed so that each answer option is plausible. Work through each response option and eliminate those you know are incorrect.

Exam success skills

The following questions are examples of the sorts of questions you could see in your exam. For these questions, we will also focus on the following exam success skills:

*   **Managing information.** It is easy for the amount of information contained in a particular question to feel a little overwhelming. Active reading is a useful technique to avoid this. This involves focusing on the requirements first on the basis that, until you have done this, the detail in the question will have little meaning and will seem more intimidating.

*   **Efficient numerical analysis.** OT questions will contain a mix of calculation and narrative questions. When attempting numerical questions, it is important that you can identify and interpret the information in the question efficiently and can apply the information to standard calculations you are familiar with. You need to be able to work through key calculations quickly and accurately.

*   **Correct interpretation of requirements.** Identify from the requirement the type of OT question. This is especially important with multiple response options (MRO) to ensure you select the correct number of response options. It is also important for fill in the blank questions as they may tell you to give your answer to a certain number of decimal places or to the nearest thousand dollars.

*   **Good time management.** Complete all questions in the time available. Each OT in Section A is worth 2 marks and should be allocated 2.4 minutes. However, some questions may take longer than others so just make sure that you complete all of the Section A questions within 84 minutes (35 x 2.4 minutes).

Skills activity

The following questions have been selected from the FA/FFA specimen exam and FA/FFA examiner's reports as good examples of the different types of questions you might face in Section A of the exam.

STEP 1 Read the requirement first! The requirement will be stated in bold text in the exam. Identify what you are being asked to do, any technical knowledge required and what type of OT question you are dealing with. Look for key words in the requirement such as 'Which TWO of the following...', 'Which of the following is NOT...'

Multiple choice activity

A company has prepared its bank reconciliation at 30 September 20X9, taking the following information into account:

	$
Outstanding lodgements	12,000
Unpresented cheques	14,700
Dishonoured cheque not entered in the cash book	2,600

The bank statement shows that the company has an overdrawn balance of $1,280.

What[1] **should be the adjusted cash book balance per the bank reconciliation at 30 September 20X9?**

[1] Requirement

A $6,580 Dr

B $6,580 Cr

C $3,980 Dr

D $3,980 Cr

Multiple response activity

On 1 October 20X8, F Co revalued a property. As a result, the annual depreciation charge increased by $20,000 as compared to depreciation based on historical cost. The company wishes to make the allowed transfer of excess depreciation between the revaluation surplus and retained earnings in accordance with IAS 16[2] *Property, Plant and Equipment*.

[2] You will need to know the requirements of this standard to correctly answer the question.

Immediately before the transfer was made, retained earnings and the revaluation surplus were as follows:

Retained earnings $875,000

Revaluation surplus $200,000

Using the information above, which TWO[3] of the following statements are true following the transfer?

A The balance on the retained earnings is $855,000

B The balance on the retained earnings is $895,000

C The balance on the revaluation reserve is $180,000

D The balance on the revaluation reserve is $220,000

[3] The multiple response question asks you which TWO of the following and gives answer options for both the revaluation surplus and retained earnings. Reading the requirement first means you will know to focus on both of these balances when considering the information in the scenario.

STEP 2 Answer the questions you know first. If you are having difficulty answering a question, move on and come back to tackle it once you have answered all the questions you know. It is often quicker to answer discursive style OT questions first, leaving more time for calculations.

Multiple response matching activity

On 31 October 20X8, Yellow, a limited liability company, has issued share capital of $50,000 (25c ordinary shares). The company also has an investment of 50,000 50c shares in Blue, a limited liability company. The following is an extract from Yellow's ledger accounts:

DIVIDEND

	$		$
		1 April 20X9 Bank	5,000

Required

Are each of the following statements true or false[4]?

[4] No calculations are required for the multiple response matching question, so you might feel comfortable answering this one first.

	True/False
Yellow has paid an interim dividend of 5c per share.	
Yellow has received a 20% interim dividend.	
Yellow has received a 10% interim dividend.	
Yellow has paid a 10% interim dividend.	

STEP 3 Answer all questions. There is no penalty for an incorrect answer in FIA/ACCA exams so there is nothing to be gained by leaving an OT question unanswered. If you are stuck on a question, as a last resort, it is worth selecting the option you consider most likely to be correct, and moving on. Make a note of the question, so if you have time after you have answered the rest of the questions, you can revisit it.

Number entry activity

Lloyd counted his inventory on 30 December 20X1 and valued it at $24,000. On the last day of trading (31 December 20X1), he ordered inventory worth $2,400 to be delivered on 1 January 20X2 and made a cash sale at cost price of $500 of inventory.

Required

What is the value of closing inventory to be shown in Lloyd's financial statements at 31 December 20X1?

$$^5 \underline{\qquad}$$

[5] Number entry questions are often the most difficult as there are not any options presented. If you do decide to leave the number entry questions to the end, make sure you use the 'flag for review' option in the exam software.

STEP 4 Work through calculations, taking your time and reading through each answer option with care. OT questions are designed so that each answer option is plausible. Work through each response option and eliminate those you know are incorrect.

The multiple response question specifically refers to the requirement of IAS 16; therefore, you need to have awareness of the requirements of the standard to correctly answer the question.

We will now work through each of the questions considering the steps introduced in the approach to the OT questions.

Multiple choice activity

The cash book should be exactly the same as the bank statement. Any differences can be accounted for by timing differences and bank interest/charges. When answering this type of question, the other important thing to remember is that the ledger maintained by the bank is recorded the opposite way around to the cash book. Therefore, a company with an overdraft would be shown as a credit in the cash book and a debit on the bank statement.

To correctly answer this question, you need to use the relevant information given about the bank reconciliation at 30 September 20X9. The dishonoured cheque for $2,600, as it was not entered into the cash book can be ignored for the purpose of this reconciliation. Reconciliation back to the cash book balance:

	$	Dr/Cr
Overdrawn balance on bank statement	(1,280)	Cr
Add: Outstanding lodgements	12,000	Dr
Less: Unpresented cheques	(14,700)	Cr
Adjusted cash book balance	(3,980)	Cr

The correct answer is therefore $3,980 Cr.

Multiple response activity

This question tests a candidate's understanding of the treatment of depreciation on a revalued asset.

When a property has been revalued, the charge for depreciation should be based on the revalued amount and the remaining useful life of the asset. The increase of the new depreciation charge over the old depreciation charge may be transferred from the revaluation surplus to retained earnings, if an entity chooses to do so. F Co has decided to make this transfer which should be accounted for as follows:

	$	$
Dr Revaluation surplus	20,000	
Cr Retained earnings		20,000

Therefore:

Retained earnings = $895,000 ($875,000 + $20,000)

Revaluation surplus = $180,000 ($200,000 – $20,000)

Number entry activity

On this question type, candidates are advised to ensure that they correctly type their answer into the number entry box in the format required.

The figure of $24,000 needs to be adjusted to find the balance to include in the financial statements at the reporting date. A common mistake made in this question was to adjust for the order of inventory of $2,400.

The order was made on 31 December 20X1 but there is no purchase invoice and the goods have not been received and, therefore, an adjustment was not required. The cash sale of inventory will be adjusted for as the goods have been sold for cash and are no longer part of Lloyd's inventory at 31 December 20X1.

The correct closing inventory balance should be $23,500 ($24,000 – $500). You do not need to enter $ nor a comma when typing your final answer. You would simply type 23500.

Multiple response matching activity

From the information given, we can see that Yellow has a credit against dividends of $5,000 and a debit against the bank, which means that the company has **received** dividend income. The options for the correct answer are therefore narrowed down to the dividends received options. We can now calculate the return from the investment in Blue as follows:

$$\frac{\$5,000 \text{ dividend}}{50,000 \text{ shares}} = 10c \text{ dividend per share}$$

$$\frac{10c \text{ dividend}}{50c \text{ share}} = 20\% \text{ return}$$

The correct answer is therefore:

	True/False
Yellow has paid an interim dividend of 5c per share.	False
Yellow has received a 20% interim dividend.	True
Yellow has received a 10% interim dividend.	False
Yellow has paid a 10% interim dividend.	False

Exam success skills diagnostic

Every time you complete a few questions, use the diagnostic below to assess how effectively you demonstrated the exam success skills in answering the questions. The table has been completed for the 'mini exam' activity to give you an idea of how to complete the diagnostic.

Exam success skills	Your reflections/observations
Managing information	Did you read each of the five requirements first? Did you actively read the scenario for each question making a note of relevant points? For example, in the multiple choice question, did you note that the company was in an **overdrawn** position?
Correct interpretation of requirements	Did you identify the correct technical knowledge needed to answer each requirement? Did you identify what type of OT question you were dealing with? For example, knowing that TWO answers were required in the multiple response question and that you should select one of the revaluation response options and one of the retained earnings options.
Efficient numerical analysis	Did you use the information in the question and the requirement to work out what calculations to perform? For example, in the number entry question, did you accurately calculate the required ratios?
Good time management	Did you manage to answer all four questions within 9.6 minutes? Did you manage your time well by answering the questions you find easiest first?
Most important action points to apply to your next question	

Summary

Being able to answer OT questions is very important for the FA/FFA exam. Key skills to focus on throughout your studies will include:

- Always reading the requirements first to identify what you are being asked to do and what type of OT question you are dealing with;
- Actively reading the scenario, making a note of key data needed to answer each requirement; and
- Answering OT questions in a sensible order, dealing with any easier discursive style questions first.

From trial balance to financial statements

Learning objectives

On competition of this chapter, you should be able to:

	Syllabus reference no.
Identify the purpose of a trial balance.	E1(a)
Extract ledger balances into a trial balance.	E1(b)
Prepare extracts of an opening trial balance.	E1(c)
Identify and understand the limitations of a trial balance.	E1(d)
Understand and apply the accounting equation.	C1(d)

Exam context

Questions on this chapter may require you to derive missing figures (for example, profit for the period) using the accounting equation, identify the correct double entry to record transactions such as drawings or determine whether balances in a trial balance should be reported in the statement of financial position or the statement of profit or loss.

Chapter overview

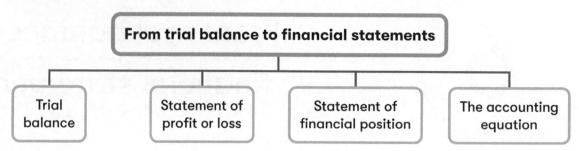

BPP
LEARNING
MEDIA

1 Introduction

In the previous chapters:

*   Transactions were categorised into books of prime entry;
*   The totals from the books of prime entry were posted to the ledger accounts; and
*   The ledger accounts were balanced off and the balances brought down.

Now we are going to move onto the next stage: transferring the balances on the ledger accounts to the trial balance.

2 The trial balance

> **Trial balance:** A trial balance is a list of ledger balances shown in debit and credit columns.

The trial balance consists of a list of balances brought down on each ledger account, separated into debits and credits as below.

Miss Smith – trial balance as at 31 December 20X7

Account	Debit	Credit
	$	$
Cash	720	
Capital		500
Sales		2,200
Purchases	1,100	
Furniture	500	
Electricity	120	
Telephone	60	
Drawings	200	
TOTAL	**2,700**	**2,700**

A trial balance **should** balance, ie **TOTAL DEBITS = TOTAL CREDITS**

If the two columns of the trial balance are not equal, there must be an error. A trial balance, however, will not disclose the following types of errors.

(a) The complete omission of a transaction, because neither a debit nor a credit is made

(b) The posting of a debit or credit to the correct side of the ledger, but to a wrong account

(c) Compensating errors (eg an error of $100 is exactly cancelled by another $100 error elsewhere)

(d) Errors of principle (eg cash from receivables being debited to trade accounts receivable and credited to cash at bank instead of the other way around)

The trial balance should reveal errors where the rules of double entry have been broken, such as:

(a) One-sided entries

(b) Where an entry has been posted as a credit to one account and a credit to a second account and no debit entry has been made (or two debits and no credits)

If the basic principle of double entry has been correctly applied throughout the period, it will be found that the total credit balances equal the total debit balances. If the trial balance does not balance, then an error must have occurred. We shall see how to correct these errors later in the Workbook.

Activity 1: Ron Knuckle – trial balance

Using the ledger accounts that you prepared for Ron Knuckle in the previous Workbook chapter, prepare the trial balance as at 31 March 20X7.

Solution

3 The statement of profit or loss

The statement of profit or loss is part of the double entry system and can be shown as a T-account.

3.1 The profit or loss ledger account

At the end of the period or year, the balances on the income and expenditure T-accounts are transferred to the profit or loss ledger account.

In this ledger account, a business summarises its results for the period by gathering together all the ledger account balances relating to the statement of profit or loss. This account is still part of the double entry system, so the basic rule of double entry still applies: every debit must have an equal and opposite credit entry.

Once the balances have been transferred to the profit or loss ledger account, the income and expenditure accounts will be closed and new accounts will be created for each income and expenditure item next year. Income and expenditure balances do not get carried into the next period or year.

Activity 2: Ron Knuckle – profit or loss ledger account

Using the trial balance from Activity 1, prepare the profit or loss ledger account.

Solution

4 The statement of financial position

The balances on all remaining ledger accounts (including the profit or loss account) can be listed and rearranged to form the statement of financial position.

The statement of financial position:

- Lists all the ledger accounts with balances remaining, ie all **assets, liabilities** and **capital;** and
- Is **not** part of the double entry system, so these balances are not transferred out. The closing balance at the end of one period becomes the opening balance at the start of the next period, eg closing cash at 31 December becomes opening cash at 1 January.

At the end of the period, the balances on the statement of profit or loss and drawings ledger accounts are cleared to the capital account. This is because the owner of the business is entitled to the cumulative profits made by the business.

Activity 3: Ron Knuckle – preparation of financial statements

Using the information in Activity 1 and Activity 2, prepare a statement of financial position and a statement of profit or loss for Ron Knuckle as at 31 March 20X7.

Solution

Ron Knuckle Statement of profit or loss for the period ended 31 March 20X7

	$	$
Sales		
Less cost of sales:		
Purchases	_____	
		_____
Gross profit		
Less expenses:		

	$	$
Rent		
Bank loan interest		
Other expenses	_____	
		_____
Net profit		=============

Ron Knuckle Statement of financial position as at 31 March 20X7

	$	$
Non-current assets		
Shop fittings		
Current assets		
Cash at bank		_____
Total assets		=============
Capital and liabilities		
Proprietor's capital		
Profit for the year		
Drawings	_____	
Non-current liabilities		
Bank loan		
Total capital and liabilities		=============

Activity 4: The capital account

Using the information from the previous activities, transfer the profit and drawings to the capital account.

DRAWINGS

	$		$
Cash	1,500	Bal c/d	1,500
Bal b/d	1,500	Capital	1,500

STATEMENT OF PROFIT OR LOSS

	$		$
Purchases	5,000	Sales	12,500
Gross profit c/d	7,500		–

	$		$
	12,500		12,500
Rent	3,500	Gross profit b/d	7,500
Loan interest	100		
Other expenses	1,900		
Net profit c/d	2,000		
	7,500		7,500
Capital	2,000	Net profit b/d	2,000

Solution

CAPITAL

	$		$
Balance c/d	5,000	Cash	5,000
		Balance b/d	5,000

4.1 Drawings

Drawings are amounts being taken out of a business by its owner. Drawings are generally in the form of cash, but an owner may also take inventory out of the business. Drawings of inventories are recorded at the cost of the inventories not the sales price.

Essential reading

See Chapter 6 of the Essential reading for more detail on the steps from ledger accounts to financial statements.

The Essential reading is available as an Appendix of the digital edition of the Workbook.

Activity 5: Opening trial balance

Alpha has the following opening balances on its ledger accounts:

	$
Fixtures	5,000
Trade receivables	2,000
Bank account	1,000
Loan	3,000

Required

What is the total assets figure?

○ $6,000

○ $5,000

○ $8,000

○ $3,000

PER alert

Two of the requirements of Performance Objective 6 (P06), 'Record and process transactions and events' are:

*   Implement or operate systems to record and process accounting data using emerging technology where appropriate or feasible.
*   Verify, input and process routine financial accounting data within the accounting system using emerging technology where appropriate or feasible.

5 The accounting equation

The accounting equation is:

Formula to learn

ASSETS = CAPITAL + LIABILITIES

KEY TERM

Business entity concept: Regardless of how a business is legally set up, for accounting purposes, a business is always treated separately from its owner(s).

Example: Liza sets up a business with $2,500 of her own money. The business is a separate entity in accounting terms and so it owes the money to Liza as **capital.**

KEY TERM

Capital: In accounting, capital is an investment of money (funds) with the intention of earning a return. A business proprietor invests capital with the intention of earning profit. As long as that money is invested, accountants will treat the capital as money owed to the proprietor by the business.

In the case of Liza, the accounting equation will now be:

$2,500 (cash asset) = $2,500 (capital) + $0 (liabilities)

As the business grows, this equation will keep changing.

Example continued: Over the next month, Liza makes the following transactions:

Buys a stall for $1,800

Buys flowers and plants for $650

Takes out a bank loan of $500

Her equation will now be:

Assets	=	Capital	+	Liabilities
Stall $1,800		$2,500		$500
Flowers (inventory) $650				

Assets	=	Capital	+	Liabilities
Cash at bank $550				

Note. You must remember that each transaction needs two entries (double entry).

Liza had cash of $2,500 but spent $1,800 on a stall and $650 on flowers, leaving her with $50 before taking out the bank loan of $500. The bank loan creates an asset and a corresponding liability as the money is owed back to the bank.

5.1 Profit and drawings and the accounting equation

> **Drawings:** Drawings are amounts of money taken out of a business by its owner.

Example continued: As the year progresses, Liza sells flowers and pays herself a wage (drawings).

These transactions will affect the accounting equation and, at this point, it is important to remember how the capital section looks in the statement of financial position.

ASSETS = CAPITAL + LIABILITIES

This equation can be extended to:

ASSETS = (OPENING CAPITAL + PROFIT – DRAWINGS) + LIABILITIES

OPENING CAPITAL + PROFIT – DRAWINGS is referred to as **proprietor's (owner's) interest.**

Example continued: Liza sells all of the flowers for $1,000 and draws cash of $300 for her own use.

The accounting equation will now be:

Assets	=	Capital	+	Profit	–	Drawings	+	Liabilities
Stall $1,800	=	2,500	+	350	–	300	+	500
Flowers $0								
Bank £1,250*								

*$550 + $1,000 – $300

Activity 6: The accounting equation (1)

Which of the following is correct?

- ○ Assets = opening capital + profit – drawings – liabilities
- ○ Assets – liabilities = opening capital + profit – drawings
- ○ Assets + liabilities = opening capital + profit – drawings
- ○ Assets = opening capital + loss – drawings + liabilities

Activity 7: The accounting equation (2)

The profit earned by a business in 20X7 was $72,500. The proprietor injected new capital of $8,000 during the year and withdrew goods for his private use which had cost $2,200.

Required

If net assets at the beginning of 20X7 were $101,700, what were the closing net assets?

- ○ $35,000
- ○ $39,400
- ○ $168,400
- ○ $180,000

Chapter summary

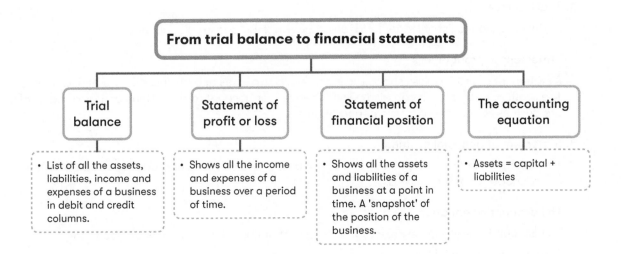

From trial balance to financial statements

Trial balance
- List of all the assets, liabilities, income and expenses of a business in debit and credit columns.

Statement of profit or loss
- Shows all the income and expenses of a business over a period of time.

Statement of financial position
- Shows all the assets and liabilities of a business at a point in time. A 'snapshot' of the position of the business.

The accounting equation
- Assets = capital + liabilities

Knowledge diagnostic

1. Trial balance

A trial balance is a list of ledger balances shown in debit and credit columns.

2. Statement of profit or loss

A statement of profit or loss shows the income and expenses of a business over a period of time. The profit or loss account can also be shown in ledger account format. Think of it as a 'video' of the business transactions over a period of time.

3. Statement of financial position

The statement of financial position shows the assets and liabilities of a business at a point in time. It is a 'snapshot' of the business.

4. The accounting equation

The accounting equation expresses the statement of financial position as an equation.

Assets = capital + liabilities

5. Drawings

Drawings represent money or goods that have been taken out of the business by the owner for personal use.

6. Capital

Capital is the amount invested in the business by the owner and is expected to be repaid to the owner at some point in the future.

Further study guidance

Question practice

Now try the following from the Further question practice bank (available in the digital edition of the Workbook):

Questions 16 and 19

Activity answers

Activity 1: Ron Knuckle – trial balance

Ron Knuckle – Trial balance as at 31 March 20X7

	Debit	Credit
	$	$
Cash at bank	6,500	
Capital		7,000
Bank loan		1,000
Purchases	5,000	
Trade payables		–
Rent	3,500	
Shop fittings	2,000	
Sales		12,500
Trade receivables	–	
Bank loan interest	100	
Other expenses	1,900	
Drawings	1,500	
TOTAL	**20,500**	**20,500**

Activity 2: Ron Knuckle – profit or loss ledger account

STATEMENT OF PROFIT OR LOSS

	$		$
Purchases	5,000	Sales	12,500
Gross profit c/d	7,500		
	12,500		**12,500**
Rent	3,500	Gross profit b/d	7,500
Loan interest	100		
Other expenses	1,900		
Net profit c/d	2,000		
	7,500		**7,500**
		Net profit b/d	2,000

Activity 3: Ron Knuckle – preparation of financial statements

Ron Knuckle Statement of profit or loss for the period ended 31 March 20X7

	$	$
Sales		12,500
Less cost of sales:		
Purchases	5,000	
		(5,000)
Gross profit		7,500
Less expenses:		
Rent	3,500	
Bank loan interest	100	
Other expenses	1,900	
		(5,500)
Net profit		2,000

Ron Knuckle Statement of financial position as at 31 March 20X7

	$	$
Non-current assets		
Shop fittings		2,000
Current assets		
Cash at bank		6,500
Total assets		8,500
Capital and liabilities		
Proprietor's capital	7,000	
Profit for the year	2,000	
Drawings	(1,500)	
Non-current liabilities		
Bank loan		
Total capital and liabilities		8,500

BPP
LEARNING
MEDIA

Activity 4: The capital account

CAPITAL				
	$			$
Balance c/d	5,000	Cash		5,000
Drawings	1,500	Balance b/d		5,000
Balance c/d	5,500	Net profit		2,000
	7,000			**7,000**

Activity 5: Opening trial balance

The correct answer is: $8,000

Assets = Fixtures + Trade receivables + Bank account

Activity 6: The accounting equation (1)

The correct answer is: Assets – liabilities = opening capital + profit – drawings

Activity 7: The accounting equation (2)

The correct answer is: $180,000

Increase in net assets = profit + new capital – drawings

= $(72,500 + 8,000 – 2,200)

= $78,300

Therefore, closing net assets = $(101,700 + 78,300) = $180,000.

Alternatively:

Closing net assets = opening net assets + capital introduced + profit – drawings

$180,000 = $101,700 + $8,000 + $72,500 – $2,200.

Inventory

Learning objectives

On competition of this chapter, you should be able to:

	Syllabus reference no.
Recognise the need for adjustments for inventory in preparing financial statements.	D3(a)
Record opening and closing inventory.	D3(b)
Identify the alternative methods of valuing inventory.	D3(c)
Understand and apply the IASB requirements for valuing inventories.	D3(d)
Recognise which costs should be included in valuing inventories.	D3(e)
Understand the use of continuous and period end inventory records.	D3(f)
Calculate the value of closing inventory using 'first in, first out' and 'average cost' – both periodic weighted average and continuous weighted average.	D3(g)
Understand the impact of accounting concepts on the valuation of inventory.	D3(h)
Identify the impact of inventory valuation methods on profit and on assets.	D3(i)

Exam context

Accounting for inventories and inventory valuation is a basic principle that affects any business. Examination questions are likely to test your understanding of the terms 'cost' and 'net realisable value'. You should also expect calculations on this area and be able to make adjustments for both opening and closing inventory.

Chapter overview

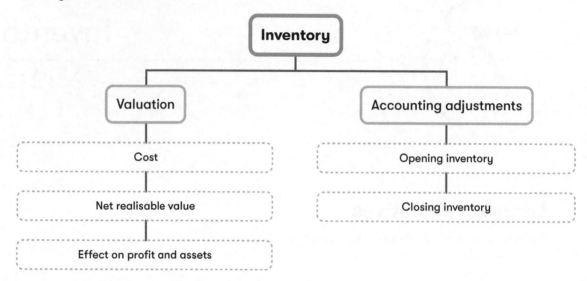

1 Introduction

KEY TERM

Inventory: Inventories are assets:
- Held for sale in the ordinary course of business;
- In the process of production for such sale; or
- In the form of materials or supplies to be consumed in the production process or in the rendering of services.

For example:
- Raw materials
- Work-in-progress
- Finished goods

For some businesses, for example manufacturing entities, inventory can be a significant figure.

It impacts the financial statement in two ways:
- A potentially large balance within current assets
- Opening and closing inventory have a direct impact on cost of sales and therefore profits.

Businesses must therefore ensure that their financial statements account for inventory accurately in terms of:
- The accounting adjustment
- Its valuation

Different types of businesses will count their inventory in different ways. For example, a very large business with huge warehouses would have an automated inventory system that records the movement of stock in and stock out throughout the year. This would then produce a closing inventory figure automatically at the year end.

Smaller businesses are more likely to carry out a physical inventory count at the end of the year. For example, a small shop selling stationery would close the shop for a day and carry out a physical count of all the items in the shop at the year end, eg 200 black pens, 197 blue pens, etc; and then they would have to assign a value to those items. We will see that a bit later in this chapter.

1.1 Unsold goods in inventory at the end of an accounting period

Goods might be unsold at the end of an accounting period and will therefore still be held in inventory. As financial statements are prepared on an accruals basis, the purchase cost of these goods should not be included in the cost of sales of the period. The reason for this is that the purchases need to be matched with the sales revenue generated by these purchases. If the inventory is not sold in the year, the sales revenue from this inventory will not be included in the statement of profit or loss until the following year. Therefore, closing inventory is removed from the statement of profit or loss for the current year and then taken back to the statement of profit or loss as opening inventory in the new year when it will be matched with the sales revenue produced from its sale.

1.2 The cost of goods sold

The cost of goods sold is found by applying the following formula:

Formula to learn

Cost of goods sold:

Opening inventory + purchases (or costs of production if manufacturing industry) − **closing inventory**.

This is shown in the statement of profit or loss as follows and is referred to as the 'trading account'.

	$
Opening inventory	1,000
Add: costs of purchase/production	6,000
	7,000
Less: closing inventory	(2,000)
Cost of goods sold	**5,000**

In other words, to **match** 'sales' and the 'cost of goods sold', it is necessary to adjust the cost of goods manufactured or purchased to allow for increases or reduction in inventory levels during the period.

The 'formula' above is based on a logical idea. You should learn it, because it is a fundamental principle of accounting.

Illustration 1: Cost of goods sold

Eddie has a business selling phones. At the beginning of the month, he had seven phones in inventory which had cost $20 each. During the month, the price of phones has remained the same so Eddie buys a further 50 phones for $20 each, and sells 35 for $30 each.

Required

Prepare the trading account for Eddie.

Solution

	$	$
Sales		1,050
Cost of sales:		
Opening inventories	140	
Purchases	1,000	
Less: closing inventories	(440)	(700)
Gross profit		350

The trading account shows a profit of $350 which relates to 35 phones sold at a profit of $10 per phone ($30 sales price – $20 purchase price).

2 Accounting for inventory

Inventory is generally accounted for as a year-end adjustment via **a journal** entry.

2.1 Opening inventory

The trial balance produced by the entity at the end of the year will show an inventory figure.

This amount generally relates to the opening inventory, ie the goods held by the business at the beginning of the year.

Such goods will have been sold during the year. They are no longer an asset of the entity but will form part of the costs that should be matched against sales revenue when determining profit.

The accounting entry is:

Dr Cost of sales (SPL)

Cr Inventories (SOFP)

This double entry moves inventory from the statement of financial position to cost of sales in the statement of profit or loss.

2.2 Closing inventory

The goods held by the business at the end of the year must be included as an asset in the statement of financial position and as a deduction within cost of sales in the statement of profit or loss.

The accounting entry is:

Dr Inventories (SOFP)

Cr Cost of sales (SPL)

This double entry moves inventory out of cost of sales in the statement of profit and loss and onto the statement of financial position as a current asset.

2.3 Calculating the value of inventory

The inventories figure comprises two elements:

Quantity is normally ascertained by an inventory count at the end of the accounting period or by continuous inventory records.

Valuation is much more subjective, so guidance is provided in IAS 2.

INVENTORY = QUANTITY × VALUATION

2.4 Inventory overview

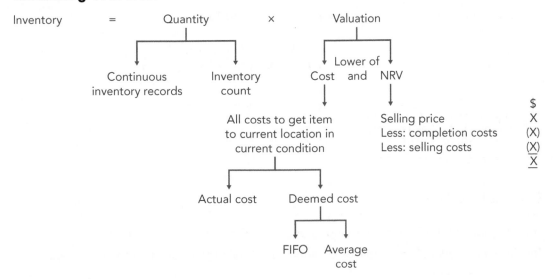

3 Valuation

The basic rule per IAS 2 *Inventories* is:

"Inventories should be measured at the lower of cost and net realisable value (NRV)."

This is an example of **prudence** in presenting financial information. As a general rule, assets should not be carried at amounts greater than those expected to be realised from their sale or use. In the case of inventories, this amount could fall below cost when items **are damaged or become obsolete,** or where the **costs to completion have increased** in order to make the sale.

The principal situations in which NRV is likely to be less than cost are:

- An **increase in costs** or a **fall in selling price**
- A **physical deterioration** in the condition of inventory
- **Obsolescence** of products

- A decision as part of the company's marketing **strategy** to manufacture and **sell** products at a **loss**
- **Errors** in production or purchasing

If the inventory is not expected to be sold at a profit:

- Value at **cost**
- Do not **anticipate** profit

If the inventory is expected to be sold at a loss:

- Value at **net realisable value**
- **Do** provide for the future loss

4 Cost

The cost of an item of inventory includes:

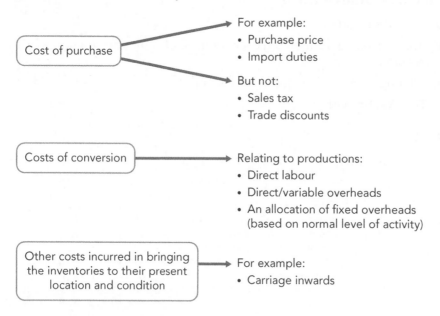

Cost of purchase

For example:
- Purchase price
- Import duties

But not:
- Sales tax
- Trade discounts

Costs of conversion

Relating to productions:
- Direct labour
- Direct/variable overheads
- An allocation of fixed overheads (based on normal level of activity)

Other costs incurred in bringing the inventories to their present location and condition

For example:
- Carriage inwards

Essential reading

See Chapter 7 of the Essential reading for more detail on the cost of inventories.

The Essential reading is available as an Appendix of the digital edition of the Workbook.

Activity 1: IAS 2 *Inventories*

According to IAS 2 *Inventories*, which of the following should **not** be included in determining the cost of the inventories of an entity?

☐ Labour costs

☐ Transport costs to deliver goods to customers

☐ Administrative overheads

☐ Depreciation on factory machine

5 Net realisable value (NRV)

Net realisable value: "Net realisable value is the estimated selling price in the ordinary course of business less the estimated costs of completion and the estimated costs necessary to make the sale" (IAS 2, para. 6).

It is calculated as:

	$
Estimated selling price	X
Less: estimated costs to completion	(X)
Less: estimated selling and distribution costs	(X)
	X

Activity 2: Net realisable value

Jessie is trying to value her inventory. She has the following information available:

	$
Selling price	35
Costs incurred to date	20
Cost of work to complete item	12
Selling costs per item	1

Required

What is the net realisable value of Jessie's inventory?

$ [   ]

6 No netting off

The IAS 2 rule 'lower of cost and net realisable value' should be applied as far as possible on an item-by-item (or line-by-line) basis.

Illustration 2: No netting off

Suppose an entity has four items of inventories on hand at the year end. Their costs and NRVs are as follows:

Inventory item	Cost	NRV	Lower of cost and NRV
	$	$	$
1	27	32	27
2	14	8	8
3	43	55	43
4	29	40	29

Inventory item	Cost	NRV	Lower of cost and NRV
	$	$	$
	113	135	107

Required

Calculate the value of closing inventory.

Solution

It would be incorrect to compare total cost of $113 with total NRV of $135 and state inventories as $113.

A loss on Item 2 of $6 can be foreseen and should therefore be recognised.

The comparison should be made for each item of inventory and thus a value of $107 would be attributed to inventories.

This would be accounted for by the journal entry:

Dr Inventories (SOFP) $107

Cr Cost of sales (SPL) $107

7 Theoretical methods of estimating cost

7.1 Issue

If various batches of inventories have been purchased at different times during the year and at different prices, it may be impossible to determine precisely which items are still held at the year end and therefore what the actual purchase cost of the goods was. IAS 2, therefore, allows an entity to approximate the cost of its inventories. There are two methods examinable:

- First in, first out (FIFO)
- Last in, first out (LIFO) – not permitted by IAS 2
- Average cost

7.1.1 FIFO

Under FIFO, it is assumed that:

- First goods purchased/produced will be the first to be sold
- Remaining inventories are from the most recent purchases/production

7.1.2 Average cost (AVCO)

There are two average costs available:

- **Periodic (or simple) average cost:** The cost of all purchases/production during the year is divided by the total number of units purchased.
- Continuous w**eighted average cost:** The weighted average of the cost of similar items is recalculated each time a new item is purchased/produced during the period (IAS 2 requires the weighted average to be used). Alternatively, the weighted average cost could be calculated periodically, for example at the end of each month.

Note. Make sure you read the question carefully to identify which AVCO you are being asked to calculate – periodic or continuous.

Activity 3: Valuing closing inventory

On 1 January 20X7, a company held 200 units of finished goods valued at $10 each. During January, the following transactions took place:

Date	Units purchased	Cost per unit
10 January	300	$10.85
20 January	350	$11.50
25 January	250	$13.00

Sales during January were as follows:

Date	Units sold	Sales price per unit
14 January	280	$18.00
21 January	400	$18.00
28 January	80	$18.00

Required

Determine the valuation of closing inventories and cost of sales using:

(a) FIFO

(b) Weighted average cost (AVCO)

Solution

(a)

Closing inventories (FIFO)

	Opening inventories	Purchases 10 Jan	Purchases 20 Jan	Purchases 25 Jan
Sales				
14 Jan				
21 Jan				
28 Jan				
Cost per unit				
Cost of closing inventory				

Closing inventories = $1,035 + $3,250 = $ [   ]

Cost of sales (FIFO)

$

Opening inventories [   ]

Purchases

Less: closing inventories

(b)

Closing inventories and cost of sales (AVCO)

		Units	Cost	Average unit cost	Total cost	Cost of sales
			$	$	$	$
1.1.X2	b/f					
10.1.X2	Purchase	_____			_____	
14.1.X2	Sale	_____			_____	
20.1.X2	Purchase	_____			_____	
21.1.X2	Sale	_____			_____	
25.1.X2	Purchase	_____			_____	
28.1.X2	Sale	_____			_____	_____
		_____			_____	_____

Note. To calculate average cost: Average unit cost/total units.

Closing inventory: $ [   ]

Cost of sales: $ [   ]

8 Advantages and disadvantages

FIFO: More 'realistic' value on statement of financial position

Average cost: Can be complex as weighted average is required by IAS 2

9 Inventory valuations and profit

Different methods of inventory valuation will provide different profit figures. In the activity, we saw that FIFO produced a closing inventory value of $4,285 whilst AVCO produced a figure for closing inventories of $4,160.

FiFO therefore produced a cost of sales figure of $8,245 compared to AVCO's cost of sales figure of $8,370.

Assuming there were sales of $18,000, FIFO would produce a profit of $9,755 and AVCO would produce a profit of $9,630.

Activity 4: Periodic weighted average cost

A business has opening inventory of 100 units which cost $10 each. It then buys 30 units at $12 each and another 40 units at $12.50. During the period it sells 120 units for $20 each.

Required

What is the value of closing inventory using the periodic weighted AVCO?

$ _____

Chapter summary

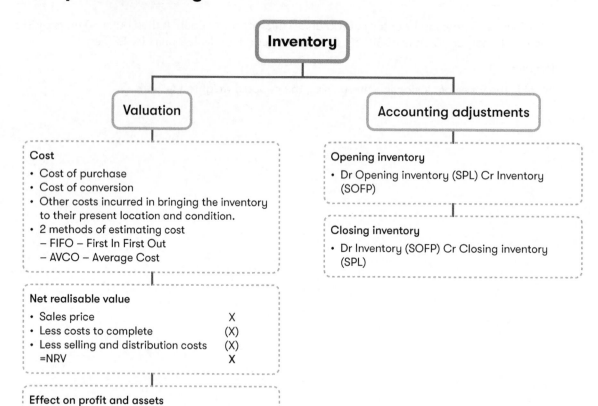

Inventory

Valuation

Cost
- Cost of purchase
- Cost of conversion
- Other costs incurred in bringing the inventory to their present location and condition.
- 2 methods of estimating cost
  - FIFO – First In First Out
  - AVCO – Average Cost

Net realisable value
- Sales price   X
- Less costs to complete   (X)
- Less selling and distribution costs   (X)
  - =NRV   X

Effect on profit and assets
- In times of rising prices, FIFO produces a higher closing inventory figure, a lower cost of sales figure and therefore a higher profit figure than AVCO.

Accounting adjustments

Opening inventory
- Dr Opening inventory (SPL) Cr Inventory (SOFP)

Closing inventory
- Dr Inventory (SOFP) Cr Closing inventory (SPL)

Knowledge diagnostic

1. Accounting adjustment

The statement of profit or loss matches the sales revenue earned in a period with the cost of sales incurred to generate that revenue. There are therefore two inventory adjustments: the opening inventory adjustment and the closing inventory adjustment.

2. Valuation

Inventories should be valued at the lower of cost and net realisable value.

3. Cost

The cost of inventory includes the cost of purchase, costs of conversion and any other costs necessary to bring the inventory to its present location and condition.

4. Net realisable value (NRV)

Net realisable value is the estimated selling price less the costs to completion and any selling and distribution costs.

5. Theoretical methods of estimating cost

Methods available to estimate the cost of inventories are first in, first out (FIFO) and average cost. Under FIFO, the inventories held at the year end are the most recent purchases but, under average cost, the cost of all inventories purchased during the year is weighted to produce an average figure.

6. Valuation effects on profit and assets

In times of rising prices, using FIFO will mean the financial statements show higher inventory values and higher profits.

Further study guidance

Question practice

Now try the following from the Further question practice bank (available in the digital edition of the Workbook):

Questions 29 to 33

Activity answers

Activity 1: IAS 2 Inventories

The correct answers are:

- Transport costs to deliver goods to customers
- Administrative overheads

Transport costs to deliver goods to customers are an example of carriage outwards and should not be included. Administrative overheads do not relate to production and cannot therefore be included.

The depreciation of the factory machine is a production overhead and should be included.

Activity 2: Net realisable value

$ 22

$35 – $12 – $1 = $22

Activity 3: Valuing closing inventory

(a)

Closing inventories (FIFO)

	Opening inventories	Purchases 10 Jan	Purchases 20 Jan	Purchases 25 Jan
	200	300	350	250
Sales				
14 Jan	(200)	(80)		
21 Jan		(220)	(180)	
28 Jan			(80)	
	Nil	Nil	90	250
Cost per unit			$11.50	$13.00
Cost of closing inventory			$1,035	$3,250

Closing inventories = $1,035 + $3,250 = $4,285

Cost of sales (FIFO)

	$
Opening inventories (200 × $10)	2,000
Purchases	10,350
	12,530
Less: closing inventories	(4,285)
	8,245

(b)

Closing inventories and cost of sales (AVCO)

		Units	Cost	Average unit cost	Total cost	Cost of sales
			$	$	$	$
1.1.X2	b/f	200	10.00		2,000	
10.1.X2	Purchase	300	10.85		3,255	
		500		10.51	5,255	
14.1.X2	Sale	(280)		10.51	(2,943)	2,943
		220			2,312	
20.1.X2	Purchase	350	11.50		4,025	
		570		11.12	6,337	
21.1.X2	Sale	(400)		11.12	(4,448)	4,448
		170			1,889	
25.1.X2	Purchase	250	13.00		3,250	
		420		12.24	5,139	
28.1.X2	Sale	(80)		12.24	(979)	979
		340			4,160	8,370

Note. To calculate average cost: Average unit cost/total units.

Closing inventory: $4,160

Cost of sales: $8,370

Activity 4: Periodic weighted average cost

$ 547

Periodic weighted average cost is calculated as total purchase cost divided by the total purchases in units.

Total purchase cost is (100 × $10) + (30 × $12) + (40 × $12.50) = $1,860

Total units purchased = 100 + 30 + 40 = 170

Total periodic weighted average cost per unit is $10.94 ($1,860/170)

Closing inventory is, therefore, units held in inventory at the year end multiplied by periodic weighted AVCO.

170 units less sale of 120 units = 50 units in closing inventory.

Closing inventory value is, therefore, 50 units × $10.94 = $547.

8

Tangible non-current assets

Learning objectives

On competition of this chapter, you should be able to:

	Syllabus reference no.
Define non-current assets.	D4(a)
Recognise the difference between current and non-current assets.	D4(b)
Explain the difference between asset and expense items.	D4(c)
Classify expenditure as asset or expenses charged to profit or loss.	D4(d)
Prepare ledger entries to record the acquisition and disposal of non-current assets.	D4(e)
Calculate and record profits or losses on disposal of non-current assets in the statement of profit or loss including part exchange transactions.	D4(f)
Record the revaluation of non-current assets in ledger accounts, the statement of profit or loss and other comprehensive income and in the statement of financial position.	D4(g)
Calculate the profit or loss on disposal of a revalued asset.	D4(h)
Illustrate how non-current asset balances and movements are disclosed in financial statements.	D4(i)
Explain the purpose and function of an asset register.	D4(j)
Understand and explain the purpose of depreciation.	D5(a)
Calculate the charge for depreciation using the straight line and reducing balance methods.	D5(b)
Identify the circumstances where different methods of depreciation would be appropriate.	D5(c)
Illustrate how depreciation expense and accumulated depreciation are recorded in ledger accounts.	D5(d)
Calculate depreciation on a revalued non-current asset including the transfer of excess depreciation between the revaluation surplus and retained earnings.	D5(e)
Calculate the adjustments to depreciation necessary if changes are	D5(f)

	Syllabus reference no.
made in the estimated useful life and/or residual value of a non-current asset.	
Record depreciation in the statement of profit or loss and statement of financial position.	D5(g)

Exam context

Tangible non-current assets and depreciation are an important part of the syllabus and you should expect several objective test questions on this area. It could also feature as part of the accounts preparation multi-task question in Section B of the exam. Questions are likely to focus on areas such as calculating depreciation and asset values (both on assets held at historic cost and revalued amounts), profits or losses on disposal of assets and the components that can be included in the cost of a non-current asset.

Chapter overview

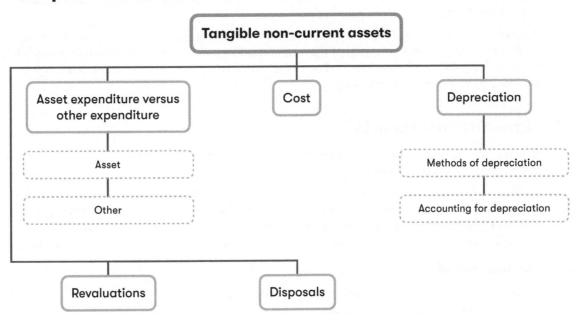

1 Introduction

The purchase of a non-current asset is often a significant cost to a business which will have a large impact on its financial statements.

Data about each non-current asset is recorded in an asset register. This asset register is used as an internal check on the accuracy of the nominal ledger (in relation to non-current assets). It is separate from the nominal ledger and contains much more detail (eg purchase date, cost, location, serial number, description).

2 Non-current assets

A statement of financial position contains both non-current assets and current assets, but what is the difference between the two?

> **Non-current assets:** Non-current assets are assets which are intended to be used by the business on a continuing basis and include both tangible and intangible assets.

2.1 Current assets

A business should classify an asset as **current** when:

- It expects to realise, sell or consume the asset in its normal operating cycle;
- It holds the asset primarily for the purpose of trading;
- It expects to realise the asset within twelve months after the reporting period; or
- The asset is cash or a cash equivalent.

All other assets should be classified as **non-current**.

2.2 IAS 16 *Property, Plant and Equipment* – key definitions

IAS 16 *Property, Plant and Equipment* is the International Financial Reporting Standard (IFRS) that should be followed when accounting for tangible non-current assets. The key concepts that we will cover in the next few sections come from IAS 16 and are very important.

IAS 16 gives a large number of definitions that you need to be aware of:

> **Property, plant and equipment:** "Property, plant and equipment are tangible items that:
> - Are held for use in the production or supply of goods or services, for rental to others, or for administrative purposes; and
> - Are expected to be used during more than one period."
>
> **Cost:** "Cost is the amount of cash or cash equivalents paid or the fair value of the other consideration given to acquire an asset at the time of its acquisition or construction."
>
> **Fair value:** "Fair value is the amount for which an asset could be exchanged between knowledgeable, willing parties in an arm's length transaction."
>
> **Carrying value:** "Carrying amount is the amount at which an asset is recognised after deducting any accumulated depreciation and impairment losses."
>
> (IAS 16, para. 6)

Activity 1: Idea generation

What examples of tangible non-current assets can you think of?

Solution

2.3 Recognition

Recognition simply means incorporation of the asset in the business's accounts. The recognition of property, plant and equipment depends on two criteria.

- "It is probable that future economic benefits associated with the asset will flow to the entity."
- "The cost of the asset to the entity can be measured reliably."

(IAS 16, para. 7)

Property, plant and equipment can amount to substantial amounts in financial statements, affecting both the presentation of the company's statement of financial position and the profitability of the entity as shown in the statement of profit or loss. Smaller items such as tools are often written off as expenses of the period. Most companies have their own policy on this; items below a certain value are charged as expenses instead of being capitalised.

2.4 Asset expenditure vs other expenditure

KEY TERM

> **Asset:** Asset expenditure is expenditure which results in the acquisition of non-current assets, or improvements to existing non-current assets.

In order to tackle the subject of non-current assets, you need to be familiar with an important distinction, the distinction between asset and other expenditure.

(a) Asset expenditure: results in the **acquisition, replacement** or **improvement** of non-current assets.

(b) Other expenditure: for the trade of the business, or to **repair, maintain** and **service** non-current assets.

Asset expenditure results in the appearance of a **non-current asset** in the statement of financial position of the business.

Other expenditure results in an **expense** in the statement of profit or loss.

Think of asset expenditure as expenditure that provides long-term benefits (eg a building, item of machinery) and other expenditure as trading costs relating to the short term (eg electricity, wages).

Illustration 1: Asset and other expenditure

A business purchases a building for $30,000 and incurs legal costs of $2,000. It then adds an extension to the building at a cost of $10,000. The building needs to have a few broken windows mended, its floors polished and some missing roof tiles replaced. These cleaning and maintenance jobs cost $900.

Required

Which costs can be capitalised as non-current asset and which are statement of profit or loss expenses?

Solution

The original purchase ($30,000) and the cost of the extension ($10,000) are asset expenditure, because they are incurred to acquire and then improve a non-current asset. The legal costs ($2,000) can also be capitalised because the building purchase would not have been completed if the legal costs had not been paid.

The other costs of $900 are statement of profit or loss expenditure, because these merely maintain the building and thus the 'earning capacity' of the building.

2.4.1 Why is the distinction between asset expenditure and other expenditure important?

Expenditure is usually shown in the **statement of profit or loss** and results from the purchase of goods and services for one of the following reasons:

- To be used fully in the accounting period in which they are purchased, and so be a cost or expense in the statement of profit or loss, eg inventory purchased and sold in the year.
- To result in a current asset as at the end of the accounting period because the goods or services have not yet been consumed or used. The current asset would be shown in the statement of financial position and is not yet a cost or expense in the statement of profit or loss, eg inventory purchased in the year but not sold in the current accounting period.

Asset expenditure is shown in the **statement of financial position** and results in the purchase or improvement of non-current assets, which are assets that will provide benefits to the business in more than one accounting period, and which are not acquired with a view to being resold in the normal course of trade. The cost of purchased non-current assets is not charged in full to the statement of profit or loss of the period in which the purchase occurs. Instead, the non-current asset is gradually depreciated over a number of accounting periods in accordance with the accruals concept.

For example, if you purchase a machine, you would expect it to be of use to the business for a number of years. Therefore, you would not classify it as an expenses in the year of purchase. You would hold it as an asset in the statement of financial position and take the cost to the statement of profit or loss over the years in which it is used by the business to make goods which are then sold. This is an example of the **matching** concept. The cost of the machine is matched with the revenue it helps to generate over the life of the asset.

Since expenditure can be accounted for in different ways, the correct and consistent calculation of **profit** for any accounting period depends on the correct and consistent classification of items as asset expenditure and statement of profit and loss expenditure.

For example, if we wrote off the cost of a $500,000 machine in the year of purchase, in a company that had profits of $400,000, this would have a dramatic effect on the profit figure for the year and seriously affect the decisions made by the users of the financial statements.

Activity 2: Asset or expense

State whether each of the following items should be classified as 'asset' or 'expense' or income for the purpose of preparing the statement of profit or loss and the statement of financial position of the business.

(1) The purchase of a property (eg an office building)

(2) The annual depreciation of such a property

(3) Solicitors' fees in connection with the purchase of such a property

(4) The costs of adding extra storage capacity to a computer used by the business

(5) Computer repairs and maintenance costs

(6) Profit on the sale of an office building

(7) Revenue from sales by credit card

(8) The cost of new plant

(9) Customs duty charged on the plant when imported into the country

(10) The 'carriage' costs of transporting the new plant from the supplier's factory to the premises of the business purchasing the plant

(11) The cost of installing the new plant in the premises of the business

(12) The wages of the machine operators

Solution

Exam focus point

Exam questions on the distinction between asset and other expenditure are highly likely.

2.5 IAS 16 *Property, Plant and Equipment*

Under IAS 16, tangible non-current assets should initially be recorded at cost.

IAS 16 lists the components that make up the cost of an item of property, plant and equipment as follows:

- **Purchase price,** excluding sales tax and trade discounts but including import duties
- Initial estimate of the **costs of dismantling and removing** the item and **restoring the site** on which it is situated
- **Directly attributable** costs to bring the asset to its intended location and ready to use, including:
  - Initial delivery and handling costs

- Installation and assembly costs
- Costs of testing whether the asset is working properly
- Professional fees

The asset can then be kept at cost and depreciated, or the entity may choose to revalue its tangible non-current assets.

The following costs may **not** be included:

- The cost of maintenance contracts
- Start up and similar pre-production costs
- Staff training costs
- Administration and other general overhead costs
- Expenses of operations that are incidental to the construction or development of the item

All of these items will be recognised as an **expense** rather than as part of the cost of the asset.

Exam focus point

Only staff costs arising directly from the construction or acquisition of the asset can be capitalised as part of the cost of the asset.

The costs of training staff to use a new asset cannot be capitalised because it is not probable that economic benefits will be generated from training the staff, as we cannot guarantee that those staff will stay and use the asset. The costs of training staff should be expensed. Watch out for this in your exam!

2.6 Subsequent expenditure

Subsequent expenditure is added to the carrying amount of the asset, but only when it is probable that future economic benefits, in excess of the originally assessed standard of performance of the existing asset, will flow to the enterprise (IAS 16, para. IN6). All other subsequent expenditure is simply recognised as an expense in the period in which it is incurred (IAS 16, para. 12).

The important point here is whether any subsequent expenditure on an asset improves the condition of the asset beyond the previous performance. The following are examples of such improvements.

- **Modification** of an item of plant to extend its useful life, including increased capacity
- **Upgrade** of machine parts to improve the quality of output
- Adoption of a **new production process** leading to large reductions in operating costs

Activity 3: Costs

On 10 December 20X7, an entity bought a machine.

The breakdown on the invoice showed:

	$
Cost of machine	20,000
Delivery costs	200
One year maintenance contract	900
	21,100

Further installation costs of $500 were also incurred.

Required

At what amount should the machine be capitalised in the entity's records?

- $20,000
- $20,700
- $20,200
- $21,600

2.7 Depreciation

The need to **depreciate** non-current assets arises from the **accruals** assumption. If money is expended in purchasing an asset, the amount expended must at some time be charged against profits.

Depreciation is a means of **spreading the cost** of a non-current asset over its useful life in order to match the cost of the asset with the consumption of the asset's economic benefits.

Land normally has an unlimited useful life and is therefore **not depreciated**. Buildings have a limited life and, therefore, are depreciable assets.

> **Depreciation:** "Depreciation is the systematic allocation of the depreciable amount of an asset over its useful life."
>
> **Depreciable amount:** "Depreciable amount is the cost of an asset or other amount substituted for historical cost, less its estimated residual value."
>
> **Useful life:** "Useful life is either:
> - the period over which an asset is expected to be available for use by an entity; or
> - The number of production or similar units expected to be obtained from the asset by an entity."
>
> (IAS 16; para. 6)

The following factors should be considered when estimating the useful life of a depreciable asset:
- Expected usage
- Expected physical wear and tear
- Obsolescence
- Legal or other limits on the use of the assets

(IAS 16, para. 56)

Once decided, the useful life should be reviewed at least each financial year end (IAS 16, para. 51) and depreciation rates adjusted for the current and future periods if expectations vary significantly from the original estimates. The effect of the change should be disclosed in the accounting period in which the change takes place.

The assessment of useful life requires judgement based on previous experience with similar assets or classes of asset (IAS 16, para. 57). When a completely new type of asset is acquired (ie through technological advancement or through use in producing a brand new product or service), it is still necessary to estimate useful life, even though the exercise will be much more difficult.

The physical life of the asset might be longer than its useful life to the enterprise in question. One of the main factors to be taken into consideration is the physical wear and tear the asset is likely to endure. This will depend on various circumstances, including the number of shifts for which the asset will be used and the enterprise's repair and maintenance programme. Other factors to be considered include obsolescence (due to technological advances/improvements in production/reduction in demand for the product/service produced by the asset) and legal restrictions, eg length of a related lease.

2.8 Residual value

> **Residual value:** "The residual value of an asset is the estimated amount that an entity would currently obtain from disposal of the asset, after deducting the estimated costs of disposal if

the asset were already of the age and in the condition expected at the end of its useful life"
(IAS 16, para. 6).

In most cases the residual value of an asset is likely to be immaterial. If it is likely to be of any significant value, that value must be estimated at the date of purchase or any subsequent revaluation. The amount of residual value should be estimated based on the current situation with other similar assets, used in the same way, which are now at the end of their useful lives. Any expected costs of disposal should be offset against the gross residual value. For example:

- A non-current asset costing $20,000 which has an expected life of five years and an expected residual value of nil should be depreciated by $20,000 in total over the five-year period.
- A non-current asset costing $20,000 which has an expected life of five years and an expected residual value of $3,000 should be depreciated by $17,000 in total over the five-year period.

2.9 Methods of depreciation

There are two main methods for calculating depreciation:

- **Straight line method**
- **Reducing balance method**

2.9.1 Straight line method

The depreciation charge is the **same every year**.

Formula to learn

$$\text{Depreciation} = \frac{(\text{cost} - \text{residual value})}{\text{useful life (years)}} \text{ or (costs} - \text{residual value)} \times \%$$

where:

Residual value = expected proceeds/scrap value at the end of the asset's useful life

Useful life = the number of years the business expects to make use of the asset

This method is suitable for assets which are used up evenly over their useful life.

Activity 4: Straight line depreciation

A business buys a machine for $2,500. It is expected to have a useful life of three years after which time it will have a scrap value of $250.

Required

(1) Calculate the annual depreciation charge.

(2) Calculate the cost, accumulated depreciation and carrying amount (CA) for each year of the asset's life.

Note. CA = cost – accumulated depreciation to date

Solution

Year	Cost	Accumulated depreciation	Carrying Amount (CA)
	$	$	$
1			
2			
3			

2.9.2 Reducing balance depreciation

This method is suitable where the benefits obtained by the business from using the asset decline over time; for example, a machine which may become progressively less efficient as it gets older.

Under this method the depreciation charge will be higher in the earlier years and reduce over time.

Note. This method does not take account of any residual value, since the CA under this method will never reach zero. The depreciation rate percentage will be provided in the question.

> **Formula to learn**
>
> Depreciation = depreciation rate (%) × carrying amount (CA)
>
> CA = cost – accumulated depreciation to date

Activity 5: Reducing balance depreciation

A business buys a machine costing $6,000. The depreciation rate is 40% on a reducing balance basis.

Required

Calculate depreciation expense, accumulated depreciation and carrying amount of the asset for the first three years.

Solution

Year	CA b/d	Depreciation rate	Depreciation expense	Accumulated depreciation	CA c/d
	$	$	$	$	$
1					
2					
3					

2.9.3 Change in depreciation method

It is up to the business concerned to decide which method of depreciation to apply to its non-current assets. Once that decision has been made, the chosen method of depreciation should be applied **consistently from year to year**. However, IAS 16 requires that the depreciation **method should be reviewed** at least **each financial year end**. If there has been a significant change in the expected pattern of economic benefits from those assets, the method should be changed to suit this new pattern. When such a change in depreciation method takes place, the remaining carrying amount is depreciated under the new method, ie only current and future periods are affected; the change is not retrospective.

(IAS 16, para. 61)

So, in the previous activity, if the depreciation method was changed to straight line over two years from Year 4, the remaining balance (CA) $1,296 would be depreciated over two years giving a $648 depreciation charge per annum.

3 Accounting for depreciation

3.1 Dual effect

Depreciation has a dual effect which needs to be accounted for:

- It **reduces the value of the asset** in the statement of financial position.
- It is an **expense** in the statement of profit or loss.

The asset remains at its **original cost in the asset account**.

Two accounts are set up to record depreciation:

> **Dr Depreciation expense**
>
> **Cr Accumulated depreciation**

Depreciation will either be charged:

- On a monthly pro-rata basis ('proportionate depreciation in the year of purchase and disposal'); or
- A full year in the year of purchase and none in the year of disposal.

> ### Exam focus point
>
> The question will tell you which policy to apply.

3.2 Accumulated depreciation

The accumulated depreciation account is used to provide for the reduction in value of the asset.

It reduces the original cost of the asset on the statement of financial position. (The balance on the account is offset against the cost account for the corresponding asset.)

Note. The cost account and the accumulated depreciation accounts are always two separate ledger accounts.

A separate accumulated depreciation account is kept for each class of asset (eg motor vehicles, buildings, plant and machinery).

Activity 6: Accounting for depreciation

Using the information in Activity 5, show:

(a) The journal entry which would have been written at the end of the first year.

Dr [   ]   Cr [   ]

(b) The treatment of depreciation for all years in the relevant ledger accounts

(c) The relevant statement of profit or loss and statement of financial position extracts for each year

Solution

(b)

MACHINE COST (SOFP)

	$		$

DEPRECIATION EXPENSE (SPL)

	$		$

	$			$
	___			___

ACCUMULATED DEPRECIATION (SOFP)

	$			$
	___			___
	___			___
	___			___
	___			___
	___			___

(c)

Statement of profit or loss (extracts)

	Year 1	Year 2	Year 3
	$	$	$
Expenses			
Depreciation			

Statement of financial position (extracts)

		Cost	Accumulated depreciation	Net Book Value
		$	$	$
Year 1	Machine			
Year 2	Machine			
Year 3	Machine			

Exam focus point

If you are expected to use the reducing balance method in the exam, you will be given the percentage rate to apply; you will not have to calculate it.

If an exam question gives you the purchase date of a non-current asset which is part way through an accounting period, you should generally assume that depreciation should be calculated in this way as a 'part-year' amount, unless the question states otherwise.

4 Disposal of non-current assets

4.1 Profit or loss on disposal

When a non-current asset is disposed of, its carrying amount (CA) needs to be removed from the statement of financial position.

The sales proceeds received are unlikely to be exactly the same as the asset's carrying amount (CA) and so a profit or loss on disposal will arise.

If:

Sales proceeds > CA = profit on disposal

Sales proceeds < CA = loss on disposal

This is not a 'true' profit or loss, but rather a book adjustment to reflect the fact that the depreciation charged over the asset's life was not completely accurate.

4.2 Accounting treatment

Everything to do with the disposal is transferred to a disposal account.

Step 1   Remove the cost of the asset:

Dr   Disposal account

Cr   Non-current asset

Step 2   Remove the accumulated depreciation charged to date:

Dr   Accumulated depreciation

Cr   Disposal account

Step 3   Account for the sales proceeds:

Dr   Cash

Cr   Disposal account

Step 4   Balance off the disposal account to find the profit or loss on disposal.

A **gain** on disposal is shown in the **statement of profit or loss as sundry income**, a **loss** as an **expense**.

Note. Steps 1 and 2 have effectively transferred the CA of the asset to the disposal account.

Activity 7: Disposal

A machine costing $26,000 with accumulated depreciation of $24,000 is sold for $3,000. No depreciation is charged in the year of disposal.

Required

Calculate the profit or loss on disposal and state the double entry required to record the disposal.

[   ] on disposal $ [   ]

Disposal of machine

Dr [   ] $ [   ]

Cr [   ] $ [   ]

Remove accumulated depreciation

Dr [   ] $ [   ]

Cr [   ] $ [   ]

Account for the cash received

Dr [   ] $ [   ]

Cr [   ] $ [   ]

4.3 Part exchange allowance

Instead of receiving sales proceeds as cash, a part exchange allowance could be offered against the cost of a replacement asset.

The part exchange allowance is calculated as: cost of new asset – any cash paid.

The gain or loss on part exchange is calculated as: part exchange allowance – carrying amount of old asset.

The journal entry that would be used to record the new asset in a part exchange is:

Dr New asset account (cost of new asset)

Cr Disposal account (part exchange allowance)

Cr Bank (cash paid)

The disposal of the old asset would be recorded as normal.

Activity 8: Part exchange

Simon has a car that he purchased for $35,000 and which has accumulated depreciation of $25,000.

He decides to buy a new car and trade in his current car. The new car costs $40,000 and he pays cash of $32,000.

Required

What is the profit or loss on disposal?

O   Profit on disposal $2,000

O   Profit on disposal $8,000

O   Loss on disposal $3,000

O   Loss on disposal $2,000

5   Revaluations

IAS 16 allows entities to revalue non-current assets to fair value.

When a non-current asset is revalued, depreciation is charged on the revalued amount, with excess depreciation being transferred between the revaluation surplus and retained earnings. Excess depreciation is the difference between the old depreciation charge and the new depreciation charge. This will be looked at in more detail in the company accounts chapters of this Workbook.

Essential reading

See Chapter 8 of the Essential reading for more detail about revaluations.

The Essential reading is available as an Appendix of the digital edition of the Workbook.

5.1 Revaluations – steps and accounting treatment

When an asset is revalued, the following steps need to be followed:

Step 1 Adjust cost account to revalued amount

Dr Non-current asset cost (SOFP)

Cr Revaluation surplus (SOFP)

Step 2 Remove the accumulated depreciation to date because the asset has not fallen in value.

Dr Accumulated depreciation (SOFP)

Cr Revaluation surplus (SOFP)

Depreciation should now be based on the revalued amount.

The amount in the revaluation surplus is the difference between the new revalued amount and the carrying amount of the asset prior to the revaluation.

Activity 9: Revaluation

A building costing $100,000 on which depreciation of $20,000 has been charged is to be revalued to $150,000.

Required

Show the double entry to record the revaluation and make the postings to the ledger accounts.

Solution

Dr Non-current asset building [   ] $ [   ]

Dr Accumulated depreciation $ [   ]

Cr Revaluation surplus $ [   ]

BUILDING (SOFP)

	$		$
Balance b/d	100,000		

ACCUMULATED DEPRECIATION (SOFP)

	$		$
		Balance b/d	20,000
			–

REVALUATION RESERVE (SOFP)

	$		$

	$		$

Activity 10: Depreciation after revaluation

A building with a useful life of 20 years was purchased for $100,000 five years ago. The building is to be revalued to $150,000 at the start of the financial year with no change in the remaining useful life.

Required

What is the new depreciation charge for the year?

- ○ $7,500
- ○ $10,000
- ○ $5,000
- ○ $8,333

5.2 Disposal of a revalued non-current asset

The disposal of a revalued non-current asset is accounted for in exactly the same way as disposal of an asset that has not been revalued, using the same proforma to calculate profit or loss on disposal:

Proceeds	$X
Less: CA	$(X)
Profit/loss on disposal	X

However, any balance in the revaluation surplus is transferred to retained earnings on disposal of the revaluated asset.

Activity 11: Profit or loss on disposal

Imagine that the building in the previous activity was sold one year after revaluation for $170,000.

Required

Calculate the profit or loss on disposal.

Solution

6 Depreciation revisited

Depreciation is charged to allocate the wearing out of an asset (depreciable amount) to the statement of profit or loss over its useful life.

There are two main depreciation methods available:

- Straight line
- Reducing balance

The useful life and residual value of an item of property, plant and equipment should be reviewed at least every financial year end and, if expectations are significantly different from previous estimates, the depreciation charge for current and future periods should be revised.

This is achieved by writing the carrying amount (less the new residual value) off over the asset's revised remaining useful life.

Activity 12: Change in residual value and useful life

1.1.X1	Asset cost $40,000
	Estimated useful life: five years
	Residual value $5,000

| 1.1.X3 | Total useful life revised to four years |
| | Residual value revised to $4,000 |

Required

What is the depreciation charge for the year ended 31 December 20X3?

- O $11,000
- O $5,500
- O $6,000
- O $7,000

6.1 Review of depreciation method

The depreciation method should be reviewed at least every financial year end and, if there has been a significant change in the expected pattern of the asset's use, the method should be changed.

This is achieved by writing the net book amount off over the remaining useful life, using the revised method.

Activity 13: Change of depreciation method

1.1.X1	Asset cost $40,000
	Residual value $1,500
	Useful life five years
	Depreciation 25% reducing balance

1.1.X3   Change depreciation method to straight line

Required

What is the depreciation charge in the year ended 31 December 20X3?

Solution

7 Disclosure in financial statement

IAS 16 requires a reconciliation of the opening and closing carrying amounts of non-current assets to be given in the financial statements.

The disclosure requirements in IAS 16 are extensive and include both numerical and narrative disclosures. The financial statements should show a reconciliation of the carrying amount of non-current assets at the beginning and end of the period. The reconciliation should show the movement on the non-current asset balance and include the following:

- Additions
- Disposals
- Increases/decreases from revaluations
- Reductions in carrying amount
- Depreciation
- Any other movements

(IAS 16, para. 73)

The following format is commonly used.

Property, plant and equipment note

	Total	Land and buildings	Plant and equipment
	$	$	$
Cost or valuation			
At 1 January 20X4	50,000	40,000	10,000
Revaluation surplus	12,000	12,000	–

	Total	Land and buildings	Plant and equipment
	$	$	$
Additions in year	4,000	–	4,000
Disposals in year	(1,000)	–	(1,000)
At 31 December 20X4	65,000	52,000	13,000
Depreciation			
At 1 January 20X4	16,000	10,000	6,000
Charge for year	4,000	1,000	3,000
Eliminated on disposals	(500)	–	(500)
At 31 December 20X4	19,500	11,000	8,500
Carrying amount			
At 31 December 20X4	45,500	41,000	4,500
At 1 January 20X4	34,000	30,000	4,000

As well as the reconciliation above, the financial statements should disclose the following.

(a) An accounting policy note should disclose the measurement bases used for determining the amounts at which depreciable assets are stated, along with the other accounting policies.

(b) For each class of property, plant and equipment:

- Depreciation methods used

- Useful lives or the depreciation rates used

- Gross amount of depreciable assets and the related accumulated depreciation at the beginning and end of the period (IAS 16, para. 73)

(c) For revalued assets:

- Effective date of the revaluation

- Whether an independent valuer was involved

- Carrying amount of each class of property, plant and equipment that would have been included in the financial statements had the assets been carried at cost less depreciation

- Revaluation surplus, indicating the movement for the period and any restrictions on the distribution of the balance to shareholders (IAS 16, para. 77)

Activity 14: Carrying amount

Consider the following questions regarding carrying amount.

Required

1 In a statement of financial position prepared in accordance with IAS 16, what does the carrying amount represent?

2 In a set of financial statements prepared in accordance with IAS 16, is it correct to say that the carrying amount figure in a statement of financial position cannot be greater than the market (net realisable) value of the partially used asset as at the reporting date? Explain your reasons for your answer.

Solution

Chapter summary

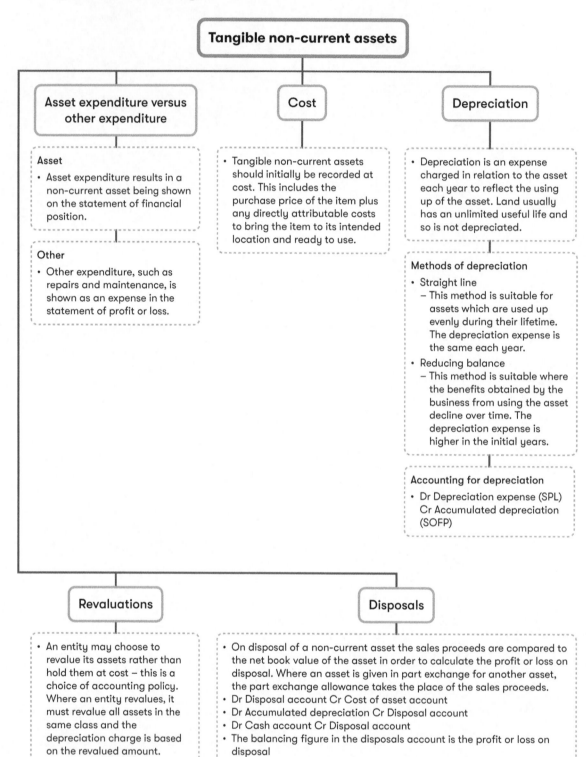

Tangible non-current assets

Asset expenditure versus other expenditure

Asset
- Asset expenditure results in a non-current asset being shown on the statement of financial position.

Other
- Other expenditure, such as repairs and maintenance, is shown as an expense in the statement of profit or loss.

Cost
- Tangible non-current assets should initially be recorded at cost. This includes the purchase price of the item plus any directly attributable costs to bring the item to its intended location and ready to use.

Depreciation
- Depreciation is an expense charged in relation to the asset each year to reflect the using up of the asset. Land usually has an unlimited useful life and so is not depreciated.

Methods of depreciation
- Straight line
  - This method is suitable for assets which are used up evenly during their lifetime. The depreciation expense is the same each year.
- Reducing balance
  - This method is suitable where the benefits obtained by the business from using the asset decline over time. The depreciation expense is higher in the initial years.

Accounting for depreciation
- Dr Depreciation expense (SPL) Cr Accumulated depreciation (SOFP)

Revaluations
- An entity may choose to revalue its assets rather than hold them at cost – this is a choice of accounting policy. Where an entity revalues, it must revalue all assets in the same class and the depreciation charge is based on the revalued amount.

Disposals
- On disposal of a non-current asset the sales proceeds are compared to the net book value of the asset in order to calculate the profit or loss on disposal. Where an asset is given in part exchange for another asset, the part exchange allowance takes the place of the sales proceeds.
- Dr Disposal account Cr Cost of asset account
- Dr Accumulated depreciation Cr Disposal account
- Dr Cash account Cr Disposal account
- The balancing figure in the disposals account is the profit or loss on disposal

Knowledge diagnostic

1. Non-current assets

Asset expenditure results in a non-current asset being shown on the statement of financial position. Other expenditure, such as repairs and maintenance, is shown as an expense in the statement of profit or loss.

2. Initial recognition

Tangible non-current assets should initially be recorded at cost. This includes the purchase price of the item plus any directly attributable costs to bring the item to its intended location and make it ready for use.

3. Depreciation

Depreciation is an expense charged in relation to the asset each year to reflect the using up of the asset.

Land usually has an unlimited useful life and so is not depreciated.

4. Methods of depreciation

Depreciation is usually calculated on a straight line or reducing balance basis.

5. Straight line method

This method is suitable for assets which are used up evenly during their lifetime. The depreciation expense is the same each year.

6. Reducing balance depreciation

This method is suitable where the benefits obtained by the business from using the asset decline over time. The depreciation expense is higher in the initial years.

7. Accounting for depreciation

Depreciation is recorded by way of a journal entry. The expense is recorded as a debit entry and reduces profit. The credit is made to the accumulated depreciation account and reduces the carrying value of the asset in the statement of financial position.

8. Disposal of non-current assets

On disposal of a non-current asset, the sales proceeds are compared to the carrying amount of the asset in order to calculate the profit or loss on disposal. Where an asset is given in part exchange for another asset, the part exchange allowance takes the place of the sales proceeds.

9. Revaluations

An entity may choose to revalue its assets rather than hold them at cost. This is a choice of accounting policy. Where an entity revalues, it must revalue all assets in the same class and the depreciation charge is based on the revalued amount.

10. Depreciation revisited

If an entity changes the method of depreciation used from straight line to reducing balance (or vice versa) or revises the useful life/residual value of an asset, it should write off the asset's carrying amount using the revised method or useful life/residual value.

Further study guidance

Question practice

Now try the following from the Further question practice bank (available in the digital edition of the workbook):

Questions 34 to 39

Activity answers

Activity 1: Idea generation

Land and buildings

Plant and equipment

Motor vehicles

Furniture and fittings

Computer equipment

Activity 2: Asset or expense

(1) Asset

(2) Expense

(3) Asset: The legal fees associated with the purchase of a property may be added to the purchase price and classified as an asset. The cost of the property in the statement of financial position of the business will then include the legal fees.

(4) Asset: The additional storage capacity is enhancing an existing non-current asset.

(5) Expense

(6) Asset income

(7) Sales income

(8) Asset

(9) Asset: If customs duties are borne by the purchaser of the non-current asset, they may be added to the cost of the machinery and classified as asset expenditure.

(10) Asset: If carriage costs are paid for by the purchaser of the non-current asset, they may be included in the cost of the non-current asset and classified as asset expenditure.

(11) Asset: Installation costs of a non-current asset are also added to the non-current asset's cost and classified as asset expenditure.

(12) Expense

Activity 3: Costs

The correct answer is: $20,700

The cost capitalised should include the purchase price ($20,000) plus all directly attributable costs (delivery and installation).

The cost of the maintenance contract should be shown as an expense in the statement of profit or loss.

Activity 4: Straight line depreciation

Year	Cost	Accumulated depreciation	Carrying Amount (CA)
	$	$	$
1	2,500	750	1,750
2	2,500	1,500	1,000
3	2,500	2,250	250

Working

Depreciation charge

$$\text{Depreciation charge} = \frac{\$2,500 - \$250}{3 \text{ years}} = \$750 \text{ per annum}$$

Activity 5: Reducing balance depreciation

Year	CA b/d	Depreciation rate	Depreciation expense	Accumulated depreciation	CA c/d
	$	$	$	$	$
1	(6,000 – 0)	× 40%	2,400	2,400	3,600
2	(6,000 – 2,400) 3,600	× 40%	1,440	3,840	2,160
3	(6,000 – 3,840) 2,160	× 40%	864	4,704	1,296

Unlike the straight-line method, this method produces a different depreciation figure each year and it will never reach a CA of zero.

Activity 6: Accounting for depreciation

(a) Dr | Depreciation expenses $2,400 | Cr | Accumulated depreciation $2,400 |

(b)

MACHINE COST (SOFP)

	$		$
Cash	6,000	Balance c/d	6,000
	6,000		**6,000**
Balance b/d	6,000		

DEPRECIATION EXPENSE (SPL)

	$		$
Year 1 Accumulated depreciation	2,400	Year 1 SPL	2,400
Year 2 Accumulated depreciation	1,440	Year 2 SPL	1,440
Year 3 Accumulated depreciation	864	Year 3 SPL	864

ACCUMULATED DEPRECIATION (SOFP)

	$		$
Balance c/d	2,400	Year 1 Depreciation expense	2,400
		Balance b/d	2,400

BPP LEARNING MEDIA

	$		$
Balance c/d	3,840	Year 2 Depreciation expense	1,440
	3,840		**3,840**
		Balance b/d	3,840
Balance c/d	4,704	Year 3 Depreciation expense	864
	4,704		**4,704**

(c)

Statement of profit or loss (extracts)

	Year 1	Year 2	Year 3
	$	$	$
Expenses			
Depreciation	2,400	1,440	864

Statement of financial position (extracts)

		Cost	Accumulated depreciation	Net Book Value
		$	$	$
Year 1	Machine	6,000	2,400	3,600
Year 2	Machine	6,000	3,840	2,160
Year 3	Machine	6,000	4,704	1,296

Activity 7: Disposal

Profit on disposal $ 1,000

Disposal of machine

Dr Disposal account $ 26,000

Cr Machine cost account $ 26,000

Remove accumulated depreciation

Dr Accumulated depreciation $ 24,000

Cr Disposal account $ 24,000

Account for the cash received

Dr Cash $ 3,000

Cr Disposal account $ 3,000

Working

Profit or loss on disposal

Cost – accumulated depreciation = CA

$26,000 – $24,000 = $2,000

Proceeds – CA = profit or loss on disposal

$3,000 – $2,000 = $1,000 Profit

Activity 8: Part exchange

The correct answer is: Loss on disposal $2,000

Working

Profit or loss on disposal

Old car CA ($35,000 – $25,000) = $10,000

Part exchange allowance ($40,000 – $32,000) = $8,000

Loss on disposal ($8,000 – $10,000) = $2,000

Activity 9: Revaluation

Dr Non-current asset building ($150 – $100)	$50,000
Dr Accumulated depreciation	$20,000
Cr Revaluation surplus	$70,000

BUILDING (SOFP)

	$		$
Balance b/d	100,000		
Revaluation surplus	50,000	Balance c/d	150,000
	150,000		**150,000**
Balance b/d	150,000		

ACCUMULATED DEPRECIATION (SOFP)

	$		$
Revaluation reserve	20,000	Balance b/d	20,000
		Balance c/d	–
	20,000		**20,000**

REVALUATION RESERVE (SOFP)

	$		$
		Building	50,000
Balance c/d	70,000	Accumulated depreciation	20,000
	70,000		**70,000**
		Balance b/d	70,000

Prior to the revaluation, the building had a CA of $80,000 ($100,000 – $20,000).

The building is revalued to $150,000 which is an increase of $70,000 ($150,000 – $80,000).

Activity 10: Depreciation after revaluation

The correct answer is: $10,000

Revalued amount/remaining useful life

$150,000/15 years = $10,000 depreciation per annum

Activity 11: Profit or loss on disposal

Revalued amount	$150,000
Less: one year's depreciation	$(10,000)
CA at date of disposal	**$140,000**

Proceeds	$170,000
CA	$(140,000)
Profit on disposal	**$30,000**

Activity 12: Change in residual value and useful life

The correct answer is: $11,000

In years X1 and X2:

($40,000 – $5,000)/5 years = depreciation of £7,000 per annum

In years X3 and X4

CA at the start of X3: $40,000 – $7,000 – $7,000 = $26,000

New depreciation charge: ($26,000 – $4,000)/2 years = $11,000 per annum

Note. The useful life has been revised to four years in total, not four years remaining. Therefore, by the start of X3, the asset only had two years remaining.

Activity 13: Change of depreciation method

In the years X1 and X2:

X1: $40,000 × 25% = $10,000

X2: ($40,000 – $10,000) × 25% = $7,500

Note. Remember that the reducing balance method does not take into account residual value or useful life.

In years X3, X4 and X5:

CA at 1.1.X3: $40,000 – $10,000 – $7,500 = $22,500

Depreciation charge for X3, X4 and X5:

($22,500 – $1,500)/3 years = $7,000 per annum

Activity 14: Carrying amount

1   In simple terms, the carrying amount of an asset is the cost of an asset less the 'accumulated depreciation'; that is, all depreciation charged so far. It should be emphasised that the main purpose of charging depreciation is to ensure that profits are fairly reported. Thus depreciation is concerned with the statement of profit or loss rather than the statement of financial position. In consequence, the carrying amount figure in the statement of financial

position can be quite arbitrary. In particular, it does not necessarily bear any relation to the market value of an asset and is of little use for planning and decision making.

An obvious example of the disparity between carrying amount and market value is found in the case of buildings, which may be worth more than ten times as much as their carrying amount.

2   Carrying amount can in some circumstances be higher than market value (net realisable value). IAS 16 *Property, Plant and Equipment* states that the value of an asset cannot be greater than its 'recoverable amount'. However, 'recoverable amount' as defined in IAS 16 is the amount recoverable from further use. This may be higher than the market value.

This makes sense if you think of a specialised machine which could not fetch much on the second-hand market but which will produce goods which can be sold at a profit for many years.

9

Intangible non-current assets

Learning objectives

On completion of this chapter, you should be able to:

	Syllabus reference no.
Recognise the difference between tangible and intangible non-current assets.	D6(a)
Identify types of intangible assets.	D6(b)
Identify the definition and treatment of 'research costs' and 'development costs' in accordance with IFRSs.	D6(c)
Calculate amounts to be capitalised as development expenditure or to be expensed from given information.	D6(d)
Explain the purpose of amortisation.	D6(e)
Calculate and account for the charge for amortisation.	D6(f)
Draft the following disclosure notes – intangible assets.	F3(b)(i)

Exam context

Intangible non-current assets are a smaller part of the syllabus than tangible non-current assets; however, you should still expect this area to be tested. Questions are likely to focus on the difference between tangible and intangible assets, the accounting treatment for research and the capitalisation criteria for development expenditure. You should also be confident in calculating amortisation.

Chapter overview

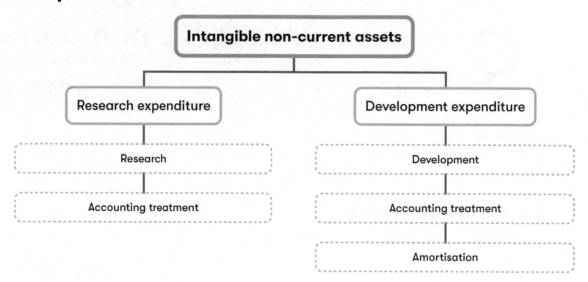

1 Intangible assets

'Intangible assets' means assets that literally cannot be touched, as opposed to tangible assets (such as plant and machinery) which have a physical existence. Intangible assets include goodwill (which we will study in the chapter on consolidated financial statements), intellectual rights (eg patents, performing rights and authorship rights), and research and development costs.

1.1 Accounting treatment

In accordance with IAS 38 *Intangible Assets*, intangible assets are capitalised in the accounts and amortised (another word for depreciation but referring specifically to intangible assets). Amortisation is intended to write off the asset over its useful life (under the accruals concept).

Illustration 1: Patent

A business buys a patent for $50,000. It expects to use the patent for the next ten years, after which it will be valueless. (A patent gives the owner the legal right to exclude others from using, making or selling an invention for a specified period. For example, if you invent a new product, a patent will stop others from copying your idea).

Required

What would the amortisation charge be?

Solution

Amortisation is calculated in the same way as for tangible assets:

(Cost – residual value)/estimated useful life

In this case, amortisation will be $5,000 per annum (50,000/10).

The double entry treatment is similar to that for depreciation. The entries for the amortisation calculated above will be:

Debit Amortisation account (statement of profit or loss) $5,000

Credit Accumulated amortisation account (statement of financial position) $5,000

2 Definitions

Intangible asset: "An intangible asset is an identifiable non-monetary asset without physical substance."

Research: "Research is original and planned investigation undertaken with the prospect of gaining new scientific or technical knowledge and understanding."

Development: "Development is the application of research findings or other knowledge to a plan or design for the production of new or substantially improved materials, devices, products, processes, systems or services prior to the commencement of commercial production or use."

Amortisation: "Amortisation is the systematic allocation of the depreciable amount of an intangible asset over its useful life."

Depreciable amount: "Depreciable amount is the cost of an asset, or other amount substituted for cost, less its residual value."

Useful life: "Useful life is:

- The period over which an asset is expected to be available for use by an entity; or
- The number of production or similar units expected to be obtained from the asset by an entity.'
  (IAS 38, para. 8)

The following are examples of intangible assets:

- Development expenditure
- Goodwill
- Concessions, patents, licences and trade marks

The syllabus only requires knowledge of the accounting treatment of research and development expenditure.

The difference between tangible and intangible non-current assets is that tangible assets have physical substance whereas intangible assets do not.

3 Research and development expenditure

Many companies, such as pharmaceutical companies, spend huge amounts on research and development every year in order to maintain or enhance their competitive position.

Companies need to account for these costs and, whilst the credit entry will be to either cash (if paid) or a current liability (if owed), the question remains as to where the debit entry should be shown.

The choices are:

- To debit the statement of profit or loss with an expense; or
- To debit the statement of financial position with an intangible non-current asset.

An intangible non-current asset should only be recorded when the entity is **confident** that the expenditure will **generate future profit**.

4 IAS 38 *Intangible Assets*

The standard gives examples of activities which might be included in either research or development, or which are neither but may be closely associated with both.

- **Research**
    - Activities aimed at obtaining new knowledge
    - The search for applications of research findings or other knowledge
    - The search for product or process alternatives
    - The formulation and design of possible new or improved product or process alternatives

    (IAS 38, para. 56)

- **Development**
    - The design, construction and testing of pre-production prototypes and models
    - The design of tools, jigs, moulds and dies involving new technology
    - The design, construction and operation of a pilot plant that is not of a scale economically feasible for commercial production
    - The design, construction and testing of a chosen alternative for new/improved materials

    (IAS 38, para. 59)

4.1 Components of R&D costs

R&D costs will include all costs that are **directly attributable to R&D activities**, or that can be allocated on a reasonable basis.

IAS 38 lists the costs which may be included in R&D, where applicable (note that selling costs are excluded).

- Salaries, wages and other employment related costs of personnel engaged in R&D activities
- Costs of materials and services consumed in R&D activities
- Depreciation of property, plant and equipment to the extent that these assets are used for R&D activities

- Overhead costs, other than general administrative costs, related to R&D activities; these costs are allocated on bases similar to those used in allocating overhead costs to inventories (see IAS 2 *Inventories*)
- Other costs, such as the amortisation of patents and licences, to the extent that these assets are used for R&D activities

5 Accounting treatment

5.1 Research costs

Research costs should be recognised as an expense in the period in which they are incurred (IAS 38, para. 54). They should not be recognised as an asset in a later period (IAS 38, para. 71).

5.2 Development costs

Development expenditure must be recognised as an intangible asset if, and only if, the business can demonstrate that all of the criteria in IAS 38 have been met (IAS 38, para. 57). The recognition criteria are as follows.

The entity must demonstrate:

- **P** – How the intangible asset will generate Probable future economic benefits (This is demonstrated by the existence of an external market or by how the asset will be useful to the business if it is to be used internally.)
- **I** – Its Intention to complete the intangible asset and use or sell it
- **R** – The availability of adequate technical, financial and other Resources to complete the development and to use or sell the intangible asset
- **A** – Its Ability to use or sell the intangible asset
- **T** – The Technical feasibility of completing the intangible asset so that it will be available for use or sale
- **E** – Its ability to measure reliably the Expenditure attributable to the intangible asset during its development (IAS 38, para. 57)

There is also an important point about the carrying amount of the asset and recoverability. The development costs of a project recognised as an asset should not exceed the amount that it is probable will be recovered from related future economic benefits, after deducting further development costs, related production costs, and selling and administrative costs directly incurred in marketing the product.

Exam focus point

The recognition criteria can be summarised by the mnemonic PIRATE which makes it easier to learn for your exam.

Activity 1: Research and development

Z Co incurred the following costs during the year ended 31 August 20X8:

(1) $20,000 on salaries for market research staff sent out to canvass drivers' opinions on a potential new car.

(2) $100,000 to purchase a machine to manufacture components for the new car. It has an estimated useful life of ten years.

(3) $25,000 on materials to manufacture a prototype and $50,000 on salaries relating to its design and manufacture. The new car is expected to go on sale in 20X9.

Required

How should each of the above items be shown in the financial statements for the year ended 31 August 20X8?

Solution

6 Amortisation of capitalised development expenditure

A tangible non-current asset, such as a machine, is capitalised and then depreciated over its useful life. This is to match the cost of the asset with the consumption of its economic benefits.

In the same way, the development expenditure must be spread on a systematic basis to reflect the pattern in which the related economic benefits are recognised.

This is called amortisation.

Amortisation should begin when the asset is ready for use.

It is an expense in the statement of profit or loss and is accounted for using the following entry:

Dr Amortisation expense (SPL)

Cr Accumulated amortisation (SOFP)

Activity 2: Research and development expenditure

Development Co incurs the following expenditure in years 20X1–20X5.

	Research	Development
	$	$
20X1	35,000	55,000
20X2	0	65,000
20X3	0	0
20X4	0	0
20X5	38,000	0

The development expenditure meets the IAS 38 criteria that require capitalisation ('PIRATE'). The item developed in 20X1 and 20X2 goes on sale on 1.1.X3 and it will be three years from then until any competitor is expected to have a similar product on the market.

Required

Show statement of profit or loss and statement of financial position extracts for the years 20X1–20X5 inclusive.

Solution

SPL (extracts)

	X1	X2	X3	X4	X5
	$	$	$	$	$
Expenses					
Research expenditure					
Amortisation of development expenditure					

SOFP (extracts)

	X1	X2	X3	X4	X5
	$	$	$	$	$
Non-current assets					
Development expenditure					
Amortisation					
NBV					

7 Disclosure in financial statements

The disclosure requirements in IAS 38 are extensive and include both numerical and narrative disclosures.

The financial statements should show a reconciliation of the carrying amount of intangible assets at the beginning and at the end of the period. The reconciliation should show the movement on intangible assets, including:

- Additions
- Disposals
- Reductions in carrying amount
- Amortisation
- Any other movements

(IAS 38, para. 118)

The following format is commonly used:

Intangible assets note

	Total	Development costs	Patents
	$	$	$
Cost			
At 1 January 20X4	40,000	30,000	10,000
Additions in year	19,000	15,000	4,000
Disposals in year	(1,000)	–	(1,000)
At 31 December 20X4	58,000	45,000	13,000
Amortisation			
At 1 January 20X4	11,000	5,000	6,000
Charge for the year	4,000	1,000	3,000
Eliminated on disposals	(500)	–	(500)
At 31 December 20X4	14,500	6,000	8,500
Carrying amount			
At 31 December 20X4	43,500	39,000	4,500
At 1 January 20X4	29,000	25,000	4,000

As well as the reconciliation above, the financial statements should also disclose the following:

(a) The financial statements should disclose the accounting policies for intangible assets that have been adopted.

(b) For each class of intangible assets (including development costs), disclosure is required of the following:

- The method of amortisation used

- The useful life of the assets or the amortisation rate used

- The gross carrying amount, the accumulated amortisation and the accumulated impairment losses as at the beginning and the end of the period

- The carrying amount of internally generated intangible assets

- The line item(s) of the statement of profit or loss in which any amortisation of intangible assets is included

(IAS 38, para. 118)

Activity 3: Tangible vs intangible non-current assets

Which of the following statements best describes the difference between tangible and intangible non-current assets?

O Tangible non-current assets are of a long-term nature; intangible non-current assets are of a short-term nature.

O Tangible non-current assets must be depreciated but intangible non-current assets should not be amortised.

O Tangible non-current assets are always recognised initially in the statement of financial position; intangible assets are always recognised initially in the statement of profit or loss.

O Tangible non-current assets are perceptible by touch; intangible non-current assets are not.

Activity 4: Amortisation

Which of the following statements best explains the purpose of amortisation of intangible non-current assets?

○ To show the true value of the intangible non-current assets in the statement of financial position.

○ To improve the profit figure in the year of purchase of the asset by spreading the cost of the asset's useful life.

○ To match the cost of the asset to the related economic benefits generated by the asset.

○ To record the replacement cost of an intangible asset in profit or loss.

Chapter summary

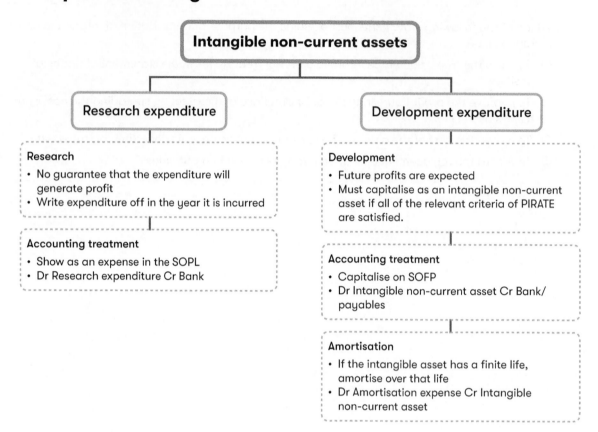

Intangible non-current assets

Research expenditure

Research
- No guarantee that the expenditure will generate profit
- Write expenditure off in the year it is incurred

Accounting treatment
- Show as an expense in the SOPL
- Dr Research expenditure Cr Bank

Development expenditure

Development
- Future profits are expected
- Must capitalise as an intangible non-current asset if all of the relevant criteria of PIRATE are satisfied.

Accounting treatment
- Capitalise on SOFP
- Dr Intangible non-current asset Cr Bank/ payables

Amortisation
- If the intangible asset has a finite life, amortise over that life
- Dr Amortisation expense Cr Intangible non-current asset

BPP LEARNING MEDIA

Knowledge diagnostic

1. Intangible assets

Intangible assets are non-current assets with no physical substance.

2. Research expenditure

Expenditure on research must always be written off in the period in which it is incurred (IAS 38, para. 54).

3. Development expenditure

If the criteria laid down by IAS 38 are satisfied, development expenditure must be capitalised as an intangible asset. If the criteria in IAS 38 are not satisfied, development expenditure must be written off in the period in which it is incurred.

4. Amortisation

If the intangible asset has a finite useful life, it should then be amortised over that life.

5. Disclosures

IAS 38 requires both numerical and narrative disclosures for intangible assets.

Further study guidance

Question practice

Now try the following from the Further question practice bank (available in the digital edition of the Workbook):

Questions 40 to 42

Activity answers

Activity 1: Research and development

(1) Market research would take place at an early stage in any development process. Its purpose is to gather information about whether there may be interest in a potential product. At this point in time, an entity cannot be certain that the expenditure will lead to profits and so the costs are research costs. $20,000 should be shown as an expense in the statement of profit or loss.

(2) A machine is a tangible, non-current asset and is accounted for under IAS 16 regardless of its use. The $100,000 should be capitalised as a tangible non-current asset and depreciated over its useful life of ten years.

(3) Material costs and design and manufacture salaries are part of the development process. They should be capitalised as an intangible non-current asset provided that all of the 'PIRATE' criteria are met.

The costs should be amortised in 20X9 once the car is available to be sold on the market.

Activity 2: Research and development expenditure

SPL (extracts)

	X1	X2	X3	X4	X5
	$	$	$	$	$
Expenses					
Research expenditure	35,000				38,000
Amortisation of development expenditure			40,000	40,000	40,000

SOFP (extracts)

	X1	X2	X3	X4	X5
	$	$	$	$	$
Non-current assets					
Development expenditure	55,000	120,000	120,000	120,000	120,000
Amortisation			(40,000)	(80,000)	(120,000)
NBV	**55,000**	**120,000**	**80,000**	**40,000**	**0**

Activity 3: Tangible vs intangible non-current assets

The correct answer is: Tangible non-current assets are perceptible by touch; intangible non-current assets are not

Tangible non-current assets have physical substance and intangible non-current assets do not. Statement one is incorrect because both tangible and intangible non-current assets are of a long-term nature. Statement two is incorrect because intangible non-current assets must be amortised if they have a finite useful life. Statement three is incorrect because some intangibles are initially recognised in the statement of financial position.

Activity 4: Amortisation

The correct answer is: To match the cost of the asset to the related economic benefits generated by the asset

The purpose of amortisation is to match the cost of the intangible non-current asset to the related economic benefits generated by the asset.

Skills checkpoint 2

Approach to multi-task questions (MTQs)

Overview

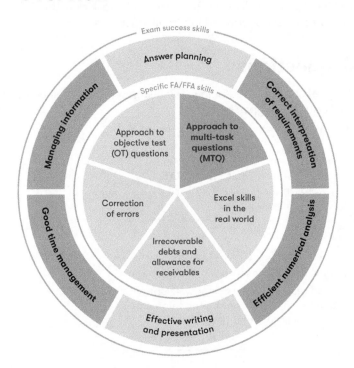

Introduction

The exam contains two sections. Section A consists of 35 objective test (OT) questions worth 2 marks each and Section B contains two multi-task questions worth 15 marks each. The multi-task questions test you understanding and application of financial accounting skills in more depth.

Multi-task questions

MTQs in Section B might ask you to prepare financial statements for a single entity or for a group of companies. There may also be some element of ratio calculation/interpretation. You may not always be required to prepare the full financial statement and may instead be asked to complete a partial statement. In this situation, there will be additional elements to the question.

You will complete the MTQs using a range of the following question types:

Question type	Explanation
Number entry (NE)	This question type requires you to type a numerical answer into a box. The unit of measurement (eg $ or $'000) will sit outside the box and if there are specific rounding requirements, these will be stated in the question.

Question type	Explanation
	Eg Q37 Task 4 of the specimen exam
Multiple response matching (MRM)	This question type requires you to select a response for a number of statements, often to identify whether the statements are true or false. You must provide a response for each statement. Eg Q37 Task 1 of the specimen exam
Drop down lists (DDL)	This question type requires you to select one answer from a drop-down list. Eg Q37 Task 5 of the specimen exam

The OT question skills discussed in Skills Checkpoint 1 will be useful in the multi-task questions. In this skills checkpoint, we will focus on the specific skills required in a multi-task question.

Approach to multi-task questions

A step-by-step technique for approaching MTQs is outlined below. Each step will be explained in more detail when we consider the different question types below.

> **STEP 1: Read the requirement first!**
> The requirement will be stated in bold text in the exam. Identify what you are being asked to do, any technical knowledge required and **what type of OT question** you are dealing with. Look for key words in the requirement such as "Which **TWO** of the following," or "Which of the following is **NOT**".

> **STEP 2: Apply your technical knowledge to the data presented in the question.**
> Work through calculations taking your time and read through each answer option with care. Ensure you double check information such as whether the opening and closing balances are debits or credits, whether any accounting has taken already taken place, dates and rates.

> **STEP 3: Answer the parts you know first.**
> Within each MTQ, there will be some easier parts and some parts you find more challenging. It is good for time management and your confidence to answer the parts you find easiest first. Normally parts that don't require calculations will be quickest and easiest to answer.

> **STEP 4: Answer all parts.**
> There is no penalty for an incorrect answer in ACCA exams; there is nothing to be gained by leaving an OT question unanswered. If you are stuck on a question, as a last resort, it is worth selecting the option you consider most likely to be correct and moving on. Make a note of the question, so if you have time after you have answered the rest of the questions, you can revisit it.

Exam success skills

The following questions are examples of the sorts of questions you could see in your exam. For these questions, we will also focus on the following exam success skills:

- **Managing information.** It is easy for the amount of information contained in a particular question to feel a little overwhelming. Active reading is a useful technique to avoid this. This involves focusing on the requirements first on the basis that, until you have done this, the detail in the question will have little meaning and will seem more intimidating.
- **Correct interpretation of requirements.** Identify from the requirement the type of question you are addressing; you will see three different question types in the MTQ. Ensure you perform plenty of question practice of MTQs when preparing for your exam so you understand the common requirements and know how to tackle them. Pay particular attention to number entry questions as they may tell you to give your answer to a certain number of decimal places or to the nearest thousand dollars.
- **Efficient numerical analysis.** There is a lot of information in the MTQs and a number of questions will require you to calculate balances for inclusion in calculations or the financial statements. It is important that you can identify and interpret the correct information from the scenario and work through calculations efficiently.
- **Good time management.** Complete all questions in the time available. Each MTQ in Section B is worth 15 marks and should be allocated 18 minutes. Each task will have an allocated number of marks and you should work on the basis of 1.2 minutes per mark to allocate time to each task.

Skills activity

The following is from the extra MTQs available on the ACCA website. We shall use this question to explain the approach that should be taken when tackling MTQs.

MTQ – Gasta Co

On 1 January 20X3, Gasta Co acquired 75% of the share capital of Erica Co for $1,380,000. The retained earnings of Erica Co at that date were $480,000. Erica Co's share capital has remained unchanged since the acquisition.

The following draft statements of financial position for the two companies have been prepared at 31 December 20X9.

	Gasta Co	Erica Co
	$'000	$'000
Investment in Erica Co	1,380	0
Other assets	4,500	2,400
Total assets	5,880	2,400
Equity share capital	2,000	1,000
Retained earnings	2,040	660
Liabilities	1,840	740
Total equity and liabilities	5,880	2,400

The non-controlling interest (NCI) was valued at $450,000 as at 1 January 20X3.

1   **Complete the following to determine the goodwill arising on acquisition.**

$'000

Value of investment at acquisition

Investment in Erica Co held by Gasta Co   (1)

	$'000
(2)	(1)
Total value of investment at acquisition **(A)**	1,830
Fair value of Erica Co's net assets at acquisition	
Equity chare capital	(3)
(4)	(3)
Total fair value of Erica Co's net assets at acquisition **(B)**	1,480
Goodwill at acquisition expressed as a formula	(5)

Pull down list 1
- 1,380
- 450
- 1,000
- 660
- 480

Pull down list 2
- Investment in Erica Co held by Gasta Co
- NCI at acquisition
- Other assets
- Retained earnings
- Equity share capital

Pull down list 3
- 660
- 740
- 480
- 2,400
- 1,000

Pull down list 4

Equity share capital

Retained earnings

Other assets

Liabilities

Pull down list 5
- A + 100% of B
- A – 75% of B
- A – 100% of B
- A + 75% of B

2   **Are each of the following statements relating to consolidation correct?**

	Yes/No
The process of consolidation results in a single separate legal entity.	
Goodwill is recalculated using the most recent fair values at each reporting period end.	
NCI will always feature within consolidated financial statements.	

3 **Select the formula which correctly calculates NCI as at 31 December 20X9, in accordance with IFRS 10** *Consolidated Financial Statements.*

A   25% of net assets at 31 December 20X9

B   Fair value of NCI at acquisition + 25% of post-acquisition profits

C   Fair value of NCI at acquisition + 25% of retained earnings as at 31 December 20X9

4 **Calculate the following figures which will be reported in Gasta's consolidated statement of financial position as at 31 December 20X9.**

	S'000
	1,380
Investment	
Other assets	6,900
Share capital	2,000
Retained earnings	2,175
Non-controlling interest	495
Liabilities	2,580

We will now work through each of the questions considering the steps introduced in the approach to the answering MTQs.

STEP 1 Read the requirement first! The requirement will be stated in bold text in the exam. Identify what you are being asked to do, any technical knowledge required and what type of OT question you are dealing with. Look for key words in the requirement such as 'Which TWO of the following...' and 'Which of the following is NOT...'

Reading each requirement will help you to identify which task you feel most comfortable with before you begin to work through the scenario in detail.

STEP 2 Answer parts you know first. Within each MTQ, there will be some easier parts and some parts you find more challenging. It is good for time management and your confidence to answer the parts you find easiest first. Normally, parts that do not require calculations will be quickest and easiest to answer.

STEP 3 Answer all parts. There is no penalty for an incorrect answer in FIA/ACCA exams so there is nothing to be gained by leaving part of an MTQ unanswered. If you are stuck on a question, as a last resort, it is worth selecting the option you consider most likely to be correct, and moving on. Make a note of the question so, if you have time after you have answered the rest of the questions, you can revisit it.

There are several number entry questions in this MTQ and these are often the most difficult as there are not any options presented. If you are struggling with a number entry question, it is still worth a sensible guess using the numbers within the question.

STEP 4   Work through calculations taking your time, and read through each answer option with care. Ensure you double check information such as whether the opening and closing balances are debits or credits, whether any accounting has already taken place, dates and rates.

 This is particularly true in a question such as this that contains a lot of information. Make sure you are clear what date the financial statements are at, what the date of consolidation is and what information relates to the parent and what information relates to the subsidiary.

Let's work through each of the tasks in detail:

Task 1 – Complete the following to determine the goodwill arising on acquisition

This question tests your technical knowledge of the goodwill calculation. It contains a range of number entry and drop-down list questions and is worth 4.5 marks in total.

Goodwill is calculated as follows:

	$'000	Explanation
Investment in Erica Co	1,380	This is shown in the statement of financial position of Gasta Co as the investment in Erica. You need to be careful to select the correct amount when scrolling through the options in the dropdown list.
NCI at acquisition	450	This information is given in the question. Again, you need to be careful to select the correct amount.
Total value of investment	1,830	The clue is in the word 'total' in the description. This should indicate to you that you are adding the investment and NCI. This was a number entry question. Make sure you enter your answer in $'000 in accordance with the column heading.
Share capital	1,000	The question states that the share capital has not changed since acquisition, so we take the amount from Erica Co's statement of financial position.
Retained earnings	480	There were two parts to this. You had to correctly select retained earnings from a dropdown list and select the correct amount. You should know that the net assets of the subsidiary at acquisition is equal to the equity, hence why retained earnings is added to share capital. The amount is at the date of acquisition; a common error is to use the retained earnings as shown in the statement of financial position which is incorrect.
Goodwill at acquisition	350	You are asked to identify the correct formula from the dropdown list. Remember what goodwill represents. It is the excess value in a company, so the amount paid over and above its net assets.

Task 2 – Are each of the following statements relating to consolidation correct?

This is a multiple response matching question in which you are asked to consider each statement and determine whether they are correct.

Within such a question, you should read each statement in isolation and determine your answer independently of other answers. Make sure you select yes or no for each statement.

	Yes/No	Explanation
The process of consolidation results in a single separate legal entity	No	Consolidated financial statements present a group as if it was a separate entity. It does not create a separate entity as such. You need to read this question carefully.
Goodwill is recalculated using the most recent fair values at each	No	Goodwill is calculated at the date of acquisition and is not updated at each

	Yes/No	Explanation
reporting period end		reporting period end.
NCI will always feature within consolidated financial statements	No	NCI is only needed when a subsidiary is not 100% owned by the parent.

Do not be distracted by the fact that all answers are 'No'. There will not necessarily be a range of different answers in this type of question.

Task 3 – Select the formula that correctly calculates NCI as at 31 December 20X9

This is a simple multiple-choice question, as was discussed in Skills Checkpoint 1.

The question tests your understanding of how to calculate non-controlling interest at the year-end date. It is calculated as NCI at acquisition + NCI share of the post-acquisition profits of the subsidiary. In this type of question, all answer options are intended to be plausible, so you will need to carefully read each option and consider the differences between the options and what is consistent with your understanding. Even if you think you identify the correct answer quite quickly, you should read the incorrect answers and justify to yourself why they are incorrect.

Task 4 – Calculate the figures for inclusion in Gasta Co's consolidated statement of financial position as at 31 December 20X9

This is another task that has a mix of number entry and drop-down list questions. It tests your ability to prepare the consolidated statement of financial position. The consolidated statement of financial position is calculated by taking the statement of financial position of the parent + subsidiary +/- any adjustments. In this case, you need to take account of adjustments for goodwill and non-controlling interest of post- acquisition profits of the subsidiary. The correct answer is as follows:

	$'000	Explanation
Investment	0	The investment in the subsidiary is eliminated on consolidation and is therefore not included in the consolidated statement of financial position.
Other assets	6,900	Other assets is the sum of the parent and subsidiary and therefore requires a simple calculation ($4,500 + $2,400).
Share capital	2,000	Share capital is that of the parent company only.
Retained earnings	2,175	Retained earnings is probably the most difficult balance to calculate. Retained earnings is calculated as the retained earnings of the parent ($2,040) plus the group share (75%) of the post-acquisition profits of the subsidiary. The post-acquisition profits of the subsidiary is calculated by comparing the retained earnings of the subsidiary at the period end with the retained earnings at the date of acquisition (660 – 480). The calculation is therefore $2,040 + (75% × ($660 – $480)) = $2,175.
Non-controlling interest	495	Non-controlling interest is the NCI at acquisition

	$'000	Explanation
		($450) plus the NCI share of the post-acquisition profits of the subsidiary. The calculation is therefore $450 + (25% × ($660 – $480)) = $495.
Liabilities	2,580	Liabilities is the sum of the parent and subsidiary and therefore requires a simple calculation ($1,840 + $740.

Exam success skills diagnostic

Every time you complete a few questions, use the diagnostic below to assess how effectively you demonstrated the exam success skills in answering the questions. The table has been completed below for the 'mini exam' activity to give you an idea of how to complete the diagnostic.

Exam success skills	Your reflections/observations
Managing information	Did you read the requirements for each task first? Did you actively read the scenario for each task making a note of relevant points? Eg In the calculation of goodwill, did you pick up the retained earnings at the date of acquisition rather than at the reporting date?
Correct interpretation of requirements	Did you identify the correct technical knowledge needed to answer each requirement? Did you identify what the task was asking you to do? Eg when identifying whether each statement regarding consolidation was correct, did you address each of the statements?
Good time management	Did you manage to answer the entire task in 18 minutes? There is a lot of information to get through and it is easy to overrun on number entry questions. Keep an eye on the clock and move on at the end of the allocated time.
Efficient numerical analysis	How did you deal with the volume of numerical information in this question? Did you remember the formula for the key calculations and were you able to use your calculator to perform the calculations efficiently?
Most important action points to apply to your next question.	

Summary

Being able to answer multi-task questions is very important for the FA/FFA exam. Key skills to focus on throughout your studies will include:

- Always reading the requirements first to identify what each task asks you to do and in which order you would like to answer the questions.
- Actively reading the scenario, making a note of key data needed to answer each task.
- Answering the tasks in a sensible order, dealing with any easier discursive style questions first.

10

Accruals and prepayments

Learning objectives

On completion of this chapter, you should be able to:

	Syllabus reference no.
Understand how the matching concept applies to accruals and prepayments.	D7(a)
Identify and calculate the adjustments needed for accruals and prepayments in preparing financial statements.	D7(b)
Illustrate the process of adjusting for accruals and prepayments in preparing financial statements.	D7(c)
Prepare the journal entries and ledger entries for the creation of an accrual or prepayment.	D7(d)
Understand and identify the impact on profit and net assets of accruals and prepayments.	D7(e)

Exam context

Accruals and prepayments are key accounting adjustments and you should expect them to be tested in the exam. You may be asked to calculate the statement of financial position amount for accruals and prepayments and/or the relevant expense that would be shown in the statement of profit or loss. Alternatively, you may be asked to determine the appropriate journal entries to record accruals and prepayments. Note that questions on accruals and prepayments may well relate to both income and expenses.

Chapter overview

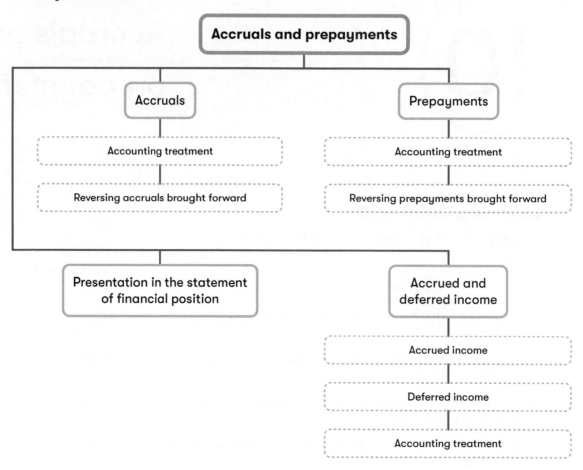

Accruals and prepayments

- Accruals
  - Accounting treatment
  - Reversing accruals brought forward
- Prepayments
  - Accounting treatment
  - Reversing prepayments brought forward

- Presentation in the statement of financial position
- Accrued and deferred income
  - Accrued income
  - Deferred income
  - Accounting treatment

1 Introduction

This chapter is designed to enable you to apply accounting concepts and principles in relation to the calculation of, and adjustments for, accruals and prepayments.

IAS 1 requires financial statements to be prepared on an **accruals basis.** This is so that transactions and events are recognised when they occur (even if the resulting cash receipts and payments occur in a different period) and they are recorded in the accounting records and reported in the financial statements of the period to which they relate.

Accrual accounting is also required in reporting financial performance by the IASB's *Conceptual Framework*.

We have already seen that the gross profit for a period should be calculated by matching sales and the cost of goods sold. In the same way, the profit for the year for a period should be calculated by charging the expenses which relate to that period. For example, in preparing the statement of profit or loss of a business for a period of, say, six months, it would be appropriate to charge six months' expenses for rent and local taxes, insurance costs and telephone costs, etc.

Expenses might not be paid for during the period to which they relate. For example, a business rents a shop for $20,000 per annum and pays the full annual rent on 1 April each year. If we calculate the profit of the business for the first six months of the year 20X7, the correct charge for rent in the statement of profit or loss is $10,000, even though the rent paid is $20,000 in that period. Similarly, the rent charge in the statement of profit or loss for the second six months of the year is $10,000, even though no rent was actually paid in that period.

1.1 Accruals

> **Accrued expenses (accruals):** Accrued expenses (accruals) are expenses which are charged against the profit for a particular period, even though they have not yet been paid for. They are shown in the statement of financial position as a liability.

You may have noticed that accruals and trade payables are separate balances within liabilities on a statement of financial position.

Accruals generally represent liabilities to pay for goods or services that have been received in a period, but that have not yet been invoiced for by the suppliers. Although most accrued expenses are for purchases of goods or services from suppliers, accruals can cover all types of expense, eg bonuses for the year ended 20X4 paid to staff in 20X5, should be accrued for in 20X4.

Trade payables are liabilities to pay for goods or services received in a period that have been invoiced for by the suppliers.

Illustration 1: Accrued expenses

Fred prepares accounts to 31 December each year. On 1 January 20X8, he pays a telephone bill of $60 which relates to the period October–December 20X7.

Required

How should the telephone bill received in January 20X8 be treated in the financial statements of 20X7?

Solution

Although the payment does not go through the cash book until 20X8, this expense must be included in the accounts for the year ended 31 December 20X7, as it was incurred during this period.

1.2 Prepayments

> **Prepayments:** Prepayments are payments which have been made in one accounting period, but should not be charged against profit until a later period, because they relate to that later period. They are shown in the statement of financial position as an asset.

Illustration 2: Prepayments

On 20 December 20X7, Fred pays for insurance on his business premises for the 12 months commencing 1 January 20X8.

Required

How should the insurance payment made in December 20X7 be treated in the financial statements of 20X7?

Solution

Although the payment was made in 20X7, the expense should not appear in the accounts for 20X7. The accounts for 20X7 will show a prepayment in current assets in the SOFP for the full amount of the insurance cost and the expense will be recorded in the SPL in 20X8.

2 Accounting treatment

2.1 Year-end adjustments

Adjustments for accruals and prepayments tend to occur at the end of the year and are made by way of a journal entry. The required entries are:

Accruals

Dr Expense (SPL)

Cr Accruals (SOFP)

Prepayments

Dr Prepayments (SOFP)

Cr Expenses (SPL)

2.2 Presentation in the statement of financial position

Accruals:

Sub-heading under 'current liabilities'.

Prepayments:

Sub-heading under 'current assets'.

Transaction	Debit	Credit	Description
Accrual	Expense	Liability	Expense incurred in period, not recorded
Prepayment	Asset	(Reduction in) Expense	Expense recorded in period, not incurred until next period

Activity 1: Year-end adjustments

Fiona set up a business on 1 January 20X7. Her cash payments for the year to 31 December 20X7 included:

	Date paid	Amount	Period
		$	
Electricity	10.3.X7	96	Two months to 28 February 20X7
	12.6.X7	120	Quarter to 31 May 20X7
	14.9.X7	104	Quarter to 31 August 20X7
	10.12.X7	145	Quarter to 30 November 20X7
Rent			
	1.2.X7	375	Three months to 31 March 20X8
	6.4.X7	1,584	12 months to 31 March 20X8

Note. On 6 March 20X8, Fiona received an electricity bill for $168 for the quarter to 28 February 20X8.

Required

1 Calculate the amount of any accruals/prepayments at the end of the year.

2 Calculate the expense incurred by Fiona for electricity and rent for the year ended 31 December 20X7.

3 State the journal entry required for the year-end adjustments.

Solution

Activity 2: Ledger accounts

Using the figures from the previous activity, complete the necessary entries in Fiona's ledger accounts as at 31 December 20X7.

Solution

ELECTRICITY EXPENSE (SPL)

	$		$
10.3.X7 Cash	96		
12.6.X7 Cash	120		
14.9.X7 Cash	104		
10.12.X7 Cash	145		

RENT EXPENSE (SPL)

	$		$
1.2.X7 Cash	375		
6.4.X7 Cash	1,584		

ACCRUALS (SOFP)

	$		$

PREPAYMENTS (SOFP)

	$		$

3 Reversing out accruals and prepayments

3.1 Problem

Using the figures from the previous activities, what is Fiona's rent expense for the year to 31 December 20X8, assuming that on 10 April 20X8, she paid rent of $1,740 for the 12 months commencing 1 April 20X8?

Her cash expense for rent in 20X8 would be $1,740. However, this relates to nine months of 20X8 and three months of 20X9.

Therefore, Fiona only needs to include nine months of the $1,740 payment – $1,305.

But, she now only has nine months' rent expense for a 12-month period.

To correct this, Fiona will need to reverse the opening prepayment of $396 for January, February and March 20X8.

This will leave a rent expense for 20X8 of $1,701 ($1,305 + $396).

3.2 Double entry

Accruals and prepayments brought forward at the start of the year must be reversed.

Reverse the opening prepayment:

Dr Rent expense	$396
Cr Prepayments	$396

Reverse the opening accrual:

Dr Accruals	$56
Cr Electricity expense	$56

3.3 Approach to questions

There are four steps to follow:

(a) Reverse opening accrual/prepayment
(b) Post cash paid during the year
(c) Post closing accrual/prepayment
(d) Balance off the accounts

Activity 3: Reversing accruals

In 20X8, Fiona paid the following electricity bills:

Date paid	Amount	Period
	$	
12.3.X8	168	Quarter to 28 February 20X8
9.6.X8	134	Quarter to 31 May 20X8
12.9.X8	118	Quarter to 31 August 20X8
12.12.X8	158	Quarter to 30 November 20X8

During March 20X9, Fiona received an electricity bill for $189 for the quarter to 28 February 20X9.

Required

Calculate the electricity expense and accrual for the year ended 31 December 20X8 and complete the ledger accounts.

Solution

ELECTRICITY EXPENSE (SPL)

	$		$
12.3.X8 Cash	168		
9.6.X8 Cash	134		
12.9.X8 Cash	118		
12.12.X8 Cash	158		
	——		——

ACCRUALS (SOFP)

	$		$
		1.1.X8 Balance b/d	56
	——		——

Activity 4: SPL expense

The following transactions related to Colin's gas expense ledger account for the year ended 31 December 20X8:

	$
Prepayment b/d	1,100
Cash paid	10,800
Accrual c/d	1,300

Required

What amount should be charged to the statement of profit or loss in the year ended 31 December 20X8 for gas?

- O $10,800
- O $13,200
- O $10,600
- O $11,000

Activity 5: Profit and net assets

At the year end, a company decides that an accrual of $750 is required for telephone expenses and a prepayment of $200 for insurance. There are no brought forward accruals or prepayments on these expense accounts.

Required

What impact will the recording of this accrual and prepayment have on profit and net assets?

○ A decrease in profit of $550; a decrease in net assets of $550.

○ An increase in profit of $550; an increase in net assets of $550.

○ A decrease in profit of $950; an increase in net assets of $950.

○ An increase in profit of $950; a decrease in net assets of $950.

Exam focus point

You will almost certainly have to deal with accruals and/or prepayments in the exam. Make sure you understand the logic, then you will be able to do whatever question comes up.

3.4 Effect on profit and net assets

The previous activity tested your knowledge of the link between accruals, prepayment, profit and net assets.

You may find the following table a useful summary of the effects of accruals and prepayments.

	Effect on income and expenses	Effect on profit	Effect on assets/liabilities
Accruals	Increases expenses	Reduces profit	Increases liabilities
Prepayments	Reduces expenses	Increases profit	Increases assets

4 Accrued income and deferred income

Accruals and prepayments relate to when expenses are paid in arrears or advance. Income may also be received in arrears or advance.

4.1 Accrued income

This relates to when income has been earned during the accounting period but not invoiced or received.

Accrued income is shown as an asset in the SOFP.

Illustration 3: Accrued income

Jenny owns a property which she rents out for $3,000 per quarter. The property was occupied all year; however, Jenny only received $9,000 in rent because she forgot to send out the final invoice of the year.

As the property was let for 12 months, Jenny's statement of profit or loss should show income of $12,000 (4 × $3,000) as this is what she has earned.

She will therefore need to accrue the 'missing' income of $3,000 as a year-end journal and also show a receivable for 'rent in arrears'.

Required

What accounting adjustment should Jenny make at the year end?

Solution

The adjustment is:

Dr	Rent in arrears (SOFP Current Asset)	$3,000
Cr	Rental income (SFP Income)	$3,000

4.2 Deferred income

This relates to when income is received in advance of it being earned.

Deferred income is shown as a liability in the SOFP.

Illustration 4: Deferred income

Ben has a year end of December and rents out his property for $1,000 per month. His tenant pays on time each month and, during December 20X7, paid Ben $2,000 as he would be away when the January 20X8 payment was due.

Ben has received income of $13,000 but only $12,000 of this relates to the current year. He must therefore remove $1,000 of income from this year's accounts because it relates to next year. A liability will also be shown for 'rent in advance'.

Required

What entries should Ben post to the ledger accounts at the year end?

Solution

Dr	Rental income (SPL decrease income)	$1,000
Cr	Rent in advance (SOFP current liabilities)	$1,000

4.3 Approach to questions

The approach for accrued income and deferred income is exactly the same as for accruals and prepayments.

There are four steps to follow:

(a) Reverse opening rent in arrears/advance

(b) Post cash received during the year

(c) Post closing rent in arrears/advance

(d) Balance off the accounts

Activity 6: Rental income

A company receives rent from a large number of properties. The total received in the year ended 30 June 20X7 was $962,400.

The following were amounts of rent in advance and in arrears at 30 June 20X6 and 30 June 20X7:

	30 June 20X6	30 June 20X7
Rent received in advance	$57,400	$62,400
Rent in arrears (all subsequently received)	$42,400	$36,800

Required

What amount of rental income should appear in the company's statement of profit or loss for the year ended 30 June 20X7?

O $973,000

O $921,800

O $1,003,000

O $951,800

Chapter summary

Accruals and prepayments

Accruals

Accounting treatment
- Accruals increase expenses and are shown as a liability on the statement of financial position at the year end.
- Dr Expense (SPL) Cr Accruals (SOFP)

Reversing accruals brought forward
- Dr Accruals (SOFP) Cr Expense (SPL)

Prepayments

Accounting treatment
- Prepayments reduce expenses and are an asset on the statement of financial position.
- Dr Prepayments (SOFP) Cr Expense (SPL)

Reversing prepayments brought forward
- Dr Expense (SPL) Cr Prepayments (SOFP)

Presentation in the statement of financial position

- Current assets - prepayments
- Current liabilities - accruals

Accrued and deferred income

Accrued income
- Income owing at the year end.

Deferred income
- Income received in advance.

Accounting treatment
- Accrued income: Dr Accrued income Cr Income
- Deferred income: Dr Income Cr deferred income

Knowledge diagnostic

1. IAS 1

An entity should produce its financial statements using the accruals basis in accordance with IAS 1 and the *Conceptual Framework*.

Accruals are made when expenses are paid in **arrears**, whereas **prepayments** arise when expenses are paid for in **advance.**

2. Accruals

Accruals increase expenses and are shown as a liability on the statement of financial position at the year end.

3. Prepayments

Prepayments reduce expenses and are an asset on the statement of financial position.

4. Reversing out accruals and prepayments

Accruals and prepayments from the previous year are reversed at the beginning of the next accounting period so that the current year expense is correct.

5. Accrued income

An entity will accrue income where it has earned the income during the period but not yet invoiced for it. This will increase income and be shown as a receivable at the year end.

6. Deferred income

Where an entity has received income in advance of it being earned, it should be deferred to the following period. This will reduce income and be shown as a payable at the year end.

7. Double entry summary for accruals and prepayments

Accruals adjustment:

> Dr Expense (SPL)
> Cr Accruals (SOFP)

Prepayments adjustment:

> Dr Prepayments (SOFP)
> Cr Expense (SPL)

Approach to questions (four steps):

(1) Reverse opening accrual/prepayment:

> Accruals:
> Dr Accruals (SOFP)
> Cr Expense (SPL)
>
> Prepayments:
> Dr Expense (SPL)
> Cr Prepayments (SOFP)

(2) Post cash paid during the year.

(3) Post closing accrual/prepayment.

(4) Balance off the ledger accounts.

Further study guidance

Question practice

Now try the following from the Further question practice bank (available in the digital edition of the Workbook)

Questions 43 to 46

Activity answers

Activity 1: Year-end adjustments

1   Electricity accrual $56 December 20X7

Rent prepayment $396 (January to March 20X8)

2   Electricity expense: Cash paid $465 ($96 + $120 + $104 + $145) + $56 (1/3 × $168) = $521

Note. The SPL should show the expense for the 12 months to 31 December 20X7, therefore we need to include one month of the invoice received after the year end as Fiona had only paid 11 months of electricity by the end of the year.

Rent expense: Cash paid $1,959 (375 + 1,584) − $396 (3/12 × $1,584) = $1,563

Fiona has paid 13 months of rent in 20X7; therefore, three months need to be removed so leave 12 months of expense in the SPL. January, February and March 20X8 need to be removed.

3   **Accrual**

Dr Electricity expense $56

Cr Accruals $56

Prepayment

Dr Prepayments $396

Cr Rent expense $396

Activity 2: Ledger accounts

ELECTRICITY EXPENSE (SPL)

	$		$
10.3.X7 Cash	96		
12.6.X7 Cash	120		
14.9.X7 Cash	104		
10.12.X7 Cash	145		
31.12.X7 Accruals	56	31.12.X7 to SPL	521
	521		**521**

RENT EXPENSE (SPL)

	$		$
1.2.X7 Cash	375	31.12.X7 Prepayments	396
6.4.X7 Cash	1,584	31.12.X7 to SPL	1,563
	1,959		**1,959**

ACCRUALS (SOFP)

	$		$
31.12.X7 Balance c/d	56	31.12.X7 Electricity	56
		1.1.X8 Balance b/d	56

PREPAYMENTS (SOFP)

	$		$
31.12.X7 Rent	396	Balance c/d	396
1.1.X8 Balance c/d	396		

Activity 3: Reversing accruals

ELECTRICITY EXPENSE (SPL)

	$		$
12.3.X8 Cash	168	1.1.X8 Accrual reversed	56
9.6.X8 Cash	134	31.12.X8 to SPL	585
12.9.X8 Cash	118		
12.12.X8 Cash	158		
31.12.X8 Accrual (1/3 × $189)	63		
	641		641

ACCRUALS (SOFP)

	$		$
1.1.X8 Accrual reversed	56	1.1.X8 Balance b/d	56
31.12.X8 Balance c/d	63	31.12.X8 Electricity accrual	63
	119		119
		1.1.X9 Balance b/d	63

Activity 4: SPL expense

The correct answer is: $13,200

A prepayment that is brought forward from the previous year will be an expense in the current year.

An accrual at the end of the current year will be an expense in the current year.

Therefore, the gas expense for the year will be $13,200 ($1,100 + $10,800 + $1,300).

Activity 5: Profit and net assets

The correct answer is: A decrease in profit of $550; a decrease in net assets of $550.

The accrual will increase expenses by $750 but the prepayment will decrease expenses by $200, resulting in a net increase in expenses of $550 ($750 – $200). A $550 increase in expenses will result in profit decreasing by $550.

The accrual is a liability and the prepayment is an asset. When netted off, this results in a net liability of $550 ($750 liability less $200 asset). This net liability will result in a decrease in net assets of $550.

Activity 6: Rental income

The correct answer is: $951,800

To answer this question, you need to think about it logically and say to yourself, does this income relate to 20X7 or a different year? If it relates to a different year, we do not want to include it in the income figure for the year.

	$
Cash received in the year	962,400
Rent received in 20X6 in advance for 20X7 (relates to 20X7)	57,400
Rent received in 20X7 in arrears from 20X6 (relates to 20X6)	(42,400)
Rent received in 20X7 in advance for 20X8 (relates to 20X8)	(62,400)
Rent received in 20X8 in arrears for 20X7 (relates to 20X7)	36,800
Total income for the year	**951,800**

This can be shown in ledger account format as follows:

RENTAL INCOME (SPL)

	$		$
Accrued income b/d and reversed	42,400	Deferred income b/d and reversed	57,400
To SPL (balancing figure)	951,800	Cash received	962,400
Deferred income c/d	62,400	Accrued income c/d	36,800
	1,056,600		**1,056,600**

Note. Rent received in advance results in deferred income (a liability); rent in arrears results in accrued income (an asset).

11

Provisions and contingencies

Learning objectives

On competition of this chapter, you should be able to:

	Syllabus reference no.
Understand the definition of 'provision', 'contingent liability' and 'contingent asset'.	D9(a)
Distinguish between and classify items as provisions, contingent liabilities or contingent assets.	D9(b)
Identify and illustrate the different methods of accounting for provisions, contingent liabilities and contingent assets.	D9(c)
Calculate provisions and changes in provisions.	D9(d)
Account for the movement in provisions.	D9(e)
Report provisions in the final accounts.	D9(f)

Exam context

Questions on this area are likely to focus on identifying when a provision or contingent liability should be made or disclosed in the financial statements. You may also be required to calculate a provision.

Chapter overview

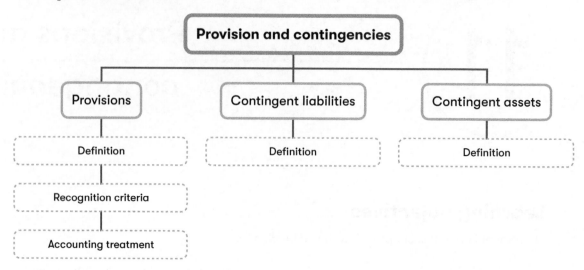

1 IAS 37 *Provisions, Contingent Liabilities and Contingent Assets*

Before the introduction of IAS 37, there was little guidance on when a provision must and must not be made.

This caused problems as entities tended to choose to make and then release provisions in order to smooth out profits, rather than making a provision where they had an obligation to incur expenditure.

IAS 37 aims to prevent this from happening in the future.

> **Exam focus point**
>
> This subject area is often highlighted by the ACCA examining team as being one of the least well answered. The examining team commented that students were not learning key definitions and displayed an inability to apply the theory to practical situations. Make sure you read this material thoroughly and work through the examples and questions to cement your understanding.

2 Provisions

> **Provision:** A provision is a liability of uncertain timing or amount.

IAS 37 distinguishes provisions from other liabilities, such as trade payables and accruals. This is on the basis that for a provision there is **uncertainty** about the timing or amount of the future expenditure.

While uncertainty is clearly present in the case of certain accruals, the uncertainty is generally much less than for provisions.

2.1 Recognition

IAS 37 states that a provision should be **recognised** (which simply means 'included') as a liability in the financial statements when **all three** of the following conditions are met.

- An entity has a **present obligation** (legal or constructive) as a result of a **past event**.
- It is **probable** (ie more than 50% likely) that a **transfer of economic benefits** will be required to settle the obligation.
- A **reliable estimate** can be made of the obligation.

(IAS 37, para. 14)

2.2 Legal obligation

A legal obligation usually arises out of a contract or a piece of legislation.

Illustration 1: Legal obligation

Grass Co sells lawnmowers and offers a one-year warranty on all models.

Required

How should Grass Co account for the warranty?

Solution

Once Grass Co sells a lawnmower (the past event), it has a legal obligation to repair any defects according to the warranty agreement.

It should therefore make an estimate of the probable costs of repair and make a provision for this amount in its financial statements.

2.3 Constructive obligation

A constructive obligation arises through past behaviour and actions where the entity has raised a **valid expectation** that it will carry out a particular action.

 Illustration 2: Constructive obligation

Seed Co also sells lawnmowers. It does not offer a warranty on its products; however, it has a reputation for making reasonable repairs free of charge to lawnmowers bought from the business. Customers buying from Seed Co all expect to receive this benefit.

Required

How should Seed Co account for the potential repairs?

Solution

Here, no warranty is offered and so Seed Co does not have a legal obligation. Its past actions however have created a constructive obligation. Based on past experience, the customers of Seed Co would expect to receive a free repair if something should go wrong with their new lawnmower. It should also therefore make a provision for the probable costs of repairs.

2.4 Probable outflow

Probable is defined as more likely than not to occur. This can be interpreted as a greater than a 50% chance of occurring.

For example, using the previous example of warranties, Seed Co will know from past experience that this will have to pay out on some of the warranties sold with the lawn mowers. Therefore, we would say that it is **more likely than not** that they will have to pay something as a result of these warranties. At the year end, they will make a best estimate of the amount based on past experience.

2.5 Measurement

The amount recognised as a provision should be the **best estimate** of the expenditure required to settle the present obligation at the end of the reporting period.

The estimates will be determined by the **judgement** of the entity's management supplemented by the **experience of similar transactions**. If the provision relates to just one item, the best estimate of the expenditure will be the most likely outcome.

When a provision involves a lot of items (for example, a warranty provision, where each item sold has a warranty attached to it), then the provision is calculated using the **expected value approach**. Using the expected value approach, the obligation is estimated by weighting all possible outcomes by their associated probabilities (IAS 37, paras. 36–39). This is illustrated in the following example.

 Activity 1: Warranty provision

Parker Co sells goods with a warranty under which customers are covered for the cost of repairs of any manufacturing defect that becomes apparent within the first six months of purchase. The company's past experience and future expectations indicate the following pattern of likely repairs.

% of goods sold	Defects	Cost of repairs $m
75	None	0
20	Minor	1.0
5	Major	4.0

Required

What should the warranty provision in Parker Co's financial statements be?

Solution

2.6 Double entry

The provision represents both a cost to the business and a potential liability:

Dr   Expense (SPL)

Cr   Provision (SOFP)

The required provision will be reviewed at each year end and increased or decreased as necessary.

To **increase** a provision:

Dr   Expense (SPL)

Cr   Provision (SOFP)

To **decrease** a provision:

Dr   Provision (SOFP)

Cr   Expense (SPL)

Activity 2: Provisions

Grass Co is reviewing its warranty obligations. Based on sales during 20X7, it has established that if all lawnmowers sold required minor repairs, this would cost $1 million whereas if major repairs were required, this would cost $6 million.

Grass Co expects that 75% of lawnmowers will have no faults, 20% will need minor repairs and 5% major repairs.

Required

What provision should be made in 20X7 and what accounting entry is needed to record it?

What entry should be made in 20X8 assuming the provision required then is $0.75m?

What entry should be made in 20X9 assuming the provision required then is $0.3m?

Solution

2.7 Disclosure for provisions

Disclosures required in the financial statements for provisions fall into two parts:

- Disclosure of details of the change in carrying amount of a provision from the beginning to the end of the year, including additional provisions made, amounts used and other movements.

- For each class of provision, disclosure of the background to the making of the provision and the uncertainties affecting its outcome, including:

   - A brief description of the nature of the provision and the expected timing of any resulting outflows relating to the provision

   - An indication of the uncertainties about the amount or timing of those outflows. Where necessary to provide adequate information, an entity shall disclose the major assumptions made concerning future events.

   - The amount of any expected reimbursement relating to the provision and whether any asset that has been recognised for that expected reimbursement

(IAS 37, paras. 84–85)

Below is an example of how a provision might be disclosed in the notes to the financial statements:

Note X: Provisions

	Warranty provision
	$'000
At 1 April 20X6	150
Increase in the provision during the year	60
Amounts used during the year	(75)
At 31 March 20X7	**135**

The warranty provision relates to estimated claims on those products sold in the year ended 31 March 20X7 which come with a three-year warranty. The expected value method is used to provide a best estimate. It is expected that the expenditure will be incurred in the next three years.

3 Contingent liabilities

A contingent liability is an uncertain liability that does not meet the three criteria for recognising a provision.

IAS 37 defines a contingent liability as the following:

> **Contingent liability:** A **possible obligation** that arises from past events and whose existence will be confirmed only the occurrence or non-occurrence of one or more uncertain future event not wholly within the control of the entity; or
>
> A **present obligation** that arises from past events but is not recognised because:
>
> * It is **not probable** that an outflow of economic resources will be required to settle the obligation; or
> * The amount of the obligation **cannot be measured** with sufficient reliability.
>
> Contingent liabilities should be **disclosed** in the notes unless probability of an outflow of resources embodying economic benefits is remote.

As a general rule, **probable** means more than 50% likely. If an obligation is probable, it is not a contingent liability – instead, a provision is needed. If the obligation is remote, it does not need to be disclosed in the accounts.

Contingent liabilities should not be recognised in financial statements but they should be disclosed in the notes (IAS 37, paras. 27–28).

Illustration 3: Contingent liability

Company A has entered into an agreement to act as guarantor on a bank loan taken out by Mr Smith. Mr Smith is a financially secure individual, and the directors are of the opinion that the chances of him defaulting on the loan are slim.

Required

How should Company A account for this guarantee?

Solution

Company A has **a present obligation** (it is **legally obliged** to honour the guarantee).

However, as the likelihood of Company A having to pay out under the guarantee is **not probable** then **no provision** for the liability should be made.

Instead, the guarantee should be **disclosed in the notes as a contingent liability** (unless considered **remote**, in which case it should be ignored altogether).

4 Provision or contingent liability

4.1 Decision tree

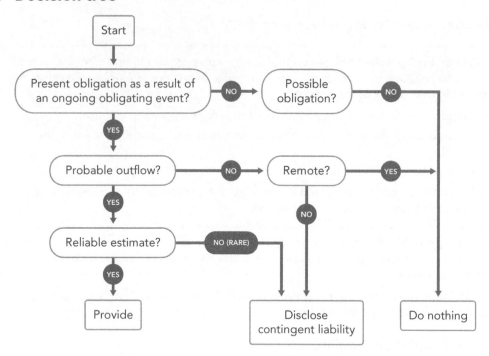

> ### Exam focus point
>
> If you learn this flow chart, you should be able to deal with most questions you are likely to meet in the exam.

Activity 3: Accounting treatment

Edward Co owns a chain of supermarkets. In the year ended 30 September 20X5, a customer slipped on a spilt yoghurt in one of the supermarkets and was seriously injured. Prior to the year end, the customer began legal proceedings seeking damages from Edward Co. Edward Co's lawyers have stated that there is a 30% chance that Edward Co will win the case and, if they lose, damages of $50,000 are likely.

Required

Which of the following is the correct accounting treatment for the legal proceedings in the financial statements for the year ended 30 September 20X5?

- ○ Edward Co should neither provide for nor disclose the legal proceedings.
- ○ Edward Co should provide for the expected cost of the damages of $50,000.
- ○ Edward Co should provide for an expected cost of $35,000.
- ○ Edward Co should disclose a contingent liability of $50,000.

Activity 4: Provisions and contingencies (1)

After a wedding in 20X0, ten people became seriously ill, possibly as a result of food poisoning from products sold by Callow Co. Legal proceedings have started seeking damages from Callow but it disputes liability. Up to the date of approval of the financial statements for the year to 31 December 20X0, Callow Co's lawyers advise that it is probable that it will not be found liable. However, when Callow prepares the financial statements for the year to 31 December 20X1, its lawyers advise that, owing to developments in the case, it is probable that it will be found liable.

Required

What is the required accounting treatment at 31 December 20X0 and at 31 December 20X1?

Solution

Activity 5: Provisions and contingencies (2)

An oil company causes environmental contamination in the course of its operations, but cleans up only when required to do so under the laws of the country in which it is operating. One country in which it has been operating for several years has up to now had no legislation requiring cleaning up. However, there is now an environmental lobby in this country. At the date of the company's year end, it is virtually certain that a draft law requiring clean up of contaminated land will be enacted very shortly. The oil company will then be obliged to deal with the contamination it has caused over the past several years.

Required

What accounting treatment is required at the year end?

Solution

---

5 Disclosure

A contingent liability should NOT be recognised in the financial statements. Instead, it is disclosed in the notes (IAS 37, paras 27–28).

The required disclosures are:

- A brief description of the nature of the contingent liability
- An estimate of its financial effect
- An indication of the uncertainties that exist
- The possibility of any reimbursement

(IAS 37, para. 86)

6 Contingent assets

Contingent assets: IAS 37 defines a contingent asset as:

"[A] possible asset that arises from past events and whose existence will be confirmed only by the occurrence or non-occurrence of one or more uncertain future events not wholly within the control of the entity" (para. 10).

A contingent asset must **not be recognised in the accounts**, but should be **disclosed** if it is **probable** that the economic benefits associated with the asset will flow to the entity (IAS 37, paras. 33–34).

A brief description of the contingent asset should be provided, along with an estimate of its likely financial effect (IAS 37, para. 89).

If the flow of economic benefits associated with the contingent asset becomes virtually certain, it should then be recognised as an asset in the statement of financial position, as it is no longer a contingent asset (IAS 37, para. 33).

For example, a company expects to receive damages of $100,000 and this is virtually certain. An asset is recognised. If, however, the company expects to probably receive damages of $100,000, a contingent asset is disclosed.

6.1 Disclosures for contingent assets

Where an inflow of economic benefits is probable, an entity should disclose:

- A brief description of its nature; and where practicable
- An estimate of the financial effect.

(IAS 37, para. 89)

Chapter summary

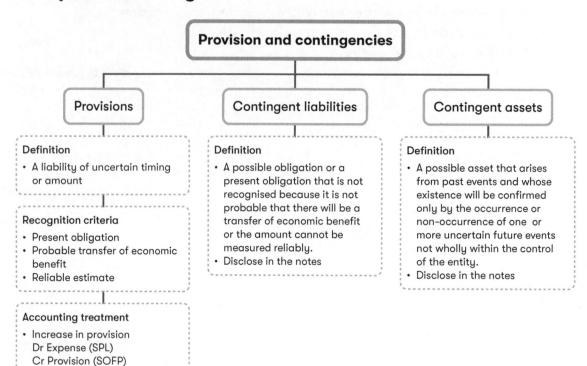

Provision and contingencies

Provisions

Definition
- A liability of uncertain timing or amount

Recognition criteria
- Present obligation
- Probable transfer of economic benefit
- Reliable estimate

Accounting treatment
- Increase in provision
  Dr Expense (SPL)
  Cr Provision (SOFP)
- Decrease in provision
  Dr Provision (SOFP)
  Cr Expense(SPL)

Contingent liabilities

Definition
- A possible obligation or a present obligation that is not recognised because it is not probable that there will be a transfer of economic benefit or the amount cannot be measured reliably.
- Disclose in the notes

Contingent assets

Definition
- A possible asset that arises from past events and whose existence will be confirmed only by the occurrence or non-occurrence of one or more uncertain future events not wholly within the control of the entity.
- Disclose in the notes

Knowledge diagnostic

1. Provision

A provision is a liability of uncertain timing or amount.

2. Accounting treatment

Increase in provision:

Dr Expense (SPL)

Cr Provision (SOFP)

Decrease in provision:

Dr Provision (SOFP)

Cr Expense (SPL)

3. Recognition

A provision should be recognised when **all three** of the following conditions are met:

- An entity has a **present obligation** (legal or constructive) as a result of a past event.
- It is **probable** (ie more than 50% likely) that a transfer of economic benefits will be required to settle the obligation.
- A **reliable estimate** can be made of the obligation.

4. Contingent liability

A contingent liability is a possible obligation that arises from past events and whose existence will be confirmed only by the occurrence or non-occurrence of one or more uncertain future events not wholly within the control of the entity; or a present obligation that arises from past events but is not recognised because:

- It is not probable that a transfer of economic benefits will be required to settle the obligation; or
- The amount of the obligation cannot be measured with sufficient reliability.

5. Contingent assets

A contingent asset is a possible asset that arises from past events and whose existence will be confirmed only by the occurrence or non-occurrence of one or more uncertain future events not wholly within the control of the entity.

Further study guidance

Question practice

Now try the following from the Further question practice bank (available in the digital edition of the Workbook):

Questions 51 to 54

Activity answers

Activity 1: Warranty provision

Parker Co should make a provision on the basis of the expected cost of the repairs under warranty.

The expected cost is calculated as (75% × $nil) + (20% × $1.0m) + (5% × $4.0m) = $400,000.

Parker Co should include a provision of $400,000 in the financial statements.

Activity 2: Provisions

20X7:

A provision should be made using expected values:

($1m × 20%) + ($6m × 5%) = $0.5m

Dr Warranty cost expense (SPL)	$0.5m	
Cr Provisions (SOFP)		$0.5m

20X8

In 20X8, the provision needs to **increase** by $0.25m ($0.75m – $0.5m).

Dr Warranty cost expense (SPL)	$0.25m	
Cr Provisions (SOFP)		$0.25m

20X9

In 20X9, the provision needs to **decrease** by $0.45m ($0.75m – $0.3m).

Dr Provisions (SOFP)	$0.45m	
Cr Warranty cost expense (SPL)		$0.45m

Activity 3: Accounting treatment

The correct answer is: Edward Co should provide for the expected cost of the damages of $50,000.

There is a present legal obligation; the outflow is probable because the lawyers believe that there is more than a 50% chance of Edward Co losing the case. As there is a single obligation, the provision should be measured at the most likely outcome of $50,000.

Activity 4: Provisions and contingencies (1)

At 31 December 20X0

On the basis of the evidence available when the financial statements were approved, there is no obligation as a result of past events. No provision is recognised. The matter is disclosed as a contingent liability unless the probability of any transfer is regarded as remote.

At 31 December 20X1

On the basis of the evidence available, there is a present obligation. A transfer of economic benefits in settlement is probable.

A provision is recognised for the best estimate of the amount needed to settle the present obligation.

Activity 5: Provisions and contingencies (2)

At the year end, there is a present obligation as a result of a past obligating event. Because it is 'virtually certain' that the law will be enacted, the past contamination becomes an obligating event. It is highly probable that an outflow of economic resources will be required to settle this. A provision should therefore be made of the best estimate of the costs involved.

12 Irrecoverable debts and allowances

Learning objectives

On competition of this chapter, you should be able to:

	Syllabus reference no.
Identify the benefits and costs of offering credit facilities to customers.	D8(b)
Understand the purpose of an aged receivables analysis.	D8(c)
Understand the purpose of credit limits.	D8(d)
Prepare the bookkeeping entries to write off an irrecoverable debt.	D8(e)
Record an irrecoverable debt recovered.	D8(f)
Identify the impact of irrecoverable debts on the statement of profit or loss and on the statement of financial position.	D8(g)
Prepare the bookkeeping entries to create and adjust an allowance for receivables.	D8(h)
Illustrate how to include movements in the allowance for receivables in the statement of profit or loss and how the closing balance of the allowance should appear in the statement of financial position.	D8(i)

Exam context

Questions on this topic are likely to require you to perform calculations dealing with writing off debts, adjusting for cash subsequently received and adjusting the allowance for receivables. You will also need to be able to determine the balances to be shown in the statement of profit or loss and the statement of financial position. This area could feature as part of the accounts preparation multi-task question in Section B.

Chapter overview

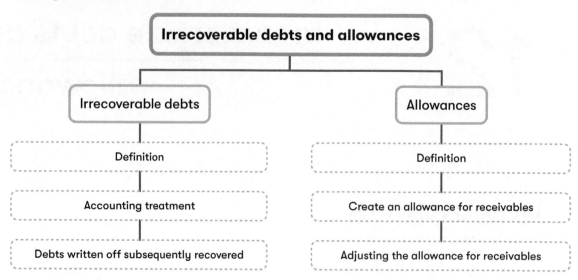

1 Introduction

Very few businesses expect to be paid immediately in cash, unless they are retail businesses on the high street. Most businesses buy and sell to one another on credit terms. This has the **benefit** of allowing businesses to keep trading without having to provide cash 'up front'. So a business will allow credit terms to customers and receive credit terms from its suppliers. Ideally, a business wants to receive money from its customers as quickly as possible, but delay paying its suppliers for as long as possible. This can lead to problems.

Most businesses aim to control such problems by means of **credit control**. A customer will be given a credit limit, which cannot be exceeded (compare an overdraft limit or a credit card limit). If an order would take the customer's account over its credit limit, it will not be actioned until a payment is received to reduce the customer's outstanding balance.

Another tool in credit control is the **aged receivables analysis**. An aged receivables analysis is a report of all receivables analysed by customer and by age of the receivable, eg balances outstanding for 30 days, 60 days and 90+ days. If a balance has been outstanding for a long period of time, it may indicate that a customer is unable to pay. Most credit controllers will have a system of chasing up payment for long outstanding invoices.

Customers might fail to pay, perhaps out of dishonesty or because they have gone bankrupt and cannot pay. Customers in another country might be prevented from paying by the unexpected introduction of foreign exchange control restrictions by their country's government during the credit period. Therefore, the costs of offering credit facilities to customers can include:

- Interest costs of an overdraft, if customers do not pay promptly
- Costs of trying to obtain payment
- Court costs

For one reason or another, a business might decide to give up expecting payment and to write the debt off.

1.1 Irrecoverable debts

Irrecoverable debts are specific debts owed to a business which it decides are never going to be paid. They are written off as an expense in the statement of profit or loss.

> **Irrecoverable debts:** An irrecoverable (or 'bad') debt is a debt which is definitely not expected to be paid. An irrecoverable debt could occur when, for example, a customer has gone bankrupt.

1.1.1 Accounting treatment

To begin with, let us recap the ledger entries when a sale on credit is made to a customer.

Dr Trade receivables (SOFP)

Cr Sales (SPL)

All being well, a few weeks later, the customer will pay the debt and cash will be received, at which point the double entry is:

Dr Cash (SOFP)

CR Trade receivables (SOFP)

But what happens if, instead, the customer goes bankrupt and then cannot pay? Remember that according to the *Conceptual Framework* an asset is a resource controlled by an entity from which future economic benefits are expected to flow. If the customer cannot pay, then no **economic benefits are expected to flow** from the trade receivable. So, the **trade receivable no longer meets the definition of an asset** and it must be removed from the statement of financial position and is charged as an expense in the statement of profit or loss.

2 Writing off irrecoverable debts

If a debt is irrecoverable, it must be removed from the statement of financial position and charged as an expense to the statement of profit or loss. Decrease assets, increase expenses.

Dr Irrecoverable debts expense (SPL)

Cr Trade receivables (SOFP)

Activity 1: Irrecoverable debts

Fight & Co has trade receivables at 31 December 20X7 of $65,000. A review of customer files indicates that two customers, Ali and Tyson, who owe $7,000 and $8,000 respectively, have gone bankrupt and their debts are considered irrecoverable.

Required

Complete the trade receivable account and the irrecoverable debt expense (SPL) account.

Solution

TRADE RECEIVABLES (SOFP)

	$		$
31.12.X7 Balance b/d	65,000		

IRRECOVERABLE DEBTS EXPENSE (SPL)

	$		$

3 Irrecoverable debts written off and subsequently recovered

An irrecoverable debt which has been written off might occasionally be unexpectedly paid (in some cases, in subsequent financial periods). Because the debt has already been written off, it no longer exists in the statement of financial position and so the cash received cannot be offset against it in the usual way. Instead, the cash received is offset against the irrecoverable debts expense.

3.1 Accounting treatment

Dr Cash (SOFP)

Cr Irrecoverable debts expense (SPL)

Activity 2: Irrecoverable debt, recovered

Using the information from Activity 1, Fight & Co subsequently receive a cheque of $7,000 from Ali.

Required

Show the treatment of this recovery in the relevant T-accounts.

Solution

TRADE RECEIVABLES (SOFP)

	$		$
Balance b/d	50,000		

IRRECOVERABLE DEBTS EXPENSE

	$		$

CASH AT BANK (SOFP)

	$		$

4 Allowance for receivables

As well as writing off irrecoverable debts, a business may make an **allowance for receivables** as a **prudent** precaution to account for the fact that some receivables balances are doubtful and might not be collectable.

Doubtful debts may occur, for example, when invoices are in dispute, or when customers are in financial difficulty.

In this situation, such **debts are not written off**, as it is not certain that they are irrecoverable. But, because there is doubt over whether they will be paid, an allowance for receivables is made against the doubtful debts.

Trade receivables in the statement of financial position are shown net of any receivables allowance (although, for bookkeeping purposes, trade receivables and the allowance for receivables are kept as two separate nominal ledger accounts).

4.1 Presentation in statement of financial position

The allowance for receivables account is usually deducted from the receivables balance and not shown separately on the SOFP. For example:

	$	$
Current assets		
Receivables	55,000	
Allowance for receivables	($5,000)	
		50,000
Cash		120,000
Total current assets		170,000

The $55,000 and the $5,000 do not need to be presented separately as above. They can simply be netted off and the receivables balance be shown as $50,000.

4.2 Determining the allowance for receivables

The methods of determining the allowance for trade receivables fall under IAS 39/IFRS 9 as part of an impairment review of trade receivables, and can be quite complex. Fortunately, these are beyond the scope of this syllabus. In this paper, the allowance for receivables is likely to be expressed simply as a percentage of trade receivables, eg 'an allowance equivalent to 2% of trade receivables'.

The allowance against the trade receivables balance is made **after** writing off any irrecoverable debts.

4.3 Creating an allowance for receivables

When an allowance is first made, the initial allowance is charged as an expense in the statement of profit or loss for the period in which the allowance is created.

4.3.1 Accounting treatment

Dr Irrecoverable debts expense (SPL)

Cr Allowance for receivables (SOFP)

Activity 3: Allowance for receivables

A company has a trade receivables balance of $100,000 but requires an allowance for receivables equivalent to 5% of the balance.

Required

Record the allowance for receivables in the accounts below and show how this would appear in extracts to the statement of profit or loss and statement of financial position.

Solution

ALLOWANCE FOR RECEIVABLES (SOFP)

	$		$

IRRECOVERABLE DEBTS EXPENSE (SPL)

	$		$

Statement of financial position (extract)

	$
Total value of receivables	
Less: allowance for receivables	
Statement of financial position value	

Statement of profit or loss

	$
Expenses	
Irrecoverable debts expense	

4.4 Adjusting the allowance for receivables at the period end

In subsequent years, adjustments may be needed to the amount of the allowance. When adjusting the allowance at the period end, the procedure is to:

- Calculate the new allowance required.

- Compare it with the existing balance on the allowance account (ie the balance b/d from the previous accounting period).
- Calculate the increase or decrease required:

  If a **higher allowance** is required now:

  Dr Irrecoverable debts expense (SPL)

  Cr Allowance for receivables (SOFP)

  with the amount of the increase.

  If a **lower allowance** is required now:

  Dr Allowance for receivables (SOFP)

  Cr Irrecoverable debts expense (SPL)

  with the amount of the decrease.

Activity 4: Changes in the allowance for receivables

A business has an allowance for receivables (SOFP) brought forward from the year end 31 December 20X2 of $5,500.

Total receivables outstanding at 31 December 20X3 are $240,000. Upon reviewing the balances, it is determined that an allowance should be made equivalent to 4% of the total balance.

Required

Complete the statements below.

The allowance for receivables to be shown in the statement of financial position at 31 December 20X3 is $ _____

The _____ in allowance for receivables included in irrecoverable debts in the statement of profit or loss for the year ended 31 December 20X3 is $ _____ .

4.5 Adjusting receivables during the year

During the year, it may be found that a debt which had previously been deemed doubtful is no longer doubtful, but definitely bad (irrecoverable). It should therefore be removed from trade receivables.

Dr Irrecoverable debts expense (SPL)

Cr Receivables (SOFP)

Note. The allowance for receivables will only be adjusted when the period end accounts are prepared. Do not post any entries to the allowance for receivables account during the year.

Activity 5: Irrecoverable debts and allowance for receivables

At 31 December 20X2, a company's receivables totalled $450,000 and an allowance for receivables of $35,000 had been brought forward from the year ended 31 December 20X1.

It was decided to write off debts totalling $22,000. The allowance for receivables is to be adjusted to 10% of receivables.

Required

What charge for irrecoverable debts expense should appear in the company's statement of profit or loss for the year ended 31 December 20X2?

O $22,000 debit

O $35,000 debit

O $7,800 debit

○ $29,800 debit

Activity 6: Irrecoverable debts

An irrecoverable debt arises in which of the following situations?

○ A customer pays part of the account

○ An invoice is in dispute

○ The customer goes bankrupt

○ The invoice is not yet due for payment

5 Terminology

There are several different ways in which the items in this chapter can be referred to so here is a summary:

Irrecoverable debt is sometimes called a bad debt.

Doubtful debt is one which is not irrecoverable yet but there is some doubt over it. This is where we would make an adjustment to the allowance for receivables.

Allowance for receivables in SOFP is sometimes called provision for doubtful debts.

Irrecoverable debts expense account is sometimes called the bad debt expense account.

In this chapter, we have taken irrecoverable debts and increases/decreases in the allowance for receivables to the SFP irrecoverable debts account. Sometimes, two accounts are used: the 'irrecoverable debts account' for the debts that have been written off in the year and the 'allowance for receivables expense account' which is where the increase/decrease in the allowance goes.

Exam focus point

In the exam, it is highly likely that you will have to calculate the increase or decrease in the allowance for receivables and show the effect of this on the statement of profit or loss.

The value of trade receivables in the statement of financial position must be shown after deducting the allowance for receivables.

The FFA/FA examining team have written a technical article entitled 'Trade receivables'. This article is helpful to your understanding of the entire process of credit sales, from the initial recording of a credit sale to the recognition of an allowance for the receivables.

https://www.accaglobal.com/in/en/student/exam-support-resources/foundation-level-study-resources/ffa/ffa-technical-articles.html

Chapter summary

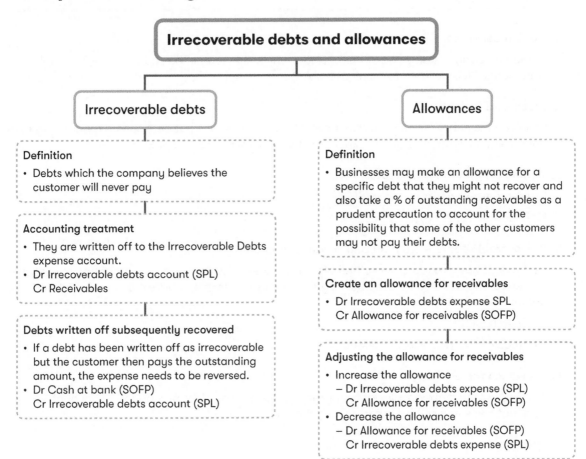

Irrecoverable debts and allowances

Irrecoverable debts

Definition
- Debts which the company believes the customer will never pay

Accounting treatment
- They are written off to the Irrecoverable Debts expense account.
- Dr Irrecoverable debts account (SPL)
  Cr Receivables

Debts written off subsequently recovered
- If a debt has been written off as irrecoverable but the customer then pays the outstanding amount, the expense needs to be reversed.
- Dr Cash at bank (SOFP)
  Cr Irrecoverable debts account (SPL)

Allowances

Definition
- Businesses may make an allowance for a specific debt that they might not recover and also take a % of outstanding receivables as a prudent precaution to account for the possibility that some of the other customers may not pay their debts.

Create an allowance for receivables
- Dr Irrecoverable debts expense SPL
  Cr Allowance for receivables (SOFP)

Adjusting the allowance for receivables
- Increase the allowance
  - Dr Irrecoverable debts expense (SPL)
    Cr Allowance for receivables (SOFP)
- Decrease the allowance
  - Dr Allowance for receivables (SOFP)
    Cr Irrecoverable debts expense (SPL)

Knowledge diagnostic

1. Trade receivables

A trade receivable is an asset of the business which should only be shown in the financial statements if it is believed to be recoverable.

2. Irrecoverable debts

Irrecoverable debts are specific debts owed to a business which it decides are never going to be paid. They are written off as an expense in the statement of profit or loss.

3. Writing off irrecoverable debts

Dr Irrecoverable debts expense (SPL)

Cr Receivables (SOFP)

4. Irrecoverable debts written off and subsequently paid

As the debt has already been written off, it no longer exists in the statement of financial position. Therefore, the cash received is offset against the irrecoverable debts expense account and NOT against receivables.

Dr Cash (SOFP)

Cr Irrecoverable debts expense (SPL)

5. Allowance for receivables

A business may make an allowance for receivables as a prudent precaution to account for the fact that some receivables balances might not be collectable.

6. Movement in an allowance for receivables

Increase:

Dr Irrecoverable debts expense (SPL)

Cr Allowance for receivables (SOFP)

Decrease:

Dr Allowance for receivables (SOFP)

Cr Irrecoverable debts expense (SPL)

Further study guidance

Question practice

Now try the following from the Further question practice bank (available in the digital edition of the Workbook):

Questions 47 to 50

Activity answers

Activity 1: Irrecoverable debts

TRADE RECEIVABLES (SOFP)

	$		$
		31.12.X7 Irrecoverable debts expense (SPL) ($7,000 + $8,000)	15,000
31.12.X7 Balance b/d	65,000	31.12.X7 Balance c/d	50,000
	65,000		**65,000**
Balance b/d	50,000		

IRRECOVERABLE DEBTS EXPENSE (SPL)

	$		$
31.12.X7 Trade receivables	15,000	31.12.X7 to SPL	15,000

The debts of Ali and Tyson no longer meet the definition of an asset as there is no expected future economic benefit and, as such, they are written off to the SPL as an expense.

Dr Irrecoverable debts expense (SPL) $15,000

Cr Trade receivables (SOFP) $15,000

Activity 2: Irrecoverable debt, recovered

TRADE RECEIVABLES (SOFP)

	$		$
Balance b/d	50,000		

IRRECOVERABLE DEBTS EXPENSE

	$		$
To SPL	7,000	Cash	7,000

CASH AT BANK (SOFP)

	$		$
Irrecoverable debts expense	7,000		

When an irrecoverable debt is written off and subsequently recovered, the entry is shown as a credit in the expense account. This reduces the balance in the irrecoverable debts expense account. For example, if Fight & Co had $60,000 in their irrecoverable debts expense account, this accounting entry would reduce that balance to $53,000.

Activity 3: Allowance for receivables

ALLOWANCE FOR RECEIVABLES (SOFP)

	$		$
		Irrecoverable debts expense (SPL)	5,000

IRRECOVERABLE DEBTS EXPENSE (SPL)

	$		$
Allowance for receivables (SOFP)	5,000		

Statement of financial position (extract)

	$
Total value of receivables	100,000
Less: allowance for receivables	(5,000)
Statement of financial position value	**95,000**

Statement of profit or loss

	$
Expenses	
Irrecoverable debts expense	5,000

Working

Calculating the allowance for receivables

Trade receivables $100,000 × 5% = $5,000

Activity 4: Changes in the allowance for receivables

The allowance for receivables to be shown in the statement of financial position at 31 December 20X3 is $ 9,600.

The increase in allowance for receivables included in irrecoverable debts in the statement of profit or loss for the year ended 31 December 20X3 is $ 4,100 debit .

Balance b/d at 1.1.X3 $5,500

Increase in allowance $4,100   Dr Irrecoverable debts expense Cr Allowance for receivables

Balance c/d at 31.12.X3 **$9,600**

Working

Allowance for receivables

Receivables as at 31.12.X3 $240,000 × 4% = $9,600

Activity 5: Irrecoverable debts and allowance for receivables

The correct answer is: $29,800 debit

Working

Irrecoverable debts expense

	$
Irrecoverable debt from the question	22,000
plus	
Increase in allowance for receivables	<u>7,800</u>
Irrecoverable debts expense	**29,800**

	$
Allowance for receivables b/d	35,000
Increase in allowance (balancing figure)	<u>7,800</u>
Allowance for receivables c/d*	**42,800**

	$
*Receivables	450,000
Less irrecoverable debts written off in the year	<u>(22,000)</u>
Remaining receivables balance	**428,000**
Allowance for receivables	10%
Allowance for receivables c/d	**42,800**

Activity 6: Irrecoverable debts

The correct answer is: The customer goes bankrupt

Options one and four – there is nothing to suggest that the customer will not pay. Option two – this may become an irrecoverable debt but, at the moment, there is just a doubt rather than a certainty over it not being paid. The company may wish to make an allowance for this debt.

Sales tax

Learning objectives

On competition of this chapter, you should be able to:

	Syllabus reference no.
Understand the general principles of the operation of a sales tax.	D1(c)
Calculate sales tax on transactions and record the consequent accounting entries.	D1(d)

Exam context

This topic is likely to be tested in two main ways. You may be asked to identify the correct journal entry to post sales and purchases transactions, including sales tax. You may also be required to consider how sales tax affects the calculation of amounts to be capitalised for non-current assets.

Chapter overview

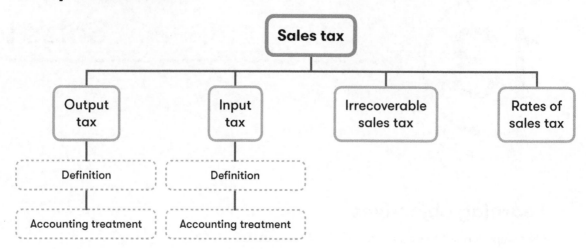

1 Introduction

This chapter is designed to enable you to prepare basic accounting entries for sales tax, known in many countries as value added tax (VAT).

2 Sales tax

> **Input and output tax:** Sales tax charged (or 'collected') on goods and services sold by a business is referred to as **output** sales tax. Sales tax paid (or 'suffered') on goods and services bought by a business is referred to as **input** sales tax.

A business' sales and purchases are often subject to sales tax. This is an indirect tax, as it is not levied directly on the individual like personal income tax. Sales tax is collected by traders who charge it on the goods they sell to the customer.

A business charges sales tax on its sales (output tax) and suffers sales tax on its purchases (input tax).

It may be easier to think of output sales tax as sales tax paid by others on goods and services going 'out' of a business and input sales tax as sales tax paid on goods and services going 'in' to a business.

A sales tax registered trader must carry out the following tasks:

- Charge sales tax on the goods and services sold at the rate prescribed by the government. This is output sales tax.
- Pay sales tax on goods and services purchased from other businesses. This is input sales tax.
- Pay to the tax authorities the difference between the sales tax collected on sales and the sales tax paid to suppliers for purchases. Payments are made at prescribed intervals. (If output sales tax is less than input sales tax in a period, the tax authorities will refund the difference to the business.)

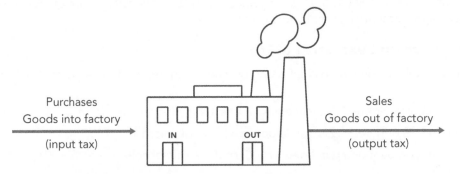

A sales tax registered business shows:

- Items of **income and expenditure net of sales tax**. This is because the sales tax is not part of the business's income or expenditure – it belongs to the tax authorities.
- **Trade receivables and trade payables gross of sales tax**

 Illustration 1: Sales tax

A business buys raw materials for $115 (inclusive of sales tax at 15%) and sells the finished product for $287.50 (inclusive of sales tax at 15%).

Required

Calculate the amounts due to or from the sales tax authority.

(The rate of sales tax will always be provided in the exam question.)

Solution

	Net	Sales tax	Gross
	$	$	$
Business buys raw materials	100	15	115
Manufactures goods and sells them	250	37.50	287.50

	$
Input tax (from sales)	37.50
Output tax (from purchases)	15.00
Net due to tax authorities	22.50

2.1 Irrecoverable sales tax

There are some circumstances in which sales tax paid on inputs cannot be reclaimed (eg where a trader is not registered for sales tax or where inputs are not related to taxable business activities). This is referred to as irrecoverable sales tax. In these cases, the trader must bear the cost of the sales tax and account for it accordingly.

For example, if a business pays $500 for entertaining expenses and suffers irrecoverable input sales tax of $75 on this amount, the total of $575 paid should be charged to the statement of profit or loss as an expense. Similarly, if a business pays $5,000 for a motor vehicle and suffers irrecoverable input sales tax of $400, the business should capitalise the full amount of $5,400 as a non-current asset in the statement of financial position.

2.2 Amounts inclusive and exclusive of tax

In business, you are likely to come across sales and purchases figures quoted as gross or net of sales tax.

The gross amount of a sale or purchase is the amount inclusive of sales tax.

The net amount of a sale or purchase is the amount exclusive of sales tax.

For example, if the net amount of a purchase is $100, and the rate of sales tax is 15%, the amounts are as follows:

	$
Net amount exclusive of sales tax:	100
Sales tax ($100 × 15%)	15
Gross amount inclusive of sales tax: ($100 + $15)	115

It is a **bit more difficult to calculate** the **net** amount, or sales tax, **from the gross** amount and the rate of tax. The net amount is equal to the gross amount/(1 + tax rate).

For example, if the gross amount of a purchase is $80, and the rate of sales tax is 15%, the sales tax and net amounts are as follows:

	$
Gross amount	80
Net amount ($80/(1 + 0.15) or ($80/1.15)	69.57
Sales tax ($80 – $69.57) or ($80/115) × 15)	10.43

Activity 1: Irrecoverable sales tax

During 20X1, Fergus buys two vans and a car each costing $10,000 plus sales tax at 15%. The car will be used 70% for business use and 30% personal use. The two vans will be used exclusively for business use. He depreciates vehicles on a straight-line basis, vans over five years and cars over six years.

In the tax regime in which Fergus operates, sales tax is only recoverable on items used wholly for business purposes.

Required

What is his depreciation expense to the nearest $ for the year?

- ○ $5,666
- ○ $5,917
- ○ $6,100
- ○ $6,517

3 Accounting for sales tax

Sales tax charged on sales is collected by the business on behalf of the tax authorities. It does not form part of the revenue of the business. For example, if a business sells goods for $600 + sales tax $90, ie for $690 total price, the sales account should only record the $600 excluding sales tax. The accounting entries to record the sale would be as follows:

Dr Cash or trade receivables	$690
Cr Sales	$600
Cr Sales tax control account (output sales tax)	$90

If input sales tax is recoverable, the cost of purchases should exclude the sales tax and be recorded net of tax. For example, if a business purchases goods on credit for $400 + sales tax $60, the transaction would be recorded as follows:

Dr Purchases	$400
Dr Sales tax control account (input sales tax recoverable)	$60
Cr Trade payables	$460

If the input sales tax is not recoverable (irrecoverable), the cost of purchases must include the tax, ie purchases would be $460 in the example above, because it is the business itself which must bear the cost of the tax.

Note. Trade **receivables** and trade **payables** are shown in the accounts **INCLUSIVE of sales tax**. The statement of financial position must reflect the TOTAL amount due from receivables and payables.

Essential reading

See Chapter 13 of the Essential reading for more detail on how to record sales tax in the day books.

The Essential reading is available as an Appendix of the digital edition of the Workbook.

4 Sales tax on the statement of financial position

The sales tax paid to the authorities each quarter is the difference between recoverable input sales tax on purchases and output sales tax on sales. For example, if a business is invoiced for input sales tax of $8,000 and charges sales tax of $15,000 on its credit sales and sales tax of $2,000 on its cash sales, the sales tax control account would be as follows:

SALES TAX CONTROL ACCOUNT

	$		$
Payables (input sales tax)	8,000	Receivables (output sales tax on invoiced sales)	15,000
Balance due to tax authorities	9,000	Cash (output sales tax on cash sales)	2,000
	17,000		**17,000**

The outstanding amount owing to the tax authorities would be a **current liability** on the SOFP.

If the input sales tax was greater than the output sales tax, the tax authorities would owe the business money and this would be shown as a **current asset** on the SOFP.

Activity 2: Sales tax

A business buys goods for $1,000 plus 15% sales tax. They then sell those goods for $1,500 plus 15% sales tax.

The purchases will cost   ($1,000 × 1.15) = $1,150

The sales will raise   ($1,500 × 1.15) = $1,725

The sales tax payable to tax authorities will be:

Payable on outputs (sales) (15% × $1,500)	$225.00
Reclaimable on inputs (purchases) (15% × $1,000)	$150.00
Net sales tax to tax authorities	**$75.00**

As the business is purely collecting the sales tax for the tax authorities, and is able to set off its sales tax suffered, it does not include sales tax as either an expense or income in the statement of profit or loss. The sales tax is accounted for when the transaction occurs.

Required

Write the double entry for the purchases and the sales, and post them to the ledger accounts.

Solution

PURCHASES

	$		$

TRADE PAYABLES

	$		$

SALES

	$		$

TRADE RECEIVABLES

	$		$

SALES TAX CONTROL ACCOUNT

	$		$

Exam focus point

The ACCA examining team have commented in the past exam, a question on calculating and accounting for sales tax had one of the lowest pass rates.

Specifically, some students accounted for sales tax on payments to credit suppliers.

This is incorrect, as the sales tax will have already been accounted for when the credit purchase was recorded.

Activity 3: Sales tax and motor vehicles

When sales tax is not recoverable on the cost of a motor vehicle, it should be treated in which of the following ways?

O   Deducted from the cost of the asset capitalised

O   Included in the cost of the asset capitalised

O   Deducted from output tax for the period

O   Written off to the statement of profit or loss as an expense

Activity 4: Sales tax owing to/from the tax authorities

A trader is registered for sales tax. During a period, they have sales of $5,750 including sales tax at 15% and purchases of $2,500 excluding sales tax at 15%.

Required

What amount is owed to or due from the tax authorities at the end of the period?

O $487.50 owed to

O $487.50 due from

O $375.00 owed to

O $375.00 due from

5   Sales tax – the main points

Sales tax – the main points

(a) Credit sales
   (i)   Include sales tax in sales day book; show it separately.
   (ii) Include gross receipts from receivables in cash book; no need to show sales tax separately.
   (iii) Exclude sales tax element from statement of profit or loss.
   (iv) Credit sales tax control account with output sales tax element of receivables invoiced.

(b) Credit purchases
   (i)   Include sales tax in purchases day book; show it separately.
   (ii) Include gross payments in cashbook; no need to show sales tax separately.
   (iii) Exclude recoverable sales tax from statement of profit or loss.
   (iv) Include irrecoverable sales tax in statement of profit or loss.
   (v)   Debit sales tax control account with recoverable input sales tax element of credit purchases.

(c) Cash sales
   (i)   Include gross receipts in cash book; show sales tax separately.
   (ii) Exclude sales tax element from statement of profit or loss.
   (iii) Credit sales tax control account with output sales tax element of cash sales.

(d) Cash purchases
   (i)   Include gross payments in cash book: show sales tax separately.
   (ii) Exclude recoverable sales tax from statement of profit or loss.
   (iii) Include irrecoverable sales tax in statement of profit or loss.
   (iv) Debit sales tax control account with recoverable input sales tax element of cash purchases.

Chapter summary

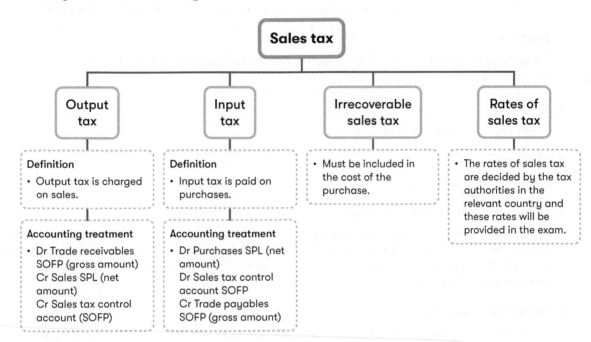

Sales tax

Output tax

Definition
- Output tax is charged on sales.

Accounting treatment
- Dr Trade receivables SOFP (gross amount)
  Cr Sales SPL (net amount)
  Cr Sales tax control account (SOFP)

Input tax

Definition
- Input tax is paid on purchases.

Accounting treatment
- Dr Purchases SPL (net amount)
  Dr Sales tax control account SOFP
  Cr Trade payables SOFP (gross amount)

Irrecoverable sales tax

- Must be included in the cost of the purchase.

Rates of sales tax

- The rates of sales tax are decided by the tax authorities in the relevant country and these rates will be provided in the exam.

Knowledge diagnostic

1. Sales tax

Sales tax is an indirect tax levied on the sale of goods and services. It is usually administered by the local tax authorities.

2. Output tax

Output tax is charged on sales.

3. Input tax

Input tax is charged in purchases.

4. Amount due to/from tax authorities

Registered businesses charge output sales tax on sales and suffer input sales tax on purchases. If output sales tax exceeds input sales tax, the business pays the difference in tax to the authorities. If output sales tax is less than input sales tax in a period, the tax authorities will refund the difference to the business.

5. Irrecoverable sales tax

Some sales tax is irrecoverable. Where sales tax is irrecoverable, it must be regarded as part of the cost of the items purchased and included in the statement of profit or loss charge or in the statement of financial position as appropriate.

6. Presentation in the financial statements

An outstanding payable for sales tax will appear as a current liability in the statement of financial position.

Further study guidance

Question practice

Now try the following from the Further question practice bank (available in the digital edition of the Workbook):

Questions 25 to 28

Activity answers

Activity 1: Irrecoverable sales tax

The correct answer is: $5,917

Sales tax on the car is not recoverable as it is not wholly used for business purposes. Sales tax is however recoverable on the vans.

	$
Vans (2 × $10,000)/5 years	4,000
Car ($10,000 × 115%)/6 years	1,917
	5,917

Activity 2: Sales tax

PURCHASES

	$		$
Trade payables	1,000		

TRADE PAYABLES

	$		$
		Purchases and sales tax	1,150

SALES

	$		$
		Trade receivables	1,500

TRADE RECEIVABLES

	$		$
Sales and sales tax	1,725		

SALES TAX CONTROL ACCOUNT

	$		$
Trade payables	150	Trade receivables	225
Balance c/d (owing to tax authorities)	75		
	225		**225**
		Balance b/d	75

Dr Purchases	$1,000
Dr Sales tax control account	$150
Cr Trade payables	$1,150

Dr Trade receivables $1,725

Cr Sales $1,500

Cr Sales tax control account $225

Note. The outstanding balance of $75 will show under current liabilities on the statement of financial position until it is paid.

Activity 3: Sales tax and motor vehicles

The correct answer is: Included in the cost of the asset capitalised

The irrecoverable sales tax should be included in the cost of the asset capitalised. The statement of financial position value will therefore include sales tax and the depreciation charge will rise accordingly.

Activity 4: Sales tax owing to/from the tax authorities

The correct answer is: $375.00 owed to

Output tax on sales $750.00 ($5,750/1.15 × 0.15) less input tax on purchases $375.00 ($2,500 × 0.15), leaves a net amount of $375.00 due to the tax authorities.

14

Control accounts

Learning objectives

On completion of this chapter, you should be able to:

	Syllabus reference no.
Understand the purpose of control accounts for accounts receivable and accounts payable.	E3(a)
Understand how control accounts relate to the double entry system.	E3(b)
Prepare ledger control accounts from given information.	E3(c)
Perform control account reconciliations for accounts receivable and accounts payable.	E3(d)
Identify errors which would be highlighted by performing a control account reconciliation.	E3(e)
Identify and correct errors in control accounts and ledger accounts.	E3(f)
Account for discounts allowed and discounts received.	D1(e/f)
Account for contras between trade receivables and trade payables.	D8(j)
Understand and record sales and purchase returns.	D1(b)
Prepare, reconcile and understand the purpose of supplier statements.	D8(k)

Exam context

Questions on this topic are likely to require you to correct the closing balance on a receivables or payables control account, including items such as contras and discounts, or calculate the correct balance per the receivables/payables ledger. You may also be required to prepare a receivables or payables ledger control account to find a missing figure.

Chapter overview

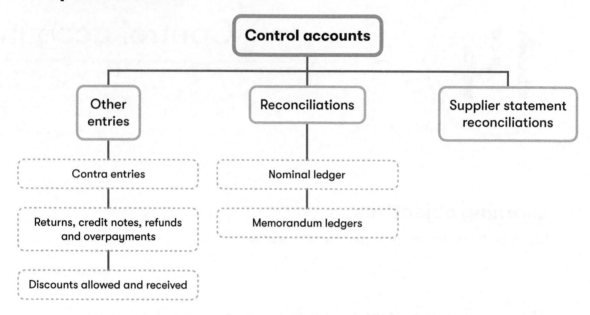

1 Recap

In Chapters 4 and 5, we saw how a business's transactions were categorised in the books of prime entry. The **totals** of these were then posted using double entry to the nominal ledger to give a summary of the information.

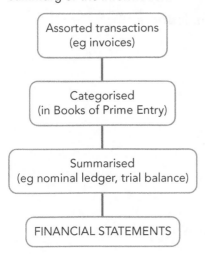

The nominal ledger contains three ledger accounts which are affected when a business sells on credit:

- Sales
- Bank
- Trade receivables – shows the **total** amount owed by **all** customers at a particular point in time. It is also called the **receivables ledger control account (RLCA)**.

In order to chase overdue debts, however, a business must know how much **each** customer owes at a particular time.

This balance could be determined by going back into the detail of the books of prime entry and extracting the information for each customer.

This is a very time consuming process and so, instead, a **memorandum ledger** is maintained for each individual customer showing invoices raised, cash received and therefore the amount owed to the business.

This memorandum ledger is called a **receivables ledger**.

The reverse is true when a business buys on credit.

1.1 Terminology

In the nominal ledger:

- Receivables ledger control account (trade receivables/RLCA): total owed by **all** credit customers
- Payables ledger control account (trade payables/PLCA): total owed to **all** credit suppliers

Memorandum ledgers:

- Receivables ledger: balance owed by each **individual** credit customer
- Payables ledger: balance owed to each **individual** credit supplier

2 The flow of information

The information in the receivables ledger control account (RLCA) and receivables ledger (RL) is posted from the **same** source documents.

BPP
LEARNING
MEDIA

Therefore, the balance on the RLCA **should equal** the sum of all balances from the RL. Similarly, the balance on the PLCA **should equal** the sum of all balances from the PL.

If the balances do not agree then an **error** has been made. This will be identified through a **control account reconciliation** (Section 5).

Activity 1: Books of prime entry and memorandum ledgers

A Co has the following information:

10 January 20X6

Sells $150 of goods to Customer A on credit.

Sells $200 of goods to Customer B on credit.

15 January 20X6

A Co purchases $100 of goods from Supplier Y on credit.

A Co purchases $1,300 of goods from Supplier Z on credit.

21 January 20X6

A Co receives full payment from Customer B and this money is used to pay Supplier Y.

Required

1 Record the above transactions in the books of prime entry and the memorandum ledgers.

2 Post the totals from the books of prime entry to the nominal ledger and balance off nominal ledger accounts.

3 Reconcile the memorandum ledgers to the control accounts.

Solution

1

Sales day book

Date	Customer	Amount
		$
		_____
		_____

Purchase day book

Date	Supplier	Amount
		$
		_____

Cash receipts book

Date	Narrative	Total	Sales	Receivables
		$	$	$
		_____		_____

Date	Narrative	Total	Sales	Receivables
		$	$	$

Cash payments book

Date	Narrative	Total	Purchases	Payables
		$	$	$

Memorandum ledgers

Receivables ledger

CUSTOMER A

	$		$

CUSTOMER B

	$		$

Payables ledger

SUPPLIER Y

	$		$

SUPPLIER Z

	$		$

2

NOMINAL LEDGER

	$		$

	$		$

PLCA (SOFP)

	$		$

BANK (SOFP)

	$		$

SALES (SPL)

	$		$

PURCHASES (SPL)

	$		$

3

Reconciliation

	$
Balance per list of balances	
Receivables ledger	
Customer A	
Customer B	
	————————
	————————
Balance per RLCA	
Payables ledger	

Balance per list of balances	$
Supplier Y	
Supplier Z	_____
	_____
Balance per PLCA	

3 Other entries

A business must ensure that any transaction recorded in the receivables ledger control account or the payables ledger control account is also reflected in the memorandum ledgers.

3.1 Contra entries

Sometimes a business may have a customer which also supplies the business with goods. The businesses may reach an agreement to offset the balances receivable and payable. This is known as a contra.

A contra entry is **always** recorded as:

Dr   PLCA

Cr   RLCA

This will reduce both receivables and payables.

Note that the memorandum ledgers will also need to be updated for the contra entry.

 Illustration 1: Recording a contra

P Co is a printing business which sells stationery to F Co, a florist. F Co supplies P Co with flowers and plants for its offices.

During October, P Co sells stationery worth $200 to F Co and F Co delivers flowers and plants to P Co worth $70.

P Co has the following amounts in its books:

	$
Receivables	200
Payables	70

The two businesses agree to offset the balances receivable and payable via a **contra**.

Required

How will the contra amount be recorded?

Solution

The contra will be for the lower of the two amounts: $70. This will **decrease both receivables and payables** by $70 and the remaining $130 can then be paid in cash.

3.2 Returns, credit notes and refunds

Sometimes, when a business has made a sale, the customer will return the goods. Equally, when the business has purchased some goods on credit, it may return them to the supplier.

3.2.1 Steps for sales returns

Step 1   Goods are sold to the customer for $250:

     Dr   RLCA $250

     Cr   Sales $250

Step 2   Customer pays for goods:

     Dr   Bank $250

     Cr   RLCA $250

     At this point, the balance on the receivables ledger control account is **nil**.

Step 3   Customer returns the goods and is issued with a credit note:

     Dr   Sales (returns) $250

     Cr   RLCA $250

     This entry reverses the original sale.

     The receivables ledger control account will show a **credit** balance reflecting that the business owes money to the customer. This could be offset against future sales or the customer may request a refund.

Step 4   The business refunds the customer:

     Dr   RLCA $250

     Cr   Bank $250

     Once again, the balance on the receivables ledger control account is **nil**.

3.2.2 Steps for purchase returns:

Step 1   Goods are purchased from the supplier for $100:

     Dr   Purchases $100

     Cr   PLCA $100

Step 2   The business pays the supplier:

     Dr   PLCA $100

     Cr   Cash $100

     At this point, the balance on the payables ledger control account is **nil**.

Step 3   The business returns the goods to the supplier and is issued with a credit note:

     Dr   PLCA $100

     Cr   Purchases (returns) $100

     This entry reverses the original purchase.

     The payables ledger control account will show a **debit** balance reflecting that the supplier owes money to the company. This could be offset against future purchases or the business may request a refund.

Step 4   The supplier refunds the business:

     Dr   Bank $100

     Cr   PLCA $100

     Once again, the balance on the payables ledger control account is **nil**.

     Again, the memorandum ledgers must also be updated.

3.2.3 Overpayment

If a customer pays too much to settle an invoice, or pays an invoice twice, the business will owe the excess to the customer.

This may be held and treated like a credit note or the monies refunded to the customer.

Equally, if the business pays too much to a supplier, the supplier will owe the excess to the business and, as for sales, this may be held and treated like a credit note or the monies refunded by the supplier.

3.2.4 Interest on overdue accounts

If a customer is late in settling their account then an entity may decide to charge them interest.

This will increase the amount they owe and will be shown as interest receivable in the statement of profit or loss.

The same could apply to late payment to suppliers.

Interest on overdue accounts is recorded using the following journal:

On trade receivables:

Dr   RLCA

Cr   Interest receivable (SPL)

On trade payables:

Dr   Interest payable (SPL)

Cr   PLCA

3.3 Discounts

There are two types of discounts:

(a) **Trade discounts**

    (i)   Given at the time of the sale/purchase, they reduce the selling price as an inducement to purchase

    (ii) Usually for regular customers or **bulk buyers**

(b) **Settlement discounts**

    (i)   Offered, but not necessarily taken, as an inducement to settle a debt early

    (ii) For example, 5% discount if settled within 14 day

> **Discounts allowed:** offered by the business to their customer
>
> **Discounts received:** received by a business from their supplier

3.3.1 Discounts allowed

Accounting treatment

Sales are always recorded **net** of (ie after) trade discounts. Therefore, trade discounts **never** appear in the financial statements.

If a customer **is expected** to take up a **settlement discount allowed**, the discount is deducted from the invoiced amount when recording the revenue for the sale.

Dr RLCA (net of discount)

Cr Revenue (net of discount)

If the customer subsequently does not take up the discount, the discount amount is then recorded as additional revenue.

Dr Cash (discount not taken)

Cr Revenue (discount not taken)

If the customer is not expected to take up the discount, the full invoiced amount is recognised as revenue when recording the sale.

Dr RLCA (full amount)

Cr Revenue (full amount)

If the customer then **does** take up the discount, revenue is reduced by the amount of the discount.

Dr Revenue (discount taken)

Cr RLCA (discount taken)

Activity 2: Sale on credit with discounts

1   On 1 January 20X7, a business made a sale on credit for $12,000. A trade discount of $2,000 was available with a further 10% settlement discount if payment was made within ten days. The business expected the customer to take up the discount.

Required

Record the initial sale.

2   On 4.1.X7, the customer pays for the goods taking advantage of the settlement discount.

Required

Record the full settlement of the amount owed.

3   How would your answer differ if the settlement discount was not taken?

Solution

1

SALES (SPL)

$		$

RCLA (SOFP)

$		$

2

BANK (SOFP)

$		$

RCLA (SOFP)

$		$

3

BANK (SOFP)

$		$

RLCA (SOFP)

$		$

	$		$

SALES (SPL)

	$		$

3.3.2 Discounts received

Accounting treatment

Purchases are recorded **net** of trade discounts but **inclusive** of settlement discounts.

Dr Purchase (SPL)

Cr PLCA (SOFP)

Again, trade discounts **never** appear in the financial statements.

Settlement discounts received are recorded as discounts received and are shown as **sundry income** in the statement of profit or loss.

Dr   PLCA (SOFP)

Cr   Discounts received (SPL)

Activity 3: Purchase on credit with discounts

Ryan Co purchases goods worth $5,000 from Austin Co. Ryan Co will receive a 5% settlement discount if the goods are paid for within seven days. Ryan Co has every intention of taking advantage of the settlement discount.

Required

In the books of Ryan:

1   Show the initial recording of the purchase.

2   Record the payment for the goods assuming Ryan pays within seven days.

3   Record the payment for the goods if payment is made after seven days.

Solution

3.4 Control account reconciliations

As mentioned previously, if we add up the balances in the receivables and payables ledgers, they should agree to the balances per the RLCA and PLCA.

If not, an error must have occurred at some point in the system.

The easiest way to identify the error is to perform a reconciliation between the two amounts.

3.4.1 Proforma control account reconciliation

	$		$
Balance b/d	X	Transposition error in posting	X
Sales day book undercast	X		
Sales omitted from SDB	X	Balance c/d	X
	—		—
	X		X
Balance b/d	X		

Activity 4: The RLCA and reconciliation with the receivables ledger

1   Post the following transactions to, and balance off, the receivables ledger control account.

(1)   Opening balance $614,000

(2)   Credit sales made during the month $302,600

(3)   Receipts from customers $311,000

(4)   Bad debts were written off $35,400

(5)   Contras against amounts due to suppliers in payables ledger $8,650

2   The receivables ledger list of balances totals to $563,900.

You have found the following errors:

(1)   The total of the sales day book was undercast by $3,600.

(2)   A credit balance of $450 was included in the list of balances as a debit.

(3)   A customer balance of $2,150 was left out when the receivables ledger list of balances was totalled.

Required

Reconcile the receivables ledger control account to the receivables ledger list of balances.

Solution

Chapter summary

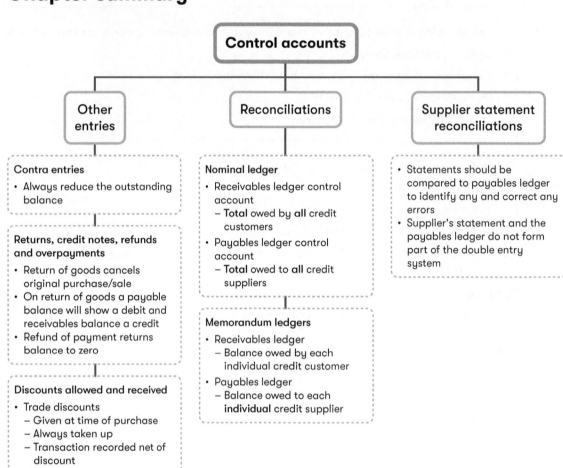

Control accounts

Other entries

Contra entries
- Always reduce the outstanding balance

Returns, credit notes, refunds and overpayments
- Return of goods cancels original purchase/sale
- On return of goods a payable balance will show a debit and receivables balance a credit
- Refund of payment returns balance to zero

Discounts allowed and received
- Trade discounts
  - Given at time of purchase
  - Always taken up
  - Transaction recorded net of discount
- Settlement discounts
  - Offered as encouragement to settle bill early
  - Not always taken up
  - Transaction recorded net of discount if discount is expected to be taken up

Reconciliations

Nominal ledger
- Receivables ledger control account
  - **Total** owed by **all** credit customers
- Payables ledger control account
  - **Total** owed to **all** credit suppliers

Memorandum ledgers
- Receivables ledger
  - Balance owed by each individual credit customer
- Payables ledger
  - Balance owed to each **individual** credit supplier

Supplier statement reconciliations
- Statements should be compared to payables ledger to identify any and correct any errors
- Supplier's statement and the payables ledger do not form part of the double entry system

Knowledge diagnostic

1. The flow of information

Information enters the accounting system from the source documents. This information flows to the nominal ledger and the memorandum ledgers.

2. Nominal ledger

- The area of the accounting system where transactions and events are entered via double entry, all elements of the financial statements have accounts in the nominal ledger.
- At each period end, the nominal ledger accounts are balanced off; assets and liabilities are transferred to the statement of financial position.
- Income and expenses are transferred to the statement of profit or loss.
- The nominal ledger reflects the total amounts of transactions and balances.

3. Memorandum ledgers

- Memorandum ledgers do not form part of the double entry system.
- The memorandum ledgers show information about each individual customer and supplier.

4. Terminology

- Control accounts (RLCA and PLCA) are the accounts from the nominal ledger; they show the total balances of receivables and payable.
- Memorandum accounts show the individual amounts relating to each receivable or payable.

5. Control account reconciliation

- The balance on the receivables ledger control account (RLCA) should agree to the sum of all individual balances in the receivables ledger.
- The balance of the payables ledger control account (PLCA) should agree to the sum of all individual balances in the payables ledger.

6. Contras

Contras between payables and receivables will always reduce the outstanding balances.

7. Discounts

- Trade discounts are given at the time of the sale/purchase; they reduce the selling price as an inducement to purchase. Amounts are always recorded net of trade discounts.
- Settlement discounts are offered, but not necessarily taken, as an inducement to settle a debt early. An assessment needs to be made of the likelihood of the settlement discount being taken up. If take up is likely, transactions are recorded net of the discount.

Further study guidance

Question practice

Now try the following from the Further question practice bank (available in the digital edition of the Workbook):

Questions 55 to 59

Activity answers

Activity 1: Books of prime entry and memorandum ledgers

1

Sales day book

Date	Customer	Amount
		$
10 Jan X6	Customer A	150
10 Jan X6	Customer B	200
		350

Purchase day book

Date	Supplier	Amount
		$
15 Jan X6	Supplier Y	100
15 Jan X6	Supplier Z	1,300
		1,400

Cash receipts book

Date	Narrative	Total	Sales	Receivables
		$	$	$
21 Jan X6	Customer B	200		200
		200		200

Cash payments book

Date	Narrative	Total	Purchases	Payables
		$	$	$
21 Jan X6	Supplier Y	100		100
		100		100

Memorandum ledgers
Receivables ledger

CUSTOMER A

	$		$
10.1.X6 Sales	150		
		Bal c/d	150
	150		150
Bal b/d	150		

CUSTOMER B

	$		$
10.1.X6 Sales	200	21.1.X6 Payment received	200
	200		200

Payables ledger

SUPPLIER Y

	$		$
21.1.X6 Payment made	100	15.1.X6 Purchases	100
	100		100

SUPPLIER Z

	$		$
Bal c/d	1,300	15.1.X6 Purchases	1,300
	1,300		1,300

2

NOMINAL LEDGER

	$		$
31.1.X6 Sales	350	31.1.X6 Bank	200
		Bal c/d	150
	350		350
Bal b/d	150		

PLCA (SOFP)

	$		$
31.1.X6 Bank	100	31.1.X6 Purchases	1,400
Bal c/d	1,300		
	1,400		1,400
		Bal b/d	1,300

BANK (SOFP)

	$		$
31.1.X6 RLCA	200	31.1.X6 PLCA	100
		Bal c/d	100
	200		200
Bal b/d	100		

SALES (SPL)

	$		$
		31.1.X6 RLCA	350

	$		$
To SPL	350		
	350		350

PURCHASES (SPL)

	$		$
31.1.X6 PLCA	1,400		
		To SPL	1,400
	1,400		1,400

3

Reconciliation

	$
Balance per list of balances	
Receivables ledger	
Customer A	150
Customer B	—
	150
Balance per RLCA	150
Payables ledger	
Supplier Y	—
Supplier Z	1,300
	1,300
Balance per PLCA	1,300

Activity 2: Sale on credit with discounts

1

SALES (SPL)

	$		$
		1.1.X7 RLCA	9,000

RCLA (SOFP)

	$		$
1.1.X7 Sales	9,000		

The sale is recorded net of the settlement discount, as the customer is expected to take it up.

($12,000 – $2,000) × (100% – 10%) = $9,000.

2

BANK (SOFP)

	$		$
4.1.X7 RLCA	9,000		

RCLA (SOFP)

	$		$
1.1.X7 Sales	9,000	4.1.X7 Bank	9,000
	9,000		9,000

3

BANK (SOFP)

	$		$
4.1.X7 RLCA	10,000		

RLCA (SOFP)

	$		$
1.1.X7 Sales	9,000	4.1.X7 Bank	10,000
4.1.X7 Sales	1,000		
	10,000		10,000

SALES (SPL)

	$		$
		1.1.X7 RLCA	9,000
		4.1.X7 RLCA	1,000

Activity 3: Purchase on credit with discounts

1

PURCHASES (SPL)

	$		$
PLCA	5,000		

PLCA (SOFP)

	$		$
		Purchases	5,000

2

BANK (SOFP)

	$		$
		PLCA	4,750

PLCA (SOFP)

	$		$
Bank	4,750	Purchases	5,000
Discounts received	250		
	5,000		5,000

DISCOUNTS RECEIVED (SPL)

	$		$
		PLCA	250

3

BANK (SOFP)

	$		$
		PLCA	5,000

PLCA (SOFP)

	$		$
Bank	5,000	Purchases	5,000

Activity 4: The RLCA and reconciliation with the receivables ledger

1

RLCA

	$		$
Balance b/d	614,000	Bank	311,000
Sales	302,600		
		Contras (PLCA)	8,650
		Bad debts	35,400
		Bal c/d	561,550
	916,600		916,600

2

RLCA

	$		$
Bal b/d (part (a))	561,550		
(i) Sales (SDB undercast)	3,600	Bal c/d	565,150
	565,150		565,150

	$	$
Balance per list of balances		563,900
(ii) Credit balance included as a debit (2 × $450)	(900)	

	$	$
Customer balance omitted	<u>2,150</u>	
		<u>1,250</u>
		<u>565,150</u>

Skills checkpoint 3

Excel skills in the real world

Overview

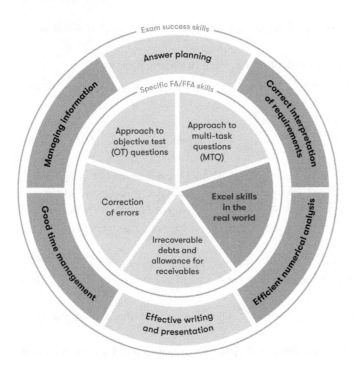

Introduction

As you move through your ACCA examinations and your accountancy career, you will need good spreadsheet skills. It is crucial that you have a good working knowledge of spreadsheets and that you are able to use them quickly and effectively. Many people do not use Excel to its full potential, for example they type in totals rather than asking Excel to sum it for them. This often leads to errors.

Spreadsheets

Why use spreadsheets?

Spreadsheets provide a tool for calculating, analysing and manipulating numerical data. Spreadsheets make the calculation and manipulation of data easier and quicker. For example, a spreadsheet can be set up to calculate the totals automatically.

Spreadsheets can be used for a wide range of tasks. Some common applications of spreadsheets are:

- Extended trial balances
- Fixed asset registers

- Reconciliations for control accounts such as receivables and payables
- Bank reconciliations
- Management accounts
- Cash flow analysis and forecasting
- Revenue analysis and comparison
- Cost analysis and comparison
- Budgets and forecasts
- What-if analysis

What-if analysis is the study of the effect on a business or model or system if variables deviate from what was expected. It allows you to explore different scenarios and the impact that they could have on the outcome. Spreadsheets are extremely useful for performing what-if analysis.

Formulae in Excel

All Excel formulae start with the equals sign =, followed by the elements to be calculated (the operands) and the calculation operators.

Formulae can be used to perform a variety of calculations. Here are some examples:

(a) =C4*5. This formula **multiplies** the value in C4 by 5. The result will appear in the cell holding the formula.

(b) =C4*B10. This **multiplies** the value in C4 by the value in B10.

(c) =C4/E5. This **divides** the value in C4 by the value in E5. (* means multiply and/means divide by.)

(d) =C4*B10-D1. This **multiplies** the value in C4 by that in B10 and then subtracts the value in D1 from the result. Note that generally Excel will perform multiplication and division before addition or subtraction. If in any doubt, use brackets (parentheses): =(C4*B10)−D1.

(e) =C4*120%. This **adds** 20% to the value in C4. It could be used to calculate a price including 20% VAT.

(f) =(C4+C5+C6)/3. Note that the **brackets** mean Excel would perform the addition first. Without the brackets, Excel would first divide the value in C6 by 3 and then add the result to the total of the values in C4 and C5.

(g) = 2^2 gives you 2 **to the power** of 2, in other words 2^2. Likewise = 2^3 gives you 2 cubed and so on.

(h) = 4^ (1/2) gives you the **square root** of 4. Likewise 27^(1/3) gives you the cube root of 27 and so on.

Without brackets, Excel calculates a formula from left to right. You can control how calculation is performed by changing the syntax of the formula. For example, the formula =5+2*3 gives a result of 11 because Excel calculates multiplication before addition. Excel would multiply 2 by 3 (resulting in 6) and would then add 5.

You may use parentheses to change the order of operations. For example =(5+2)*3 would result in Excel firstly adding the 5 and 2 together, then multiplying that result by 3 to give 21.

Extended trial balance

Preparing a set of accounts for a sole trader could begin with a trial balance that has been produced by the client's computer software. The client will have posted receipts and payments throughout the year but there will be year-end journals that still need to be posted before a set of financial statements can be produced.

It is most likely that you will use a spreadsheet to prepare these journals, post them to the client's trial balance figures and produce the final figures for the financial statements. This will involve producing an extended trial balance.

An extended trial balance will consist of several horizontal debit and credit columns and a vertical list of all the nominal ledger accounts, such as sales, purchases etc.

It is often helpful to include the credit figures as negative numbers. This way, when you sum across the spreadsheet, it will deduct them from any debits that are in that line. It also helps to ensure that you have posted both sides of the journal as the final column should always total zero.

Example extended trial balance spreadsheet

	A	B	C	D	E	F	G	H	I	J	K	L
1												
2	Mr Smith (Sole trader)											
3	Extended trial balance for year ended 31 December 20X9											
4												
5												
6		Trial balance per client		Depreciation		Accruals and prepayments		Accountancy fee		Closing trial balance		
7		Debit	Credit	Debit	Credit	Debit	Credit	Debit	Credit			
8	Sales		-55,000							-55000		
9	Purchases	35,000								35000		
10	Motor expenses	5,000								5000		
11	Telephone	400					-40			360		
12	Electricity	1050				95				1145		
13	Stationery	250								250		
14	Depreciation			3560						3560		
15	Accountancy							250		250	Profit for the year	
16										-9435		
17	Computer equipment - cost (10yrs SL)	10,000								10000		
18	Computer equipment - accumulated depreciation		-2,000		-1000					-3000		
19	Motor vehicles - cost (20% reducing balance)	20000								20000		
20	Motor vehicles - accumulated depreciation		-7,200		-2560					-9760		
21	Receivables	1500								1500		
22	Prepayments	250					-95			155		
23	Cash at bank	13000								13000		
24	Payables		-1800							-1800		
25	Accruals		-450			40			-250	-660		
26	Capital		-15000							-15000		
27	Drawings		-5000							-5000		
28												
29		86450	-86450	3560	-3560	135	-135	250	-250	0		
30												

This first spreadsheet image shows you the spreadsheet as you would normally see it: numbers in the relevant cells and totals at the bottom and at the end. The last column in this case is one single column that totals to zero so that you can check you have posted complete double entries.

Next, you want to see the formula's that you have put into the spreadsheet rather than the numbers. To do this, go to 'Formulas' and click 'Show Formulas'. This is shown in the following diagram:

Finally, you have the third diagram which shows the same spreadsheet but the cells are showing formulas where relevant.

	A	B	C	D	E	F	G	H	I	J	K
1											
2	Mr Smith (Sole trader)										
3	Extended trial balance for year ended 31 December 20X9										
4											
5											
6		Trial balance per client		Depreciation		Accruals and prepayments		Accountancy fee		Closing trial balance	
7		Debit	Credit	Debit	Credit	Debit	Credit	Debit	Credit		
8	Sales		-55000							=SUM(B8:I8)	
9	Purchases	35000								=SUM(B9:I9)	
10	Motor expenses	5000								=SUM(B10:I10)	
11	Telephone	400					-40			=SUM(B11:I11)	
12	Electricity	1050				95				=SUM(B12:I12)	
13	Stationery	250								=SUM(B13:I13)	
14	Depreciation			=-SUM(E18+E20)						=SUM(B14:I14)	
15	Accountancy							250		=SUM(B15:I15)	Profit for the year
16											=SUM(J8:J15)
17	Computer equipment - cost (10yrs SL)	10000								=SUM(B17:I17)	
18	Computer equipment - accumulated depreciation		-2000		=-SUM(B17/10)					=SUM(B18:I18)	
19	Motor vehicles - cost (20% reducing balance)	20000								=SUM(B19:I19)	
20	Motor vehicles - accumulated depreciation		-7200		=-SUM(B19*80%*80%*20%)					=SUM(B20:I20)	
21	Receivables	1500								=SUM(B21:I21)	
22	Prepayments	250					-95			=SUM(B22:I22)	
23	Cash at bank	13000								=SUM(B23:I23)	
24	Payables		-1800							=SUM(B24:I24)	
25	Accruals		-450			40			-250	=SUM(B25:I25)	
26	Capital		-15000							=SUM(B26:I26)	
27	Drawings		-5000							=SUM(B27:I27)	
28											
29		=SUM(B8:B28)	=SUM(C8:C28)	=SUM(D8:D28)	=SUM(E8:E28)	=SUM(F8:F28)	=SUM(G8:G28)	=SUM(H8:H28)	=SUM(I8:I28)	=SUM(J8:J28)	
30											

Each column is totalled with a basic SUM formula. For example, the total of Column B is summed using =SUM(B8:B28).

Cell J16 shows the sum of all of the statement of profit or loss accounts J8 to J15. The result is a credit balance (negative figure) so this tells you that the client made a profit of £9,435 in the year to 31 December 20X9.

Cell E28 is a calculation of the accumulated depreciation to date for motor vehicles. They are depreciated by 20% each year on a reducing balance basis and, therefore, if you want to know the accumulated depreciation figure for Year 3, you would reduce the cost by 80% twice and then multiply the remaining NBV figure by 20%. This is shown in the spreadsheet as:

=(B19*80%*80%*20%)

Cost £20,000 × 80% gives the NBV in Year 1. Multiply this by 80% and you get the NBV for Year 2. Multiply this 20% and you get the depreciation charge for Year 3.

Note. This is a quick way to calculate depreciation in your exam too.

Skills activity

Question 1

Computer equipment was purchased on 1.1.20X3 for £25,000. It is being depreciated on a reducing balance basis at 25%.

Which formula would be used in the spreadsheet to calculate depreciation for the year ended 31 December 20X5?

A	=(25000*75%*75%*75%)
B	=(25000*75%*25%)
C	=(25000*75%*75%*25%)
D	=(25000-10958*25%)

The correct answer is C.

Answer A would produce the carrying amount at the end of the year.

Answer B assumes we are calculating depreciation for Year 2 and not Year 3.

For Answer D to be correct, it would need to be written as =(25000-10958)*25%.

Question 2

A business sells dresses for £55 each. This figure is inclusive of a 25% mark up.

Which formula(s) would correctly calculate the selling price?

A	=(55/125)*100
B	=(55/100)*25%
C	=55*100/125
D	=55*75%

The corrects answers are A and C.

Answers B and D are both treating it as a margin and not a mark up. B calculates the profit and D calculates the net selling price.

Exam success skills diagnostic

Every time you complete a few questions, use the diagnostic below to assess how effectively you demonstrated the exam success skills in answering the questions. The table has been completed below for generic FIA questions as the topic of spreadsheets is not an exam topic.

Exam success skills	Your reflections/observations
Managing information	Did you read the requirements in full? Sometimes, when rushing, people guess at what the question is asking rather than reading it in full.
	Did you look at all of the possible answer options? Often, we get a number when plugging figures into our calculator and, if it is an option, we go for that as our answer rather than thinking - have I finished my calculation; have I answered the question? This is common in non-current asset depreciation and NBV calculations.
Correct interpretation of requirements	Did you identify the need to select TWO options?
	Did you identify the need to fill in the blanks without the $ sign?
	Did you identify the need to fill in the blanks with a number with no decimal places?
Efficient numerical analysis	Did you correctly identify the figure you needed to use to calculate your answer?
Good time management	Did you manage to attempt a set number of questions in the time allocated? For example, 10 questions in FFA FIA should take you 24 minutes as there are 1.2 minutes per mark and each short question is worth 2 marks.

Most important action points to apply to your next question (Fill in this section with areas you feel need improvement and how you intend to improve on them.)

Summary

Whilst this section is not exam focussed, spreadsheets will be a key part of your accountancy career. Future employers will always look for good core spreadsheet skills when selecting a candidate for a role.

15

Bank reconciliations

Learning objectives

On competition of this chapter, you should be able to:

	Syllabus reference no.
Understand the purpose of bank reconciliations.	E4(a)
Identify the main reasons for differences between the cash book and the bank statement.	E4(b)
Correct cash book errors and/or omissions.	E4(c)
Prepare bank reconciliation statements.	E4(d)
Derive bank statement and cash book balances from given information.	E4(e)
Identify the bank balance to be reported in the final accounts.	E4(f)

Exam context

Exam questions are likely to ask you to perform calculations to correct a bank reconciliation. Alternatively, they may ask you to state whether differences between the cash book and the bank statement should be adjusted in the cash book or in the reconciliation statement. You could also be asked to derive either the bank statement or cash book balance from given information.

Chapter overview

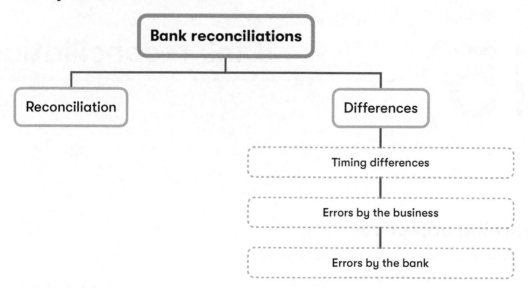

1 Introduction

This chapter is designed to enable you to explain and apply the approach to identifying and correcting errors through the use of bank reconciliations.

In theory, the entries appearing on a business's bank statement should be exactly the same as those in the business cash book. The balance shown by the bank statement should be the same as the cash book balance on the same date.

The cash book is used to record the detailed transactions of receipts and payments into and out of the bank account. These are then posted to the nominal ledger periodically using double entry. At the end of each accounting period, the balance on the cash book should equal the balance in the nominal ledger cash account.

Bank statements provide an independent record of the balance on the bank account **but** this balance is unlikely to agree exactly to the cash book balance.

When there is a difference between the cash book balance and the balance on the bank statement, this is when a bank reconciliation is performed. If the balances agree, then no reconciliation is required.

1.1 Differences between the cash book balance and the bank statement

Differences essentially occur for three reasons:

(a) **Timing differences:**

  (i) **Outstanding lodgements/deposits credited after date** (money paid into the bank by the business but not yet appearing as a receipt on bank statement)

  (ii) **Unpresented/outstanding cheques** (cheques paid out by business which have not yet appeared on bank statement)

(b) **Errors by the business (ie in the cash book):**

  (i) **Omissions**, such as standing orders, direct debits, bank charges, interest

  (ii) **Transposition errors**

  (iii) **Casting errors**

(c) **Errors by the bank.**

A word of warning

In the books of the **business**:

POSITIVE BANK BALANCE = ASSET = DEBIT

NEGATIVE BANK BALANCE (OVERDRAFT) = LIABILITY = CREDIT

But, from the **bank's** point of view:

POSITIVE BALANCE = LIABILITY = CREDIT (the bank owes you your money)

NEGATIVE BALANCE (OVERDRAFT) = ASSET = DEBIT

(You owe the bank/this is an asset for the bank.)

2 Preparing a bank reconciliation

(a) Compare the bank statement to the cash account and **tick off** all items which agree.

(b) Remaining items must represent timing differences or errors. Decide which!

2.1 Example of how to set out a bank reconciliation

CASH ACCOUNT

	$		$
Balance b/d	X	Dishonoured cheque	X
		Bank charges	X

	$		$
		Standing orders	X
Under cast error in balance b/d	X	Direct debits	X
	_	Balance c/d	X
	X		X

	$
Balance per bank statement	X
plus outstanding lodgements	X
less unpresented cheques	(X)
plus/less bank errors	X/(X)
	___
Balance per adjusted cash account	X

(a) On reconciliation, put overdrafts and payments in brackets.

(b) It is the corrected cash account balance which is shown on the statement of financial position. This figure will be the recalculated 'Balance c/d' on the cash account (or the total at the end of the reconciliation statement, which **should** be identical!).

Activity 1: Bank reconciliation (1)

The cash account of Graham showed a debit balance of $204 on 31 March 20X8. A comparison with the bank statements revealed the following:

		$
(1)	Cheques drawn but not presented	3,168
(2)	Amounts paid into the bank but not credited	723
(3)	Entries in the bank statements not recorded in the cash account	
	(i) Standing order payments	35
	(ii) Interest on bank deposit account	18
	(iii) Bank charges	14
(4)	Balance on the bank statement at 31 March 20X8	2,618

Required

Make any necessary adjustments to the cash book balance and complete the bank reconciliation statement as at 31 March 20X8.

Solution

CASH ACCOUNT

	$		$
	—		
	___		___

Bank reconciliation statement

	$
Balance per bank statement at 31 March 20X8	
Outstanding lodgements	723
Unpresented cheques	___
Balance per cash book at 31 March 20X8	

Activity 2: Bank reconciliation (2)

Whilst preparing a bank reconciliation statement at 31 December, the following items caused a difference between the bank statement balance and the cash book balance:

(1) Bank interest charged to the account in error
(2) Direct debit for $500 for insurance
(3) Bank charges of $70
(4) Cheque paid to a supplier on 29 December
(5) Receipt from a trade receivable by electronic transfer

Required

Which of these items will result in an adjustment to the balance per the bank statement?

O 2, 3, and 5
O 1 and 4
O 1, 4 and 5
O 1, 3 and 5

Activity 3: Bank reconciliation (3)

The following bank reconciliation has been prepared by a trainee accountant:

	$
Overdraft per bank statement	7,720
Less: unrepresented cheques	18,320
	10,600
Add: outstanding lodgements	33,380

	$
Cash at bank	43,980

Required

What should be the correct balance per the cash book?

O $43,980 balance at bank as stated

O $22,780 balance at bank

O $7,340 balance at bank

O $7,340 overdrawn

Activity 4: Bank reconciliation (4)

Jed is preparing his monthly bank reconciliation. The unadjusted balance per the cash book (prior to performing a bank reconciliation) is a debit balance of $2,500. The balance per the cash book and the balance per the bank statement do not agree for the following reasons:

(1)   Cheques to the value of $750 written and sent to suppliers but not yet presented by the suppliers for payment

(2)   Bank charges of $100 not yet entered in the cash book

(3)   An error by the bank in crediting to another customer's account a lodgement of $300 by Jed

(4)   A payment of $538 was recorded in the cash book as $583

Required

What was the original balance per the bank statement?

O $2,445

O $1,995

O $2,805

O $2,895

Chapter summary

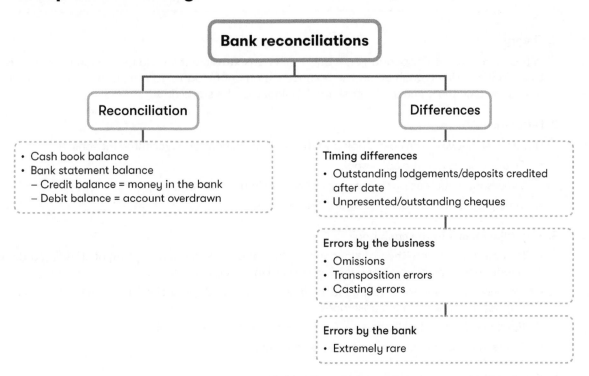

Knowledge diagnostic

1. Theory

In theory, the entries appearing on a business's **bank statement** should be exactly the same as those in the business **cash book**. The balance shown by the bank statement as on a particular date should be the same as the cash book balance at the same date.

2. Differences

Differences between the cash book and the bank statement arise for three reasons:

- Errors – usually in the cash book
- Omissions – such as bank charges not posted in the cash book
- Timing differences – such as unpresented cheques

3. Key adjustments to the cash book

- Payments made into the bank account or from the bank account by way of standing order or direct debit, which have not yet been entered in the cash book
- Dividends received (on investments held by the business), paid direct into the bank account but not yet entered in the cash book
- Bank interest and bank charges, not yet entered in the cash book
- Errors in the cash book that need to be corrected

4. Key adjustments to reconcile the bank statement

- Cheques drawn (ie paid) by the business and credited in the cash book, which have not yet been presented to the bank, or 'cleared', and so do not yet appear on the bank statement. These are commonly known as unpresented cheques or outstanding cheques.
- Cheques received by the business, paid into the bank and debited in the cash book, but which have not yet been cleared and entered in the account by the bank, and so do not yet appear on the bank statement. These are commonly known as outstanding lodgements or deposits credited after date.
- Electronic payments that have not yet been cleared.

5. Bank statement

When looking at a bank statement, assets and liabilities **appear** to be the wrong way around. Remember: If you have money in the bank, this is a liability to the bank and is shown as a credit balance. If your account is overdrawn, this is an asset to the bank and is shown as a debit balance.

Further study guidance

Question practice

Now try the following from the Further question practice bank (available in the digital edition of the Workbook):

Questions 60 to 63

Activity answers

Activity 1: Bank reconciliation (1)

CASH ACCOUNT

	$		$
Balance b/d	204	Standing order (3i)	35
Bank interest (3ii)	18	Bank charges (3iii)	14
		Balance c/d	173
	222		222

Bank reconciliation statement

	$
Balance per bank statement at 31 March 20X8	2,618
Outstanding lodgements	723
Unpresented cheques	(3,168)
Balance per cash book at 31 March 20X8	173

Activity 2: Bank reconciliation (2)

The correct answer is: 1 and 4

(1) is a bank error, (4) is an outstanding cheque and (2), (3) and (5) have all been processed correctly by the bank but need recording in the cash account.

Activity 3: Bank reconciliation (3)

The correct answer is: $7,340 balance at bank

	$
Overdraft per bank statement	(7,720)
Less: unrepresented cheques	(18,320)
	(26,040)
Add: outstanding lodgements	33,380
Cash at bank	7,340

Activity 4: Bank reconciliation (4)

The correct answer is: $2,895

ADJUSTMENT OF CASH BOOK BALANCE

	$		$
Balance b/d	2,500	Bank charges	100
Payment transposition error ($583 – $538)	45	Balance c/d	2,445
	2,545		2,545

Bank reconciliation statement

	$
Balance per bank statement (balancing figure)	2,895
Unpresented cheques	(750)
Bank error	300
Balance per corrected cash book	2,445

16

Correction of errors

Learning objectives

On competition of this chapter, you should be able to:

	Syllabus reference no.
Identify the types of error which may occur in bookkeeping systems.	E2(a)
Identify errors which would be highlighted by the extraction of a trial balance.	E2(b)
Prepare journal entries to correct errors.	E2(c)
Calculate and understand the impact of errors on the statement of profit or loss and other comprehensive income and statement of financial position.	E2(d)
Understand the purpose of a suspense account.	E5(a)
Identify errors leading to the creation of a suspense account.	E5(b)
Record entries in a suspense account.	E5(c)
Make journal entries to clear a suspense account.	E5(d)

Exam context

Questions on this area are likely to focus on three main areas. You may be asked to identify which explanations could have led to a particular difference or be asked to identify the journal entry to correct an error. You may also need to determine the effect errors may have on the profit figure.

Chapter overview

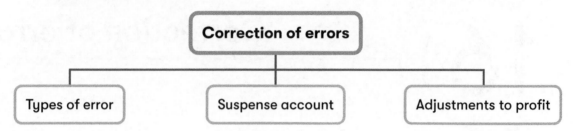

Correction of errors

- Types of error
- Suspense account
- Adjustments to profit

1 Introduction

Previous chapters showed us how the trial balance was extracted from the ledger accounts and that it should balance, ie total debits should equal total credits.

If the trial balance does not balance, then an error has definitely been made and must be corrected.

2 Types of error

The following errors will still allow the trial balance to balance:

Type of error	Definitions and examples
Error of omission	An error of omission means failing to record a transaction at all, or making a debit or credit entry, but not the corresponding double entry. If a business receives an invoice from a supplier for $250, the transaction might be omitted from the books entirely. As a result, both the total debits and the total credits of the business will be incorrect by $250. If a business receives an invoice from a supplier for $300, the payables control account might be credited, but the debit entry in the purchases account might be omitted. In this case, the total credits would not equal total debits (because total debits are $300 less than they ought to be).
Error of commission	Errors of commission are where the bookkeeper makes a mistake in carrying out their task of recording transactions in the accounts, eg putting a debit entry or a credit entry in the wrong account. For example, if telephone expenses of $540 are debited to the electricity expenses account, an error of commission would have occurred. The result is that although total debits and total credits balance, telephone expenses are understated by $540 and electricity expenses are overstated by the same amount. Errors of casting (adding up) are also examples of errors of commission. The total daily credit sales in the sales day book should be $28,425, but are incorrectly added up as $28,825. The total sales in the sales day book are then used to credit total sales and debit total receivables in the ledger accounts. Although total debits and total credits are still equal, they are incorrect by $400.
Error of principle	An error of principle involves making a double entry in the belief that the transaction is being entered in the correct accounts, but subsequently finding out that the accounting entry breaks the 'rules' of an accounting principle or concept. For example, repairs to a machine costing $150 should be treated as expenditure, and debited to a repairs account. If, instead, the repair costs are added to the cost of the non-current asset (asset expenditure) an error of principle would have occurred. As a result, although total debits still equal total credits, the repairs account is $150 less than it should be and the cost of the non-current asset is $150 greater than it should be.
Compensating error	Compensating errors are errors which are, coincidentally, equal and opposite to one another. For example, although unlikely, in theory two transposition errors of $540 might occur in extracting ledger balances, one on each side of

Type of error	Definitions and examples
	the double entry. In the administration expenses account, $2,282 might be written instead of $2,822 while, in the sundry income account, $8,391 might be written instead of $8,931. Both the debits and the credits would be $540 too low, and the mistake would not be apparent when the trial balance is cast. Consequently, compensating errors hide the fact that there are errors in the trial balance.

However, the trial balance will not balance if any of the following types of error occur:

(a) Transposition error

(b) An entry has been posted where:

   (i) Debits do not equal credits

   (ii) A debit entry has been posted and no corresponding credit made (or vice versa)

   (iii) Two debit entries or two credit entries have been posted.

These errors will be corrected by creating a **suspense account** and making a journal entry to correct the error.

3 Suspense accounts

Suspense accounts are **temporary** accounts. They **never** appear in the final accounts.

They are used for two main reasons:

(a) To account for a debit or credit entry when the accountant is unsure as to where it should go

(b) To make a preliminary trial balance when an error has been detected

Steps to clear a suspense account:

(a) Determine the original accounting entry which **was** made.

(b) Decide what entry **should** have been made.

(c) Make the required adjustment.

Illustration 1: Suspense accounts

W Co sold goods with a value of $2,500 to James, a credit customer. When recording the sale, W Co posted the transaction to the correct accounts but made two debit entries.

Required

Show the original entry and the entry necessary to correct the transaction.

Solution

Step 1   Entry made was:

Dr	Trade receivables	$2,500	
Dr	Sales		$2,500

Step 2   Entry should have been:

Dr	Trade receivables	$2,500	
Cr	Sales		$2,500

Step 3   Correction:

Dr	Suspense account	$5,000	

Cr	Sales (2 × $2,500)	$5,000

The trade receivables entry is correct but sales has been debited by $2,500 when it should have been credited by that amount.

The correction is therefore twice the original error.

Activity 1: Correction of errors

Dan, the bookkeeper of Tiffany & Co, has produced a draft trial balance for the year ended 30 April 20X7.

	$	$
Property, plant and equipment		
At cost	60,000	
Accumulated depreciation		31,000
Capital at 1 May 20X6		53,000
Profit for the year		12,300
Inventory	14,000	
Receivables ledger control account	9,600	
Payables ledger control account		6,500
Cash at bank	1,640	
	85,240	102,800

As chief accountant, you discover the following:

(1)   A rent payment of $350 in March 20X7 had been debited to the receivables ledger control account in error.

(2)   Irrecoverable debts of $500 during the year ended 30 April 20X7 have not been recorded in the books.

(3)   No entry has been made for the refund of $2,620 made by cheque to V Woolf in March 20X7, in respect of defective goods returned to Tiffany & Co. V Woolf, who had already paid for the goods, returned them on 28 February 20X7.

(4)   The total column of the cash receipts book had been overcast by $1,900 in March 20X7.

(5)   The purchase of stationery for $1,460 cash in June 20X6 has been correctly entered in the cash account, but no entry has been made to the appropriate expense account.

(6)   Capital of $35,000 has been recorded incorrectly as $53,000.

Required

Prepare:

1   Journal entries to correct the above errors.

2   A suspense account showing how it is cleared.

Solution

4 Adjustments to profit

When errors are corrected, they may affect the business's profit for the year figure.

In the example above, Item 5 tells us that a stationery expense of $1,460 has not been recorded in the expense account.

The profit for the year figure in the trial balance of $12,300 is therefore too high and needs to be corrected.

This is done by using a statement of adjustments to profit.

Proforma

	$	$	$
	–	+	
Original profit			X
Adjustment:			
(a) Over depreciation		X	
(b) Unrecorded expense	X		
(c) Unrecorded sale		X	
	(X)	X	X/(X)
Adjusted profit			X

Activity 2: Adjustment of profits

Prepare a statement of adjustments to profit for Tiffany & Co.

Solution

Adjustment of profits statement for the year ended 30 April 20X7

	Decreases	Increases	
	$	$	$
Draft profit			
Adjustments			_____
Rent (1)			
Irrecoverable debts (2)			
Stationery (5)			
Total adjustments	_____		_____
Revised profit			_____

Activity 3: Errors and profit

Z Co's statement of profit or loss showed a profit of $112,400 for the year ended 30 September 20X7. The following errors were later discovered:

(1) Sales returns of $2,700 had been recorded as a new sale.

(2) A machine which had been held for two years and had originally cost $15,000 was depreciated this year using a $33\frac{1}{3}\%$ reducing balance basis. Z Co's policy is to depreciate machines over four years.

Required

What would be the net profit after adjusting for these errors?

BPP
LEARNING
MEDIA

- ○ $103,250
- ○ $105,750
- ○ $105,950
- ○ $108,450

 Essential reading

Chapter 16 of the Essential reading provides more detail on the types of errors that can be found in accounting and the use of journal entries.

The Essential reading is available as an Appendix of the digital edition of the Workbook.

Chapter summary

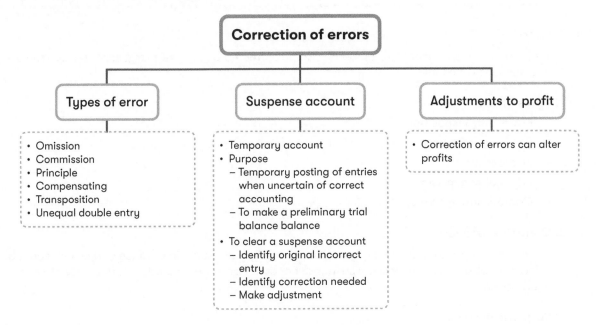

Correction of errors

Types of error

- Omission
- Commission
- Principle
- Compensating
- Transposition
- Unequal double entry

Suspense account

- Temporary account
- Purpose
  - Temporary posting of entries when uncertain of correct accounting
  - To make a preliminary trial balance balance
- To clear a suspense account
  - Identify original incorrect entry
  - Identify correction needed
  - Make adjustment

Adjustments to profit

- Correction of errors can alter profits

Knowledge diagnostic

1. Overview

There are five main types of error. Some can be corrected by journal entry; some require the use of a suspense account.

2. Types of error

- Errors of **transposition**
- Errors of **omission**
- Errors of **principle**
- Errors of **commission**
- **Compensating errors**

3. Correction of errors

Errors which leave total debits and credits in the ledger accounts in balance can be corrected by using journal entries. Otherwise, a suspense account has to be opened first, and later cleared by a journal entry.

4. Suspense accounts

Suspense accounts, as well as being used to correct some errors, are also opened when it is not known immediately where to post an amount. When the mystery is solved, the suspense account is closed and the amount is correctly posted using a journal entry.

Suspense accounts are only temporary. None should exist when it comes to drawing up the financial statements at the end of the accounting period.

5. Method

For each error, apply the following method:

- What is the correct entry?
- What entry has been made (if any)?
- What is the entry needed to correct the error?
- The other side of the entry then goes to the suspense account (eg if the entry above is a debit, then the entry in the suspense account will be a credit).

Further study guidance

Question practice

Now try the following from the Further question practice bank (available in the digital edition of the Workbook):

Questions 64 to 68

Activity answers

Activity 1: Correction of errors

1

Journal entries

		Dr $	Cr $
(1)	Rent and rates	350	
	Receivables ledger control account		350
(2)	Irrecoverable debts expense	500	
	Receivables ledger control account		500
(3)	Receivables ledger control account	2,620	
	Cash at bank		2,620
(4)	Suspense account	1,900	
	Cash at bank		1,900
(5)	Stationery and postage	1,460	
	Suspense account		1,460
(6)	Capital	18,000	
	Suspense account		18,000

2

SUSPENSE ACCOUNT

	$		$
Brought forward ($102,800 – $85,240)	17,560	Stationery and postage (5)	1,460
Cash at bank (4)	1,900	Capital (6)	18,000
	19,460		19,460

Activity 2: Adjustment of profits

Adjustment of profits statement for the year ended 30 April 20X7

	Decreases	Increases	
	$	$	$
Draft profit			
Adjustments			12,300
Rent (1)	350		
Irrecoverable debts (2)	500		
Stationery (5)	1,460		
Total adjustments	2,310		(2,310)
Revised profit			9,990

Activity 3: Errors and profit

The correct answer is: $105,750

	Decreases	Increases	
	$	$	$
Draft profit			112,400
Adjustments:			
(1) Sales returns (2 × $2,700)	5,400		
(2) Depreciation (W)	1,250	–	
	6,650		(6,650)
Adjusted profit			105,750

Working

Depreciation

The depreciation charge was:

$33^{1}/_{3}\% \times (\$15,000 \times 2/4) = \$2,500$

Depreciation charge should have been:

$15,000/4 years = $3,750

Incremental depreciation to be charged $1,250

Incomplete records

Learning objectives

On competition of this chapter, you should be able to:

	Syllabus reference no.
Understand and apply techniques used in incomplete record situations: i) Use of accounting equation ii) Use of ledger accounts to calculate missing figures iii) Use of cash and/or bank summaries iv) Use of profit percentages to calculate missing figures	F6(a)

Exam context

Questions on this chapter will require you to identify missing figures, for example sales, closing inventories and drawings.

Chapter overview

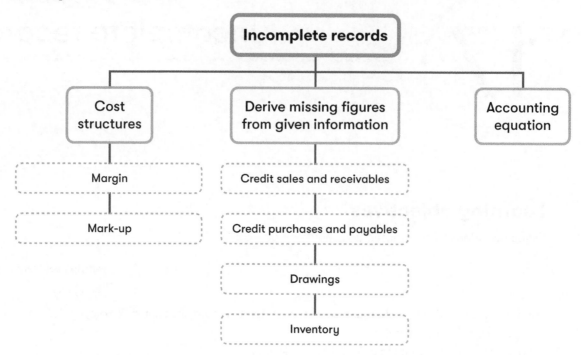

1 Issue

Individuals running small businesses such as a newsagent or greengrocer may not keep all of the accounting records we have studied or have a detailed understanding of double entry bookkeeping.

They still need to know how the business is performing and so will produce financial statements. If some necessary information is not maintained by the business, it will need to be derived from other available information.

2 Cost structures

Cost structure information is usually expressed in one of two ways, either as a margin or a mark up.

(a) **Margin.** Here, gross profit is expressed as a percentage of sales, for example a margin of 25% gives:

Sales	100%
Cost of sales	75%
Gross profit	25%

(b) **Mark-up.** Here, gross profit is expressed as a percentage of cost of sales, for example a mark up of 35% gives:

Sales	135%
Cost of sales	100%
Gross profit	35%

Remember that:

Cost of sales = opening inventories + purchases – closing inventories

Activity 1: Cost of sales

W Co has on average a profit margin of 40%. In 20X7, sales total is $476,000.

Required

What is cost of sales?

Solution

Activity 2: Calculation of purchases

Y Co operates with a standard mark up of 30% and has the following information available for 20X7:

	$
Sales	221,000
Opening inventories	43,000
Closing inventories	47,500

Required

What is the value for purchases in 20X7?

Solution

Activity 3: Inventory

On 1 January 20X7, J Co had inventory of $620,000. Sales for the month amounted to $985,000 and purchases were $700,000. At the end of January, a fire in the warehouse destroyed some inventory items. The owners salvaged inventory valued at $180,000. J Co operates with a mark up of 25%.

Required

What is the cost of inventory destroyed in the fire?

O $335,000

O $352,000

O $401,250

O $532,000

3 Credit sales and trade receivables

If a business does not keep a record of its sales on credit, the value of these sales can be derived from the opening balance of trade receivables, the closing balance of trade receivables, and the payments received from customers during the period.

Formula to learn

	$
Payments from trade receivables	X
Plus closing balance of trade receivables (since these represent sales in the current period for which cash payment has not yet been received)	X
Less opening balance of trade receivables (these represent credit sales in a previous period)	(X)
Credit sales in the period	X

Activity 4: Sales

B Co maintains a cash float of $50. In 20X7, all receipts from credit customers were banked, after the following payments from the till had been made:

	$
General expenses	4,500
Drawings	6,250

Total bankings in the year amounted to $28,454, and opening and closing trade receivables were $1,447 and $1,928 respectively.

Required

Based on the information above, what was the value of sales made during the year?

Solution

PETTY CASH

	$		$
Bal b/d		General expenses	
Receipts from trade receivables		Drawings	
		Bankings	
		Bal c/d	
	____		____

TRADE RECEIVABLES

	$		$
Bal b/d			
		Cash (deducted from petty cash a/c)	
Sales*			
		Bal c/d	
	____		____

4 Purchases and trade payables

A similar relationship exists between purchases of inventory during a period, the opening and closing balances for trade payables, and amounts paid to suppliers during the period.

If we wish to calculate an unknown amount for purchases, the amount would be derived as follows:

Formula to learn

	$
Payments to trade payables during the period	X
Plus closing balance of trade payables (since these represent purchases in the current period for which payment has not yet been made)	X
Less opening balance of trade payables (these debts, paid in the current period, relate to purchases in a previous period)	(X)
Purchases during the period	X

Illustration 1: Purchases (1)

Joe's business had trade payables of $3,728 on 1 October 20X5 and trade payables of $2,645 on 30 September 20X6. Payments to trade payables during the year to 30 September 20X6 were $31,479.

Required

What were purchases for the year?

Solution

	$
Payments to trade payables	31,479
Plus closing balance of trade payables	2,645
Less opening balance of trade payables	(3,728)
Purchases	30,396

The calculation above could be made in a T-account, with purchases being the balancing figure to complete the account:

	$		$
Cash payments	31,479	Opening balance b/d	3,728
Closing balance c/d	2,645	Purchases (balancing figure)	30,396
	34,124		34,124

Activity 5: Purchases (2)

Emma is a sole trader who does not keep full accounting records. The following details relate to her transactions with credit customers and suppliers for the year ended 31 December 20X3:

	$
Trade receivables, 1 January 20X3	65,000
Trade payables, 1 January 20X3	30,000
Cash received from customers	343,200
Cash paid to suppliers	151,400
Irrecoverable debts written off	700
Discounts received	1,480
Contra between payables and receivables ledgers	1,000
Trade receivables, 31 December 20X3	90,500
Trade payables, 31 December 20X3	42,000

Required

What figure should appear for purchases in Emma's statement of profit or loss for the year to 31 December 20X3?

○ $162,920

○ $163,880

○ $165,100

○ $165,880

---

5 Drawings

5.1 Cash drawings

Drawings would normally represent no particular problem at all in preparing a set of final accounts from incomplete records, but it is not unusual for exam questions to contain complicating situations.

(a) The business owner may pay income into their bank account which has nothing whatever to do with the business operations. For example, the owner might pay dividend income, or other income from investments into the bank, from stocks and shares which they own personally, separate from the business itself. (In other words, there are no investments in the business statement of financial position, and so income from investments cannot possibly be income of the business.) These amounts will be **credited to their drawings**.

(b) The business owner may pay money out of the business bank account for items which are not business expenses, such as life insurance premiums and a payment for their family's holidays. These will be **treated as drawings**.

> ### Exam focus point
>
> Beware of the wording in an exam question.
>
> You should note that:
>
> (a) If a question states that a proprietor's drawings during a given year are 'approximately $40 per week' then you should assume that drawings for the year are $40 × 52 weeks = $2,080.
>
> (b) However, if a question states that drawings in the year are 'between $35 and $45 per week', do not assume that the drawings average $40 per week and so amount to $2,080 for the year. You could not be certain that the actual withdrawals did average $40, and so you should treat the withdrawals figure as a missing item that needs to be calculated.

Activity 6: Drawings (1)

Bob owns and manages B Co although he does not keep detailed accounting records. All of Bob's sales are for cash. He pays certain expenses from his till and then banks the remaining funds.

Bob maintains a $1,000 float and operates with a margin of 20%. He has provided you with the following information.

	$
Purchases of goods (on credit)	20,000
Wages for clerical assistant (per week; there are 52 weeks in the year)	100
Stationery	500
Electricity	1,200
Bankings	12,800
Opening inventories	2,000
Closing inventories	3,000

Bob is unsure of the level of drawings taken during the year but estimates they were between $60 and $90 per week.

Required

What were Bob's drawings during the year?

Solution

5.2 Goods drawn by proprietor

The owners of the business may at times take goods or cash from the business for their own use. We have seen these before as drawings.

In incomplete records questions, these drawings need to be included.

Cash drawings

Dr   Drawings

Cr   Cash

Goods taken for own use

Dr   Drawings

Cr   Purchases

These are recorded at the **cost** to the business **not** at sale price.

They are taken out of purchases and **not** recorded against inventories.

Note. If you are using a trade payables T-account to calculate purchases, remember to adjust purchases for any goods taken by proprietor.

Activity 7: Drawings (2)

During the year ended 31 December 20X7, Peter, a sole trader, carried out the following transactions:

	$
Sales (40 units @ $100)	4,000
Purchases (45 units @ $60)	2,700
His inventories (at cost) were:	
1 January 20X7 (5 units @ $60)	300
31 December 20X7 (8 units @ $60)	480

During the year, he had withdrawn two units for his own use. Firstly, ignoring the drawings, an outline trading account would appear as follows:

	$	$
Sales		4,000
Cost of sales		
Opening inventories	300	
Purchases	2,700	
	3,000	
Less: closing inventories	(480)	
		2,520
Gross profit		1,480

Required

How should the drawings of goods be treated?

Solution

5.3 Accounting equation

We saw in a previous chapter that the statement of financial position can be stated as an equation:

Debits = Credits

Assets = Liabilities + Capital + Profit – Drawings

This can be rearranged as:

Assets – Liabilities (Net assets) = Capital + Profit – Drawings

Therefore, the movement in net assets can be explain by the movement in capital (ie new capital introduced + profit – drawings).

If we wish to find a missing figure, such as profit or drawings, the accounting equation can be expressed as:

Closing net assets = Opening net assets + Capital introduced + Profit – Drawings

It can then be rearranged to find a missing figure such as profit:

Profit = Closing net assets + Drawings – Capital introduced – Opening net assets

Activity 8: Calculation of profit or loss

Joe, a sole trader, set up business on 1 October 20X6 with $40,000 of his own money. During the year to 30 September 20X7, he won $50,000 on the lottery and paid $30,000 of this into his business. He took cash drawings of $5,000 during the year and, at 30 September 20X7, the net assets of the business totalled $59,000.

Required

Calculate Joe's profit or loss for the year.

O $6,000 loss

O $6,000 profit

O $16,000 loss

O $4,000 profit

Essential reading

Chapter 17 of the Essential reading goes into more detail about the cash book and how it is used in incomplete records. It also covers the impact of accruals and prepayments on incomplete records.

The Essential reading is available as an Appendix of the digital edition of the Workbook.

Chapter summary

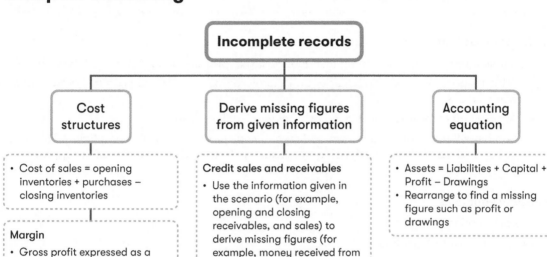

Incomplete records

Cost structures

- Cost of sales = opening inventories + purchases – closing inventories

Margin
- Gross profit expressed as a percentage of sales

Mark-up
- Gross profit expressed as a percentage of cost of sales

Derive missing figures from given information

Credit sales and receivables
- Use the information given in the scenario (for example, opening and closing receivables, and sales) to derive missing figures (for example, money received from credit customers)
- Remember to exclude cash sales from the T-account working

Credit purchases and payables
- Use the information given in the scenario (for example, opening and closing payables, and purchases) to derive missing figures (for example, payments to credit suppliers)
- Remember to exclude cash purchases from the T-account working

Drawings
- Owners of the business take goods or cash for their own use
- Where goods are withdrawn they are recorded at the cost to the business

Inventory
- Use the information given in the scenario (for example, opening and closing inventory and purchases) to derive missing figures (for example, drawings of inventory)

Accounting equation

- Assets = Liabilities + Capital + Profit – Drawings
- Rearrange to find a missing figure such as profit or drawings

Knowledge diagnostic

1. Situations tested

Incomplete records questions may test your ability to prepare accounts in the following situations:

- A trader does not maintain a ledger and therefore has no continuous double entry record of transactions.
- Accounting records are destroyed by accident, such as fire.
- Some essential figure is unknown and must be calculated as a balancing figure. This may occur as a result of inventory being damaged or destroyed, or because of misappropriation of assets.

2. Useful equations

The accounting equation:

Assets = Capital + Liabilities

The business equation:

Closing net assets = Opening net assets + Capital introduced + Profit – Drawings

3. Drawings

Drawings often feature as the missing item in an incomplete records problem. The trader has been drawing money but does not know how much.

4. Approach

The approach to incomplete records questions is to build up the information given so as to complete the necessary double entry. This may involve reconstructing control accounts for:

- Cash and bank
- Trade receivables and payables

5. Mark ups and margins

Where inventory, sales or purchases is the unknown figure, it will be necessary to use information on gross profit percentages to construct a working for gross profit in which the unknown figure can be inserted as a balance.

Further study guidance

Question practice

Now try the following from the Further question practice bank (available in the digital edition of the Workbook):

Questions 68 to 72

BPP
LEARNING
MEDIA

Activity answers

Activity 1: Cost of sales
$285,600

Working

	%	$
Sales	100	476,000
COS	60	285,600
GP	40	190,400

Activity 2: Calculation of purchases
$174,500

Workings

1 **Cost structure**

	%	$
Sales	130	221,000
COS	100	170,000
GP	30	51,000

2 **Purchases**

	$
Cost of sales	
Opening inventory	43,000
+ Purchases (balancing figure)	174,500
– Closing inventory	47,500
	170,000

Activity 3: Inventory
The correct answer is: $352,000

Cost structure: 25% mark up

				$
Sales	=	125%	=	985000
∴ COS	=	100%	=	788,000
Gross profit		25%		197,000

Cost of sales

	$
Opening inventories	620,000
Purchases	700,000
	1,320,000
Less: cost of sales	(788,000)
Closing inventories **should be**	532,000
Closing inventories **is**	(180,000)
∴ inventory lost in fire	352,000

Activity 4: Sales

PETTY CASH

	$		$
Bal b/d	50		
Receipts from trade receivables	39,204	General expenses	4,500
		Drawings	6,250
		Bankings	28,454
		Bal c/d	50
	39,254		39,254

TRADE RECEIVABLES

	$		$
Bal b/d	1,447		
Sales*	39,685	Cash (deducted from petty cash a/c)	39,204
		Bal c/d	1,928
	41,132		41,132

Activity 5: Purchases (2)

The correct answer is: $165,880

PLCA

	$		$
Cash paid	151,400	Balance b/d	30,000
Discount received	1,480		
Contra	1,000	Purchases (bal. figure)	165,880
Balance c/d	42,000		
	195,880		195,880

Activity 6: Drawings (1)

$4,050

Cost structure

			Cash		$
Sales	=		100%	=	23,750
∴ COS	=		80%	=	19,000
Gross profit			20%		4,750

Cash

	$			$
Balance b/d	1,000	Wages		5,200
		Stationery		500
Sales	23,750	Electricity		1,200
		Bankings		12,800
		∴ Drawings		4,050
		Bal c/d		1,000
	24,750			24,750

Activity 7: Drawings (2)

	$	$
Sales		4,000
Cost of sales		
Opening inventories	300	
Purchases	2,700	
Less: goods drawn by proprietor		
2 units @ $60	(120)	
	2,880	
Less: closing inventories	(480)	
		2,400
Gross profit		1,600

Activity 8: Calculation of profit or loss

The correct answer is: $6,000 loss

Profit = Closing net assets + Drawings – Capital introduced – Opening net assets

Profit = $59,000 + $5,000 – $30,000 – $40,000 = ($6,000), ie a loss

18

Preparation of financial statements for sole traders

Learning objectives

On competition of this chapter, you should be able to:

	Syllabus reference no.
Prepare extracts of an opening trial balance.	E1(c)
Prepare journal entries to correct errors.	E2(c)
Record entries in a suspense account.	E5(c)
Make journal entries to clear a suspense account.	E5(d)
Prepare a statement of financial position or extracts as applicable from given information using accounting treatments as stipulated within Sections D, E and examinable documents.	F1(d)
Prepare a statement of profit or loss and other comprehensive income or extracts as applicable from given information using accounting treatments as stipulated within Sections D, E and examinable documents.	F2(a)

Exam context

This chapter recaps some of the key skills you have learnt in the chapters covered to date. In the multi-task accounts preparation question in Section B of the exam, you could be asked to produce extracts from or a full statement of financial position or statement of profit or loss. This chapter will also help you to see how financial accounting fits together.

Chapter overview

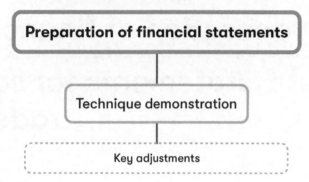

1 Introduction

The purpose of this chapter is to recap some of the skills covered in previous chapters.

In the computer-based exam, you are unlikely to have to prepare a full set of financial statements. In the multi-task accounts preparation question, you are more likely to have to perform a series of smaller tasks as part of the preparation of final financial statements. However, completing this exercise will revise your understanding of topics covered so far and enable you to see the end product: a business' transactions ordered into a set of financial statements.

Activity 1: Technique demonstration

You have been given the information below and asked to prepare the accounts of Mugg for the year ended 31 December 20X7.

Trial balance as at 31 December 20X7

	Dr	Cr
	$	$
Capital account at 1 January 20X7		2,377
Rent	500	
Inventories 1 January 20X7	510	
Electricity	240	
Insurance	120	
Wages	1,634	
Trade receivables	672	
Sales		15,542
Repairs	635	
Purchases	9,876	
Discounts received		129
Drawings	1,200	
Petty cash	5	
Bank	762	
Motor vehicles at cost	1,740	
Furniture and fixtures at cost	830	
Accumulated depreciation at 1 January 20X7		
Motor vehicles		435
Furniture and fixtures		166
Travel and entertaining	192	
Trade payables		700
Suspense account	433	
	19,349	19,349

The following information is also available:

(1) Closing inventories, valued at cost, amounts to $647.

(2) Mugg has drawn $10 a month and these drawings have been charged to wages.

(3) Depreciation is to be provided at 25% on cost on motor vehicles, and 20% on cost on furniture and fixtures.

(4) Bad debts totalling $37 are to be written off.

(5) $180 received from a credit customer was correctly entered in the trade receivables account and credited to the bank account.

(6) Mugg has taken goods from inventories for his own use. When purchased by his business, these goods cost $63 and they would have been sold for $91.

(7) The annual rental of the business premises is $600, and $180 paid for electricity in August 20X7 covers the 12 months to 30 June 20X8.

(8) A contra entry of $73 has only been recorded in the trade receivables account.

Required

1   Prepare journal entries to record items (1) – (8).

2   Clear the suspense account.

3   Produce a statement of profit or loss for the year ended 31 December 20X7 and a statement of financial position as at that date.

Solution

2

SUSPENSE ACCOUNT

	$		$
	—		—

3

Mugg Statement of profit or loss for the year ended 31 December 20X7

	$	$
Sales		
Less: cost of sales		
Opening inventories		
Purchases		
Less: closing inventories		
Gross profit		
Discounts received		
Less expenses:		

BPP
LEARNING
MEDIA

	$	$
Rent [ ]		
Electricity [ ]		
Insurance		
Wages [ ]		
Repairs		
Depreciation		
Travel and entertaining		
Bad debts		
	____	_____
Profit for the period		

Mugg Statement of financial position as at 31 December 20X7

	Cost	Accumulated depreciation	NBV
	$	$	$
Non-current assets			
Motor vehicles			
Furniture and fixtures	_____	_____	_____
Current assets			
Inventories			
Trade receivables [ ]			
Prepayments			
Cash and bank balances			
[ ]			
Total current assets			_____
Total assets			_____
Capital			
Capital as at 1 January 20X7			
Profit for the period			
Less: drawings [ ]			_____
Current liabilities			

	Cost	Accumulated depreciation	NBV
	$	$	$
Trade payables	[ ]		
Accruals			
			‾‾‾‾‾‾‾
			‾‾‾‾‾‾‾

Exam focus point

You may not be asked to prepare a full statement of profit or loss or statement of financial position in your exam. However, the 15-mark format questions are likely to ask you to prepare extracts from these statements.

In addition, the ACCA examining team has stated that it is essential that you practise preparing full financial statements so that you fully understand the concepts and principles involved. If you are moving on to study Financial Reporting (FR), practising full questions now is vital.

Essential reading

Chapter 17 of the Essential reading has an additional question for you to practice your skills in this area.

The Essential reading is available as an Appendix of the digital edition of the Workbook.

Chapter summary

Preparation of financial statements

Technique demonstration

Key adjustments
- Closing inventory
- Drawings
- Depreciation
- Irrecoverable debts
- Accruals and prepayments
- Control accounts

Knowledge diagnostic

1. Exam focus

You may not be asked to prepare a full statement of profit or loss or statement of financial position in your exam. However, the 15-mark format questions are likely to ask you to prepare extracts from these statements.

2. Dealing with the information provided

Carefully read through the information provided in the question and decide what should be included in the statement of profit and loss. Remember not everything in a trial balance may be needed.

3. Additional information

Information in the additional information will typically require an adjustment to the financial statements. Always remember to enter a full double entry for these adjustments.

4. Adjustments

You will be tested on accounting theory from other areas of the syllabus when preparing a set of financial statements. Make sure you are happy with dealing with depreciation, inventory, prepayments, accruals, irrecoverable debts, and allowances for receivables.

5. Finalising the financial statements

Remember, before you add up your statement of financial position, you will need to transfer the profit for the year into your retained earnings in the statement of financial position.

Further study guidance

Question practice

Now try the following from the Further question practice bank (available in the digital edition of the Workbook):

Question 67

Further reading

There is an article called 'Adjustments to financial statements' on the ACCA website. You are advised to read this article as part of the preparation for your exam.

Activity answers

Activity 1: Technique demonstration

1 (1)

		Dr	Cr
		$	$
Dr	Inventories (SOFP)	647	
Cr	Closing inventories (SPL)		64

Being: adjustment to record year end closing inventories

(2)

		$	$
Dr	Drawings (12 × $10) (SOFP)	120	
Cr	Wages (SPL)		120

Being: correction of cash drawings posted as wages

(3)

		$	$
Dr	Depreciation expense (SPL)	601	
Cr	Accumulated depreciation (SOFP):		
	Motor vehicles ($1,740 × 25%)		435
	Furniture and fittings ($829 × 20%)		166

Being: adjustment to record depreciation for the year

(4)

		$	$
Dr	Bad debt expense (SPL)	37	
Cr	Trade receivables (SOFP)		37

Being: write off of irrecoverable customer balance

(5)

		$	$
Dr	Bank (2 × $180) (SOFP)	360	
Cr	Suspense account		360

Being: adjustment to correct cash receipt from trade receivables

(6)

		$	$
Dr	Drawings (SOFP)	63	
Cr	Purchases (SPL)		63

Being: adjustment for goods drawn from business (removed at cost value)

(7)

		$	$
Dr	Rent expense ($ $500) (SPL)	100	
Cr	Accruals (SOFP)		100

Being: accrual of rent expense

		$	$
Dr	Prepayments ($180 × 6/12) (SOFP)	90	
Cr	Electricity expense (SPL)		90

Being: prepayment of electricity expense

(8)

		$	$
Dr	Trade payables (SOFP)	73	
Cr	Suspense account		73

Being: adjustment for contra omitted from trade payables

2

SUSPENSE ACCOUNT

	$		$
Bal b/d	433		
		(5) Bank	360
		(8) Trade payables	73
	———		———
	433		433

3

Mugg Statement of profit or loss for the year ended 31 December 20X7

	$	$
Sales		15,542
Less: cost of sales		
Opening inventories	510	
Purchases ($9,876 − $63)	9,813	
	10,323	
Less: closing inventories	647	
		(9,676)
Gross profit		5,866
Discounts received		129
		5,995
Less expenses:		
Rent ($500 + $100)	600	

	$	$
Electricity ($240 – (6/12 × $180))	150	
Insurance	120	
Wages ($1,634 – $120)	1,514	
Repairs	635	
Depreciation	601	
Travel and entertaining	192	
Bad debts	37	
		(3,849)
Profit for the period		2,146

Mugg Statement of financial position as at 31 December 20X7

	Cost	Accumulated depreciation	NBV
	$	$	$
Non-current assets			
Motor vehicles	1,740	870	870
Furniture and fixtures	830	332	498
	2,569	1,202	1,368
Current assets			
Inventories			647
Trade receivables ($672 – $37)			635
Prepayments			90
Cash and bank balances ($5 + $762 + $360)			1,127
Total current assets			2,499
Total assets			3,867
Capital			
Capital as at 1 January 20X7			2,377
Profit for the period			2,146
Less: drawings ($1,200 + $63 + $120)			(1,383)
			3,140
Current liabilities			
Trade payables ($700 – $73)			627
Accruals			100
			727
			3,867

Skills checkpoint 4

Irrecoverable debts and allowance for receivables

Overview

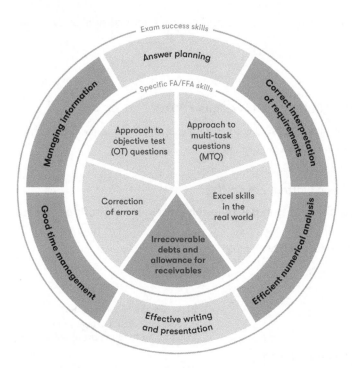

Introduction

The 2018/2019 examiners report commented that the topic of 'irrecoverable debts and allowance for receivables' continues to be an area of the syllabus where performance is mixed with many candidates not providing the correct response. There is often a lot of detail in these questions and they need to be read very carefully.

Irrecoverable debts and allowance for receivables

Here we shall recap the key areas of this topic.

Irrecoverable (bad) debts

These are debts which the business does not believe it will recover. For example, if a customer owes you $2,000 but you find out that they have closed their business and left the country, it is highly unlikely that you will recover that $2,000, therefore you will write it off as an irrecoverable (bad) debt.

To do this, you need to remove it from receivables and show it as an expense in the statement of profit or loss. The latter will then show a net figure of Nil – $2,000 sale and a $2,000 expense.

Irrecoverable (bad) debts written off and subsequently recovered

If the customer in the previous example returns to the country and pays you that $2,000 then you will need to account for cash coming in.

Cash increases and the other entry is posted to the irrecoverable debts expense account as a credit (negative expense).

That is all you would need to do for this transaction as the debt will have already been removed from receivables when it was originally written off (in our previous example).

Allowance for receivables

Usually, a business will have an idea as to how much of their receivables balance tends to go unpaid each year. For example, over the years, a business could have worked out that, as well as certain irrecoverable debts, there will be another 5% of the remaining receivables that are unlikely to pay.

The business will then make an allowance for this 5% at the end of each year after irrecoverable debts have been written off.

Illustration

Pumpkin has a receivables balance of $50,000 as at 31 December 20X0.

It has been decided to write off debts totalling $10,000 and to make an allowance for 5% of the receivables balance at 31 December 20X0.

The opening allowance for receivables was $1,500.

A customer whose debt had previously been written, pays $700.

What figure should appear for irrecoverable debts expense in the statement of profit or loss for the year ended 31 December 20X0?

STEP 1   Firstly, let's think about what has happened to receivables:

Balance at the year end	$50,000
Debts written off	$(10,000)[6]
Closing receivables	**$40,000**

[6] This amount is going to the irrecoverable debts expense account so this is going to form part of our answer.

STEP 2   Next, let's deal with the debt that has been written off and subsequently recovered:

$700 goes to cash at bank and the other entry is to **the irrecoverable dents expense account** as a credit (negative).

The running balance on our expense account is now $10,000 – $700 = **$9,300**.

STEP 3   Finally, let's take a look at the allowance for receivables account.

I would always set up my allowance working as follows:

Opening allowance for receivables	$X
Increase or decrease in allowance	$X/(X)
Closing allowance for receivables	**$X**

Using a proforma like this enables you to slot in the figures that you know for certain and then calculate the missing figure.

So far, we only know the opening allowance so we slot in the $1,500.

Next, we calculate the closing allowance for receivables using the closing receivables figure we calculated in Step 1:

5% × $40,000 = $2,000

Now, our proforma looks like this:

Opening allowance for receivables	$1,500
Increase or decrease	$?
Closing allowance for receivables	**$2,000**

The missing figure is therefore an increase of **$500**.

The double entry for this is Dr Irrecoverable debts expense and Cr Allowance for receivables.

Answer: the irrecoverable debts expenses account balance is $9,800 ($10,000 – $700 + $500).

Skills activity

Now we have had a look at an illustration, have a go at the following question:

Justin has an allowance for receivables at 1 January 20X8 of $3,000.

Receivables at the year end were $60,000.

During the year, an irrecoverable debt of $5,000 was written off.

$1,000 was subsequently recovered from a debt written off in the previous year.

The closing allowance for receivables will be 2% of receivables at the year end.

What is the irrecoverable debts expense at the 31 December 20X8?

    A $2,200

    B $5,800

    C $2,100

    D $2,800

A is the correct answer. If you chose answer C then you did not read the question properly. In this case, the irrecoverable debt had already been written off and therefore did not need to be removed from receivables before calculating the allowance for the year.

If you answered B then you added the decrease in the allowance.

If you answered D then you took the closing allowance figure of $1,200 to the irrecoverable debts expense account rather than the decrease.

Let's look at our steps:

STEP 1 Write off irrecoverable debts.

These had been written off in the year and, as such, the irrecoverable debts expense figure will currently be $5,000.

STEP 2 Account for irrecoverable debts subsequently recovered.

$1,000 to cash and $1,000 to irrecoverable debts expense as a credit balance.

Irrecoverable debts expense balance is now $4,000.

STEP 3 Adjust the allowance for receivables.

Opening allowance	$3,000
Increase or decrease in allowance	$?
Closing allowance	**$1,200**

In this case, there is a **decrease of $1,800** so this will be posted as Dr Allowance for receivables and Cr Irrecoverable debts expense (negative).

The irrecoverable debts expense balance is now $5,000 – $1,000 – $1,800 = $2,200.

Skills activity

Now, let's look at a number entry question. This question and commentary are taken from the examiner's report (September 2018 to August 2019).

Rackit had a receivables allowance of $50,000 at 31 December 20X7. At 31 December 20X8, trade receivables totalled $970,000. It has been decided to write off debts totalling $20,000 and to adjust the allowance for receivables to 10% of trade receivables at 31 December 20X8.

What figure should appear for trade receivables in the statement of financial position as at 31 December 20X8?

$_____

This question is testing both irrecoverable debts and allowances for receivables, and requires candidates to show the amount recorded for trade receivables on the statement of financial position. At the reporting date, the total for trade receivables was $970,000 but this will be subject to a write off of $20,000. Trade receivables will now be recorded at $950,000. However, there is a requirement to adjust the allowance for receivables to 10% of trade receivables at 31 December 20X8. The allowance will therefore be $95,000 ($950,000 × 10%). Trade receivables will be reported as follows on the statement of financial position:

Adjusted trade receivables ($970,000 – $20,000)	$950,000
Less: allowance for receivables	$(95,000)
Trade receivables (SOFP)	**$855,000**

Therefore, the correct number entry is the net trade receivable of **$855,000**.

Exam success skills diagnostic

Every time you complete a few questions, use the diagnostic below to assess how effectively you demonstrated the exam success skills in answering the questions. The table has been completed below for the above activities to give you an idea of how to complete the diagnostic.

Exam success skills	Your reflections/observations
Managing information	Did you take your time to read the question carefully to ensure you were answering the question set? For example, did you notice that the question said that the irrecoverable debt had been written off **during the year**?
Correct interpretation of requirements	Did you identify that the requirement was to calculate the receivables figure and not the allowance for receivables figure?
Efficient numerical analysis	Did you notice that the movement in the first activity was a decrease in the allowance for receivables and therefore needed to be deducted from the irrecoverable debts expense account rather than added?
Good time management	Did you complete the question in the allotted time? 2-mark questions should take 2.4 minutes.

Most important action points to apply to your next question. (Complete this for any learning from this checkpoint that you want to carry forward to your revision.)

Summary

Irrecoverable debts and allowance for receivables will be in every exam. They could also be in the long question where you would need to include the expense in the statement of profit or loss and the receivables figure in the statement of financial position. It is therefore crucial that you familiarise yourself with the steps involved in answering these questions and also the different ways in which these questions can be written.

19

Introduction to company accounting

Learning objectives

On competition of this chapter, you should be able to:

	Syllabus reference no.
Understand the capital structure of a limited liability company including ordinary shares, preference shares (redeemable and irredeemable) and loan notes.	D10(a)
Record movements in the share capital and share premium accounts.	D10(b)
Identify and record the other reserves which may appear in the company statement of financial position.	D10(c)
Define a bonus (capitalisation) issue and its advantages and disadvantages.	D10(d)
Define a rights issue and its advantages and disadvantages.	D10(e)
Record and show the effects of a bonus (capitalisation) issue in the statement of financial position.	D10(f)
Record and show the effects of a rights issue in the statement of financial position.	D10(g)
Record dividends in ledger accounts and the financial statements.	D10(h)
Calculate and record finance costs in ledger accounts and the financial statements.	D10(i)
Recognise the legal differences between a sole trader, a partnership and a limited liability company.	A1(c)
Identify the advantages and disadvantages of operating as a limited liability company, sole trader or partnership.	A1(d)

Exam context

Questions on this chapter are likely to focus on the calculation of share capital movements (new issues, bonus issues and rights issues), dividends and finance costs and their associated journal entries. You may also see a question comparing a sole trader and a limited company.

Chapter overview

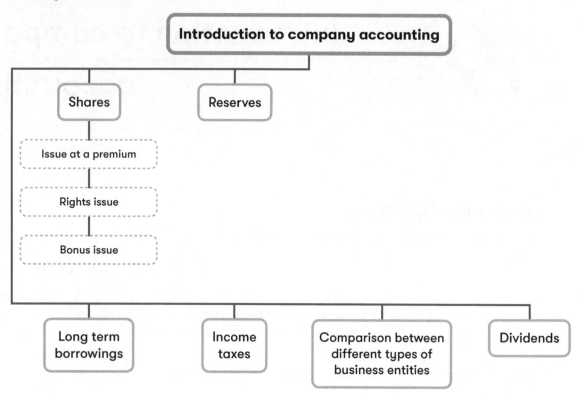

1 Introduction

We have seen how financial statements are produced for sole traders. These accounts are not subject to any specific regulation and so there is some flexibility as to how they are presented.

Companies use exactly the **same bookkeeping process** as sole traders; however, the financial statements they produce are subject to regulation and must follow a **prescribed format**.

Many of the differences are due to the **terminology** used by company financial statements.

2 Proforma financial statements

Statement of profit or loss for the year ended 31 March 20X7

	$'000
Revenue	X
Cost of sales	(X)
Gross profit	X
Other income	X
Distribution costs	(X)
Administrative expenses	(X)
Finance costs	(X)
Profit before tax	X
Income tax expense	(X)
Profit for the year	X

Statement of financial position as at 31 March 20X7

	$'000
Assets	
Non-current assets	
Property, plant and equipment	X
Intangible assets	X
	X
Current assets	
Inventories	X
Trade receivables	X
Other current assets	X
Cash and cash equivalents	X
	X
Total assets	X

	$'000
Equity and liabilities	
Equity	
Share capital	X
Share premium account	X
Retained earnings	X
Revaluation surplus	X
	X
Non-current liabilities	
Long term borrowings	X
Long term provisions	X
	X
Current liabilities	
Trade payables	X
Short-term borrowings	X
Current tax payable	X
Short term provisions	X
Total equity and liabilities	X

3 Share capital

It is necessary to be able to distinguish between the following types of share capital:

(a) Authorised share capital: Maximum number of shares the company **may issue**

(b) Issued share capital: Number of shares **actuallyissued** to shareholders

(c) Called up share capital: The amount of issued share capital the company has **asked shareholders to pay for** to date

(d) Paid up share capital: Amount of called up share capital which **has been paid for**

3.1 Types of shares

The two types of share most commonly encountered are ordinary shares and preference shares.

Ordinary share	Preference share
Equity shareholders	Fixed rate of dividends (eg 7% preference share)
Ordinary shareholders effectively own business	Receive dividend in priority to ordinary shareholders
Usually have voting rights	On winding up, receive capital in priority
No right to a fixed dividend, receive what directors decide to pay	Can be redeemable at a certain date, or irredeemable.

Ordinary share	Preference share
Holder entitled to all profits left after the payment of any preference dividend	Do not usually have voting rights

4 Share capital: accounting treatment

4.1 Issue of new shares

Rab Co started business on 1 January 20X6 issuing 100,000 ordinary shares of 50c each for 50c per share. The initial statement of financial position would be:

	$
Cash	50,000
Share capital – 50c ordinary shares	50,000

4.2 Issue of new shares at a premium

Where shares are issued for more than their nominal value, the excess must be credited to a **share premium account**.

 Activity 1: Share issue

On 1 June 20X6, Rab Co issued a further 200,000 ordinary shares of 50c each for 80c per share.

Required

Show how this issue of shares would be accounted for and what the equity section of the statement of financial position (excluding retained earnings) would look like immediately after the issue.

Solution

	Dr	Cr
	$	$
Dr Cash		
Cr Share capital		
Cr Share premium account		

Statement of financial position (extract) as at 1 June 20X0

	$
Equity	
Share capital – 50c ordinary shares	
Share premium account	

4.3 Bonus issue (capitalisation issue)

This is used when a company wishes to increase its share capital without needing to raise additional finance by issuing new shares. Any reserve may be used including the share premium account.

Advantages	Disadvantage
Bonus issue can be made from the share premium account which has few other uses.	The rationale for a bonus issue is not always understood by shareholders.
Will allow the share price to fall (without disadvantaging shareholder wealth) to make the company's shares more affordable to new investors	
Shareholders will now own more shares and could sell part of their holding.	

A bonus issue is always done at **nominal value**.

Activity 2: Bonus issue

Rab Co Statement of financial position (extract)

	$
Share capital – 50c ordinary shares	150,000
Share premium account	60,000
Retained earnings	200,000
	410,000

Several years later, Rab Co is to make a bonus issue on a 1 for 4 basis.

Required

Show how this issue of shares would be accounted for and prepare the equity section of the statement of financial position of Rab Co immediately after the issue.

Solution

	Dr	Cr
	$	$
Dr Share premium account		
Cr Share capital		

Rab Co Statement of financial position (extract)

	$
Share capital – 50c ordinary shares	_____
Share premium account	_____
Retained earnings	

$

_____

4.4 Rights issue

A rights issue is an issue of shares for cash (unlike a bonus issue) to existing shareholders for less than their market value.

'Rights' are offered to the existing shareholders who can sell them if they wish.

Advantages	Disadvantages
More cost-effective way for the company to raise finance than a fresh issue to the public	Lack of shareholder interest may reflect badly on the company.
A more time efficient way to issue shares	Unwelcome predators may try to acquire shares where not all rights are taken up.
If all rights are taken up, shareholders will maintain their existing percentage shareholding.	Effect on future dividend policy as company will have issued more shares under the rights issue than it would have under a fresh issue to the public
As shares offered at below market value, shareholders are more likely to buy them.	Will cause the share price to fall as shares are issued at below market value

Activity 3: Rights issue

One year later, Rab Co is to make a rights issue on a 1 for 5 basis. The rights price is $1.50. All shareholders take up their rights.

The following statement of financial position extract shows the position before the issue:

Rab Co Statement of financial position (extract)

	$
Share capital – 50c ordinary shares	187,500
Share premium account	22,500
Retained earnings	230,000
	440,000

Required

Show how this issue of shares would be accounted for and prepare the equity section of the statement of financial position of Rab Co immediately following the issue.

Solution

	Dr	Cr
	$	$
Dr Cash		
Cr Share capital		
Cr Share premium account		

Rab Co Statement of financial position (extract)

$

Share capital – 50c ordinary shares [   ]

Share premium account [   ]

Retained earnings

_____

_____

4.5 Preference shares

There are two types of preference shares: **redeemable** (the company is obliged to repay the nominal value of the shares at a later date) and **irredeemable** (no obligation to repay).

In substance, **redeemable preference shares** behave like debt because they contain an obligation, meeting the *Conceptual Framework* definition of a liability. Therefore, they should be treated as a **liability** (non-current until one year before redemption) in the statement of financial position; the **dividends** should be treated as a **finance cost** (ie interest) in the statement of profit or loss.

Irredeemable preference shares contain no obligation so should be treated as **equity,** ie in the same way as ordinary shares. The **dividends** should be treated as **an appropriation of profit** (see the following).

4.6 Reserves

The following reserves are commonly found in limited liability company accounts:

(a) The share premium account
   (i) Typical permitted uses:
       (1) To issue bonus shares
       (2) To write off share issue expenses
(b) The revaluation surplus (see Chapter 8)
(c) Other reserves:
   (i) As designated by the individual company, for example a 'general reserve'
(d) Retained earnings:
   (i) Cumulative undistributed profits less any losses

4.7 Dividends

Dividends: A sharing out/appropriation of retained earnings to owners/shareholders.

Illustration 1: Dividends

A company with 1,000 ordinary $1 shares in issue made a profit of $500 in its first year. The company has two choices as to what can be done with this profit:

(1) Distribute it as a **dividend** to the shareholders; or

(2) Retain it in the business.

Required

If this company decides to pay a dividend of 10c per share and retain the remaining profits, how would the financial statements appear?

Solution

Statement of profit or loss for the year ended 31 December 20X7

	$
Profit for the year	500

Statement of financial position as at 31 December 20X7 (extract)

	$
Share capital – $1 shares	1,000
Retained earnings ($500 – $100)	400
	1,400

Dividends on ordinary shares and irredeemable preference shares are **charged directly to retained earnings** as they are an **appropriation** of profits earned to date. They are **not** an expense in the statement of profit or loss.

The double entry for dividends on ordinary shares and irredeemable preference shares is:

Dr   Retained earnings (SOFP)

Cr   Cash (if paid)/Dividends payable (if declared) (SOFP)

Dividends on redeemable preference shares are treated as a finance cost (interest):

Dr   Finance costs (SPL)

Cr   Cash (SOFP)

A company may pay dividends in two stages:

(a) Interim (mid year)

(b) Final (end year)

In reality, the directors will wait until they know the company's full year profit before declaring the final dividend.

The final dividend will only be accounted for in the current year if it is declared before the year end. Otherwise, it will be disclosed in a note to the financial statements.

Activity 4: Retained earnings

ABC Co has the following share capital:

100,000	6% $1 irredeemable preference shares
200,000	50c ordinary shares

Retained earnings at the beginning of the year were $125,000.

During the year ended 31 December 20X7 it made the following profit:

	$
Profit before tax	60,000
Income tax expense	(10,000)
Profit for the year	50,000

Ordinary dividends paid and declared during the year were as follows:

Interim dividend paid	5c per share

Final dividend declared on 20 January 20X8   10c per share

Required

Show the movement in retained earnings for ABC Co for the year ended 31 December 20X7.

Solution

ABC Co Reconciliation of movement in retained earnings for year ended 31 December 20X6

	$	$
Retained earnings at beginning of year		
Profit for the year		
Dividends Irredeemable preference		
Ordinary		
Retained earnings at end of year		

5 Long term borrowings

A company may choose to raise finance by issuing shares (equity).

Alternatively, it can raise funds by issuing **debt**.

One way of raising long-term finance is for a company to issue loan notes (also called **loan stock** or **debentures**).

These loans usually carry a fixed rate of interest and have a pre-determined redemption date, for example, $50,000 10% debentures 20X6. This means the company will pay interest at 10% on the $50,000 borrowed each year. The capital amount of $50,000 will be repaid in 20X6.

6 Finance costs

The interest expense incurred on long-term borrowings will be shown as an **expense** called 'finance costs' in the statement of profit or loss.

It will be accounted for as follows:

Dr   Finance costs (SPL)

Cr   Bank (SOFP)

7 Income taxes

Companies must pay income tax on their profits. This tax is payable after the end of the financial year and so the financial statements will include an accrual for the directors' best estimate of the tax due on the profit for the period.

The tax is shown as an expense in the statement of profit or loss and a current liability in the statement of financial position and will be accounted for as follows:

Dr   Income tax expense (SPL)

Cr   Current tax payable (SOFP)

Often, the actual amount of tax paid will be different from the amount that was recorded in the financial statements.

This over or under provision is simply adjusted in the next financial statements.

Activity 5: Tax

Lauren Ltd (Lauren) has a year end of December.

When preparing its financial statements for the year ended 31 December 20X5, Lauren estimated that its income tax payable would be $62,000.

Lauren settled this tax liability on 30 September 20X6, paying $65,000. The tax estimate for the year ended 31 December 20X6 is $43,000.

Required

1   Record the tax entries for the years ended 31 December 20X5 and 20X6 in the ledger accounts.

2   Prepare the tax note which relates to the statement of profit or loss for the year ended 31 December 20X6.

Solution

1

INCOME TAX EXPENSE

	$		$

CURRENT TAX PAYABLE

	$		$

8 Comparison

The following table shows a comparison between a sole trader or partnership and a limited liability company.

	Sole trader/partnership	Company
Ownership	The proprietor(s) owns the business.	There are often a large number of owners, who are called shareholders or members.
Liability	The proprietor(s) has unlimited legal liability regarding the business.	Members/shareholders have limited liability. This means that they are only liable to the extent of their investment in the business.
Legal status	The business and the proprietor(s) share legal identity (although the business is a separate business entity for reporting purposes).	A company is a separate legal entity.
Management	The proprietor(s) usually owns and manages the business.	Members/shareholders do not usually manage the business, but appoint a board of directors to run the company on their behalf.
Profits	The proprietor(s) takes 'drawings' out of the business. Any cash amounts taken as a salary are **not** an expense of the business but drawings.	Members/shareholders receive profits in the form of dividends. The remainder of the profits are retained in the company. The directors receive a salary from the company and this is an **expense** in the statement of profit or loss.
Taxation	Business profits are taxed in the hands of the proprietor(s), using individual's tax rates.	Income tax is paid on the **company** profits.

	Sole trader/partnership	**Company**
Statement of financial position	For a sole trader, the middle of the statement of financial position is split into 'opening capital', 'profits' and 'drawings'. For a partnership, the capital is shown in an account called the 'capital account' and the profit and drawings in an account called the 'current account'.	The middle of the statement of financial position is split into 'share capital' and 'reserves'.
Legal requirements	There are no legal requirements specific to a sole trader or partnership.	There are extensive legal requirements governing limited companies (eg annual filing of financial statements).
Other	The business is closed to outside investors.	Investors can invest in a company.

 ## Essential reading

Chapter 19 of the Essential reading goes into more detail about the regulation surrounding limited companies and also expands the information given in this chapter on the various types of shares and reserves.

The Essential reading is available as an Appendix of the digital edition of the Workbook.

Chapter summary

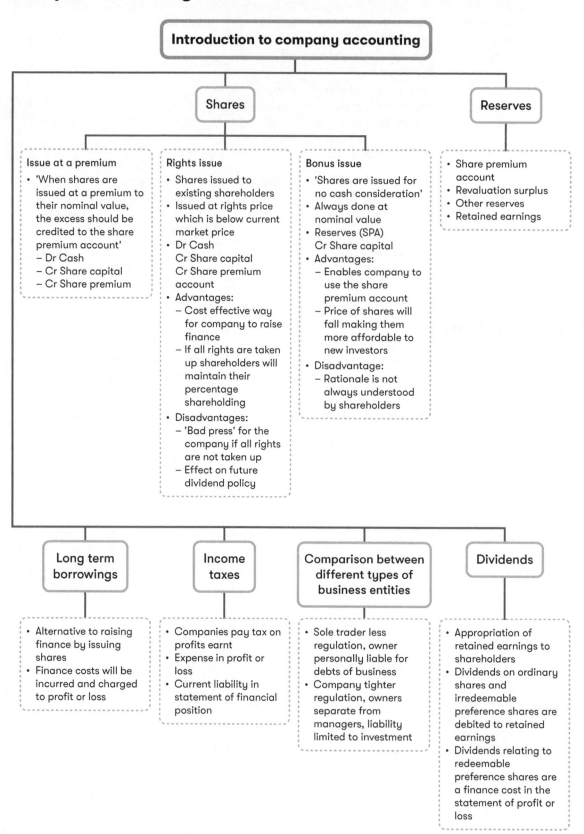

Introduction to company accounting

Shares

Reserves
- Share premium account
- Revaluation surplus
- Other reserves
- Retained earnings

Issue at a premium
- 'When shares are issued at a premium to their nominal value, the excess should be credited to the share premium account'
  - Dr Cash
  - Cr Share capital
  - Cr Share premium

Rights issue
- Shares issued to existing shareholders
- Issued at rights price which is below current market price
- Dr Cash
  Cr Share capital
  Cr Share premium account
- Advantages:
  - Cost effective way for company to raise finance
  - If all rights are taken up shareholders will maintain their percentage shareholding
- Disadvantages:
  - 'Bad press' for the company if all rights are not taken up
  - Effect on future dividend policy

Bonus issue
- 'Shares are issued for no cash consideration'
- Always done at nominal value
- Reserves (SPA)
  Cr Share capital
- Advantages:
  - Enables company to use the share premium account
  - Price of shares will fall making them more affordable to new investors
- Disadvantage:
  - Rationale is not always understood by shareholders

Long term borrowings
- Alternative to raising finance by issuing shares
- Finance costs will be incurred and charged to profit or loss

Income taxes
- Companies pay tax on profits earnt
- Expense in profit or loss
- Current liability in statement of financial position

Comparison between different types of business entities
- Sole trader less regulation, owner personally liable for debts of business
- Company tighter regulation, owners separate from managers, liability limited to investment

Dividends
- Appropriation of retained earnings to shareholders
- Dividends on ordinary shares and irredeemable preference shares are debited to retained earnings
- Dividends relating to redeemable preference shares are a finance cost in the statement of profit or loss

Knowledge diagnostic

1. Financial statements

There are some important differences between the accounts of a limited liability company and those of sole traders or partnerships.

Limited companies are governed by strict rules which prescribe how financial statements must be presented.

2. Reserves

Limited companies have 'reserves' rather than the 'capital' that you will see for a sole trader.

In preparing a statement of financial position, you must be able to deal with:

(a) Ordinary and preference share capital

(b) Reserves

(c) Loan stock

3. Share issues

Companies issue shares to raise capital, shares can be issued in a number of ways:

(a) At nominal value

    (i) Funds are credited to a share capital account.

(b) At a premium

    (i) The excess over the nominal amount is credited to a share premium account.

(c) Bonus issue

    (i) This is not a way of raising funds; shares are issued to existing shareholders free of charge.

(d) Rights issue

    (i) Existing shareholders have the right to buy shares at a price that is typically cheaper that the price of shares on the open market.

4. Dividends

Profits in a company are paid out to shareholders in the form of dividends.

Dividends are not classed as an expense; they are an appropriation of profit. Dividends are charged to retained earnings and shown in the statement of changes in equity.

5. Retained earnings

This is the **most significant reserve.**

These are **profits** earned by the company and not appropriated by dividends, taxation or transfer to another reserve account.

Provided that a company is earning profits, this reserve generally increases from year to year, as most companies do not distribute all their profits as dividends. Dividends can be paid from it; even if a loss is made in one particular year, a dividend can be paid from previous years' retained earnings.

Further study guidance

Question practice

Now try the following from the Further question practice bank (available in the digital edition of the Workbook):

Questions 73 to 76

Activity answers

Activity 1: Share issue

	Dr	Cr
	$	$
Dr Cash (200,000 × 80c)	160,000	
Cr Share capital (200,000 × 50c)		100,000
Cr Share premium account (200,000 × 30c)		60,000

Statement of financial position (extract) as at 1 June 20X0

	$
Equity	
Share capital – 50c ordinary shares (50,000 + 100,000)	150,000
Share premium account	60,000
	210,000

Activity 2: Bonus issue

	Dr	Cr
	$	$
Dr Share premium account	37,500	
Cr Share capital		37,500

Rab Co Statement of financial position (extract)

	$
Share capital – 50c ordinary shares ($160,000 + $37,500)	187,500
Share premium account ($60,000 – $37,500)	22,500
Retained earnings	200,000
	410,000

Bonus issue

There are 300,000 × 50c shares in issue. The bonus issue will create 75,000 new shares (300,000 / 4). New share capital can be created from the share premium account. The amount of new share capital is:

$$\frac{300,000}{4} \times 50c = \$37,500$$

Activity 3: Rights issue

	Dr $	Cr $
Dr Cash	112,500	
Cr Share capital		37,500
Cr Share premium account		75,000

Rab Co Statement of financial position (extract)

	$
Share capital – 50c ordinary shares (187,500 + 37,500)	225,000
Share premium account ($22,500 + $75,000)	97,500
Retained earnings	230,000
	552,500

Rights issue

There are 375,000 shares in issue ($187,500 / $0.50) and so there are 75,000 new shares created by the rights issue (375,000 / 5).

The new share capital as a result of the rights issue is:

$$\frac{375,000}{5} \times 50c = \$37,500$$

The new share premium as a result of the rights issue is:

$$\frac{375,000}{5} \times \$1 = \$75,000$$

Activity 4: Retained earnings

ABC Co Reconciliation of movement in retained earnings for year ended 31 December 20X6

		$	$
Retained earnings at beginning of year			125,000
Profit for the year			50,000
Dividends	Irredeemable preference ($100,000 × 6%)	6,000	
	Ordinary (200,000 shares × 5c)	10,000	
			(16,000)
Retained earnings at end of year			159,000

Activity 5: Tax

1

INCOME TAX EXPENSE

	$		$
31.12.X5 Current tax payable	62,000	31.12.X5 Statement of profit or loss	62,000
30.9.X6 Current tax payable	3,000		
31.12.X6 Current tax payable	43,000	31.12.X6 Statement of profit or loss	46,000

CURRENT TAX PAYABLE

	$		$
31.12.X5 Balance c/d	62,000	31.12.X5 Income tax expense	62,000
	62,000		62,000
30.9.X6 Bank	65,000	1.1.X6 Balance b/d	62,000
		30.9.X6 Income tax expense	3,000
31.12.X6 Bal c/d	43,000	31.12.X6 Income tax expense	43,000
	108,000		108,000
		1.1.X7 Balance b/d	43,000

2 Tax note for the year ended 31 December 20X6:

	$
Tax charge for the year	43,000
Under provision in respect of prior periods	3,000
	46,000

20

Preparation of financial statements for companies

Learning objectives

On competition of this chapter, you should be able to:

	Syllabus reference no.
Recognise how the accounting equation, accounting treatments and business entity concept underlie the statement of financial position.	F1(a)
Understand the nature equity reserves.	F1(b)
Identify and report equity reserves in a company statement of financial position.	F1(c)
Prepare a statement of financial position or extracts as applicable from given information.	F1(d)
Understand why the heading 'retained earnings' appears in a company statement of financial position.	F1(e)
Prepare a statement of profit or loss and other comprehensive income or extracts as applicable from given information.	F2(a)
Understand how accounting concepts apply to revenue and expenses.	F2(b)
Calculate revenue, cost of sales, gross profit, profit for the year and total comprehensive income from given information.	F2(c)
Disclose items of income and expenditure in the statement of profit or loss.	F2(d)
Record income tax in the statement of profit or loss of a company including the over and under provision of tax in the prior year.	F2(e)
Understand the inter-relationship between the statement of financial position and statement of profit or loss and other comprehensive income.	F2(f)
Identify items requiring separate disclosure on the face of the statement of profit or loss.	F2(g)
Identify the components of the statement of changes in equity.	D10(j)
Explain the purpose of disclosure notes.	F3(a)
Draft disclosure notes for tangible and intangible non-current assets, inventory, provisions and events after the reporting period.	F3(b)

	Syllabus reference no.
Illustrate how non-current asset balances and movements are disclosed in financial statements.	D4(i)
Calculate depreciation on a revalued non-current asset including the transfer of excess depreciation between the revaluation surplus and retained earnings.	D5(e)
Classify items as current or non-current liabilities in the statement of financial position.	D8(l)

Exam context

In the multi-task accounts preparation question, you might be required to produce an entire statement of profit or loss and other comprehensive income, statement of financial position or statement of changes in equity or an extract thereof. Also, you may be asked to calculate individual elements of each statement either in an objective test question or as part of the accounts preparation multi-task question. For example, you may be asked to demonstrate an understanding of what is included in the statement of changes in equity. You could also be asked to prepare a disclosure note.

Chapter overview

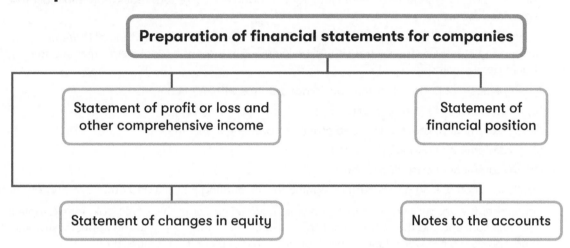

1 Introduction

The financial statements of a limited liability company are subject to regulation and must follow a prescribed format.

Much of the prescribed format is determined by IAS 1 *Presentation of Financial Statements*. This accounting standard states what should be included in a set of financial statements and how they should be presented.

A complete set of financial statements in accordance with IAS 1 comprises:

(a) A statement of financial position;

(b) A statement of profit or loss and other comprehensive income;

(c) A statement of changes in equity;

(d) A statement of cash flows; and

(e) Notes, comprising a summary of significant accounting policies and other explanatory notes.

Remember the accounting concepts that were covered earlier in this Workbook, for example the accruals concept and the separate entity concept? These also apply to the financial statements of companies so it is worth looking back over these if you can't remember them.

The accounting equation also applies to companies but instead of the proprietors' interest section, there is the capital and reserves section.

> ### PER alert
>
> This section of the Workbook will help fulfil Performance Objective 7 (PO7) of the PER, 'Prepare external financial reports'.

2 Proforma financial statements

Statement of profit or loss for the year ended 31 March 20X7

	$'000
Revenue	X
Cost of sales	(X)
Gross profit	X
Other income	X
Distribution costs	(X)
Administrative expenses	(X)
Finance costs	(X)
Profit before tax	X
Income tax expense	(X)
Profit for the year	X

Statement of financial position as at 31 March 20X7

	$'000
Assets	
Non-current assets	
Property, plant and equipment	X

	$'000
Intangible assets	X
	X
Current assets	
Inventories	X
Trade receivables	X
Other current assets	X
Cash and cash equivalents	X
	X
Total assets	X
Equity and liabilities	
Equity	
Share capital	X
Share premium	X
Retained earnings	X
Revaluation surplus	X
	X
Non-current liabilities	
Long-term borrowings	X
Long-term provisions	X
Current liabilities	
Trade payables	X
Short-term borrowings	X
Current tax payable	X
Short-term provisions	X
Total equity and liabilities	X

Note that, according to IAS 1, a liability should be classified as current when it is due to be settled within 12 months of the year end. If it is due to be settled after that, it is to be classified as non-current.

2.1 Retained earnings

It is important at this point to have a look at retained earnings. This is the most significant reserve and is variously described as:

(a) Revenue reserve

(b) Retained earnings

(c) Accumulated profits

(d) Undistributed profits

(e) Unappropriated profits

These are profits earned by the company and not appropriated by dividends, taxation or transfer to another reserve account. When we looked at sole trader financial statements we simply referred to this as profit and over the years the profits of the sole trader accumulated and, along with drawings, formed part of the capital section of the statement of financial position. In the case of the company, it earns profits and the owners take drawings but in this case, we refer to the profit as retained earnings and the drawings as dividends.

Provided that a company is earning profits, this reserve generally increases from year to year, as most companies do not distribute all their profits as dividends. Dividends can be paid from it: even if a loss is made in one particular year, a dividend can be paid from previous years' retained earnings.

For example, if a company makes a loss of $100,000 in one year, yet has unappropriated profits from previous years totalling $250,000, it can pay a dividend not exceeding $150,000. One reason for retaining some profit each year is to enable the company to pay dividends even when profits are low (or non-existent). Another reason is usually shortage of cash.

Very occasionally, you might come across a debit balance on the retained earnings account. This would indicate that the company has accumulated losses.

2.2 Illustration

Below are the statement of profit or loss and statement of financial position for Arrow Co for the year ended 30 September 20X6

Arrow Co Statement of profit or loss for the year ended 30 September 20X6

	$'000
Revenue	12,740
Cost of sales	(7,040)
Gross profit	5,700
Distribution costs	(2,060)
Administrative expenses	(2,375)
Finance costs	(72)
Profit before tax	1,193
Income tax expense	(270)
Profit for the year	923

Arrow Co Statement of financial position as at 30 September

	$'000
Assets	
Non-current assets	
Property, plant and equipment	5,000
	5,000
Current assets	
Inventories	610
Trade receivables	1,000
Cash and cash equivalents	1,170
	2,780

	$'000
Total assets	7,780

Equity and liabilities

Equity

Share capital	1,750
Share premium	585
Retained earnings	1,873
Revaluation surplus	1,400
	5,608

Non-current liabilities

Long-term borrowings	1,200
	1,200

Current liabilities

Trade payables	550
Other payables	72
Current tax payable	270
Short-term provisions	80
	972
Total equity and liabilities	7,780

The following information **was** accounted for when the above financial statements were produced:

(a) During the year, the company made a rights issue on a 1 for 6 basis. The issue was fully subscribed and the rights price was $1.27. Prior to the rights issue, Arrow Co had 3,000,000 50c ordinary shares in issue.

(b) Property, plant and equipment was revalued by $600,000 during the year.

(c) A dividend of $300,000 was paid during the year.

2.3 Statement of profit or loss and other comprehensive income

IAS 1 requires financial statements to include a **statement of profit or loss and other comprehensive income.**

This statement shows all of the **realised** gains and losses from the statement of profit or loss and the **unrealised** gains and losses from the statement of financial position in **one statement of performance.**

Statement of profit or loss	Statement of financial position
Realised	Unrealised
gains and losses	gains and losses
(posted to income or expense in SPL)	(posted directly to reserves)
eg profit for the year	eg revaluation gains
Statement of profit or loss and other comprehensive income	

The statement can be presented in one of two ways:

(a) As one single statement (Proforma 1)

(b) As two separate statements (Proforma 2)

Proforma 1 – one single statement

Statement of profit or loss and other comprehensive income for the year ended 31 March 20X7

	20X7	20X6
	$'000	$'000
Revenue	X	X
Cost of sales	(X)	(X)
Gross profit	X	X
Other income	X	X
Distribution costs	(X)	(X)
Administrative expenses	(X)	(X)
Finance costs	(X)	(X)
Investment income	X	X
Profit before tax	X	X
Income tax expense	(X)	(X)
Profit for the year	X	X
Other comprehensive income:		
Gains on property revaluation	X	X
Total comprehensive income for the year	X	X

Proforma 2 – two separate statements

Statement of profit or loss for the year ended 31 March 20X7

	20X7	20X6
	$'000	$'000
Revenue	X	X
Cost of sales	(X)	(X)
Gross profit	X	X
Other income	X	X
Distribution costs	(X)	(X)
Administrative expenses	(X)	(X)
Finance costs	(X)	(X)
Investment income	X	X
Profit before tax	X	X
Income tax expense	(X)	(X)
Profit for the year	X	X

Statement of other comprehensive income for the year ended 31 March 20X7

	20X7	20X6
	S'000	S'000
Profit for the year	X	X
Other comprehensive income:		
Gains on property revaluation	X	X
Total comprehensive income for the year	X	X

Illustration 1: Statement of profit or loss and other comprehensive income

Using the illustration, Arrow Co, prepare the statement of profit or loss and other comprehensive income for the year ended 30 September 20X6:

1   Showing the statement as one statement

Statement of profit or loss and other comprehensive income for the year ended 30 September 20X6

	S'000
Revenue	12,740
Cost of sales	(7,040)
Gross profit	5,700
Distribution costs	(2,060)
Administrative expenses	(2,375)
Finance costs	(72)
Profit before tax	1,193
Income tax expense	(270)
Profit for the year	923
Other comprehensive income:	
Gains on property revaluation	
Total comprehensive income for the year	

2   Showing the statement as two separate statements

Statement of profit or loss for the year ended 30 September 20X6

	S'000
Revenue	12,740
Cost of sales	(7,040)
Gross profit	5,700
Distribution costs	(2,060)
Administrative expenses	(2,375)

	$'000
Finance costs	(72)
Profit before tax	1,193
Income tax expense	(270)
Profit for the year	923

Statement of other comprehensive income for the year ended 30 September 20X6

	$'000
Profit for the year	923
Other comprehensive income:	
Gains on property revaluation	_____
Total comprehensive income for the year	_____

Solution

1

Statement of profit or loss and other comprehensive income for the year ended 30 September 20X6

	$'000
Revenue	12,740
Cost of sales	(7,040)
Gross profit	5,700
Distribution costs	(2,060)
Administrative expenses	(2,375)
Finance costs	(72)
Profit before tax	1,193
Income tax expense	(270)
Profit for the year	923
Other comprehensive income:	
Gains on property revaluation	600
Total comprehensive income for the year	1,523

2

Statement of profit or loss for the year ended 30 September 20X6

	$'000
Revenue	12,740
Cost of sales	(7,040)
Gross profit	5,700
Distribution costs	(2,060)

	$'000
Administrative expenses	(2,375)
Finance costs	(72)
Profit before tax	1,193
Income tax expense	(270)
Profit for the year	923

Statement of other comprehensive income for the year ended 30 September 20X6

	$'000
Profit for the year	923
Other comprehensive income:	
Gains on property revaluation	600
Total comprehensive income for the year	1,523

2.4 Statement of changes in equity

The statement of changes in equity shows the movements in the entity's equity for the period. The statement of profit or loss and other comprehensive income show the financial performance of the entity for the period. The statement of changes in equity links this with the results of transactions with the owners of the business such as share issues and dividends.

A statement of changes in equity might look like this:

	Share capital	Share premium	Retained earnings	Revaluation surplus	Total equity
	$'000	$'000	$'000	$'000	$'000
Balance at 31 March 20X6	X	X	X	X	X
Issue of share capital	X	X			X
Dividends			(X)		(X)
Total comprehensive income			X	X	X
Transfer to retained earnings	–	–	X	(X)	–
Balance at 31 March 20X7	X	X	X	X	X

The transfer from the revaluation surplus to retained earnings above is allowed by IAS 16 under two different circumstances:

(a) Annually, the difference between depreciation calculated on the revalued asset and historic cost depreciation may be transferred from the revaluation surplus to retained earnings.

(b) On disposal, the balance on the revaluation surplus may be transferred to retained earnings.

The double entry is:

Dr   Revaluation surplus

Cr   Retained earnings

Illustration 2: Excess depreciation arising on revaluation

Brian Co buys a property on 1 January 20X1 for $100,000. The property is to be depreciated on a straight-line basis over its 50-year useful life. On 31 December 20X5, the property is revalued to $135,000.

Required

How could Brian account for the excess depreciation arising on the revaluation?

Solution

Excess depreciation

	$
Depreciation based on revalued amount ($135,000 × 1/45*)	3,000
Historic cost depreciation ($100,000 × 1/50)	(2,000)
Excess depreciation	1,000

* The asset has been held for five years at the date of revaluation so has a remaining useful life of 45 years (50 years – 5 years).

Double entry for excess depreciation:

Dr Revaluation surplus $1,000

Cr Retained earnings $1,000

Activity 1: Statement of changes in equity

Arrow Co had the following equity balances at 1 October 20X5 (the beginning of the year):

	$'000
Share capital – 50c ordinary shares	1,500
Share premium account	200
Retained earnings	1,250
Revaluation surplus	800
	3,750

Required

Using the information from the illustration in Section 2.3, produce a statement of changes in equity for Arrow Co for the year ended 30 September 20X6 (assume there is no annual transfer of the excess depreciation between the revaluation surplus and retained earnings).

Solution

	Share capital	Share premium account	Retained earnings	Revaluation surplus	Total equity
	$'000	$'000	$'000	$'000	$'000
Balance at 30 September 20X5					

	Share capital	Share premium account	Retained earnings	Revaluation surplus	Total equity
	$'000	$'000	$'000	$'000	$'000
Issue of share capital					
Dividends					
Total comprehensive income	____	___	_____	_____	_____
Balance at 30 September 20X6	_____	_____	_____	_____	_____

3 Notes to the accounts

> ### Exam focus point
>
> ACCA's examining team has reported that questions on this topic have not been very well answered in previous exams. In particular, students do not appear to know the purpose or content of the notes. You should expect to see a question on this area in your exam. You are expected to have a detailed knowledge of the disclosures given below, so make sure you learn these.

Notes to the financial statements provide more detail for the users of the accounts about the information in the statement of profit or loss and other comprehensive income, the statement of financial position, the statement of cash flows and the statement of changes in equity. For example, the statement of financial position shows just the total carrying amount of property, plant and equipment owned by an entity. The notes to the financial statements then break down this total into the different categories of assets, the cost, any revaluation, the accumulated depreciation and the depreciation charge for the year. Notes are included in a set of financial statements to give users extra information. For your exam, you need to know the following disclosure requirements in detail.

(a) **Tangible non-current assets**

A reconciliation of the opening and closing amounts at the beginning and end of the period, as shown below (IAS 16, para. 73).

Property plant and equipment

	Land and buildings	Machinery	Office equipment	Total
	$	$	$	$
Carrying amount at 1 April 20X6	X	X	X	X
Additions	X	X	X	X
Revaluation surplus	X			X
Depreciation charge	(X)	(X)	(X)	(X)
Disposals	(X)	(X)	(X)	(X)
Carrying amount at 31 March 20X7	X	X	X	X

	Land and buildings	Machinery	Office equipment	Total
	$	$	$	$
At 31 March 20X7				
Cost or valuation	X	X	X	X
Accumulated depreciation	(X)	(X)	(X)	(X)
Carrying amount	X	X	X	X
At 31 March 20X6				
Cost or valuation	X	X	X	X
Accumulated depreciation	(X)	(X)	(X)	(X)
Carrying amount	X	X	X	X

An alternative version of this note is shown in the earlier Workbook chapter on non-current assets.

The following must also be disclosed in relation to property, plant and equipment:

- The accounting policies for property, plant and equipment
- For each class of property, plant and equipment:
  - Depreciation methods;
  - Useful lives or depreciation rates;
  - Total depreciation allocated for the period; and
  - Gross amount on depreciable assets and the related accumulated depreciation at the beginning and end of the period; (IAS 16, para. 73)
- For revalued assets:
  - Effective date of revaluation;
  - Whether an independent valuer was involved;
  - Carrying amount for each class of asset that would have been included in the statement of financial statements has assets been carried at cost less depreciation; and
  - Revaluation surplus, indicating the movement for the period and any restrictions on the distribution of the balance of shareholders. (IAS 16, para. 77)

(b) Intangible non-current assets

	Development expenditure
	$
Carrying amount at 1 April 20X6	X
Additions	X
Amortisation charge	(X)
Disposals	(X)
Carrying amount at 31 March 20X7	X
At 31 March 20X7	
Cost	X
Accumulated amortisation	(X)

	Development expenditure
	$
Carrying amount	X

At 31 March 20X6

	$
Cost	X
Accumulated amortisation	(X)
Carrying amount	X

The following must also be disclosed in relation to intangible assets:
- The accounting policies for intangible assets.
- For each class of intangible asset:
    - The method of amortisation;
    - The useful life of assets or the amortisation rate;
    - The gross carrying amount, the accumulated amortisation and the accumulated impairment losses at the beginning and end of the period;
    - The carrying amount of internally generated intangible assets; and
    - The line item(s) of the statement of profit or loss in which any amortisation of intangible assets is included

(c) Inventory

	$
Raw materials	X
Work in progress	X
Finished goods	X
	X

(d) Provisions

Disclosures required in the financial statements for provisions fall into two parts.
- Disclosure of details of the change in carrying amount of a provision from the beginning to the end of the year, including additional provisions made, amounts used and other movements.
- For each class of provision, disclosure of the background to the making of the provision and the uncertainties affecting its outcome, including:
    - A brief description of the nature of the provision and the expected timing of any resulting outflows relating to the provision.
    - An indication of the uncertainties about the amount or timing of those outflows and, where necessary to provide adequate information, the major assumptions made concerning future events.
    - The amount of any expected reimbursement relating to the provision and whether any asset has been recognised for that expected reimbursement.

(IAS 37, paras. 84–85)

	$
At 1 April 20X6	X
Increase in provision in the period	X
Released in period (amount of provision used in the year)	(X)
At 31 March 20X7	X

The accompanying note should look similar to this:

The warranty provision relates to estimated claims on those products sold in the year ended 31 March 20X7 which come with a three-year warranty. The expected value method is used to provide a best estimate. It is expected that the expenditure will be incurred in the next three years.

Contingent liabilities

Unless remote, disclose for each contingent liability:

(a) A brief description of its nature; and where practicable

(b) An estimate of the financial effect;

(c) An indication of the uncertainties relating to the amount or timing of any outflow; and

(d) The possibility of any reimbursement.

Contingent assets

Where an inflow of economic benefits is **probable**, an entity should disclose:

(a) A brief description of its nature; and where practicable

(b) An estimate of the financial effect.

Events after the reporting period

In respect of non-adjusting events after the reporting period, disclose:

(a) The nature of the event; and

(b) An estimate of its financial effect (or a statement that an estimate cannot be made).

Essential reading

Chapter 20 of the Essential reading explains in more detail some of the terminology used in this chapter and also includes extra practice questions.

The Essential reading is available as an Appendix of the digital edition of the Workbook.

Chapter summary

Preparation of financial statements for companies

Statement of profit or loss and other comprehensive income

- Shows the income and expenses for a period under specific headings
- Points to note:
  - SPL relates to realised gains/losses; OCI relates to unrealised gains/losses (posted directly to reserves)
  - Distribution costs: delivery costs
  - Administrative expenses: general costs that do not 'fit' under the other captions
  - Finance costs: bank interest, debenture/loan note interest
  - Income tax expense: estimate of income tax due on the profits for the period plus/minus any under/over provision in respect of prior periods

Statement of financial position

- Shows the assets and liabilities of a business at a point in time

Statement of changes in equity

- Explains the movements between the equity section of the statement of financial position at the beginning and the end of the year
- Key components:
  - Issue of share capital
  - Dividends (on ordinary shares)
  - Total comprehensive income for the year
  - Profit for the year
  - Revaluation surplus on non-current assets
  - Transfer to retained earnings

Notes to the accounts

- Examinable notes:
  - Property, plant and equipment
  - Intangible non-current assets
  - Inventory
  - Provisions
  - Contingent liabilities
  - Contingent assets
  - Events after the reporting period

Knowledge diagnostic

1. IAS 1

IAS 1 *Presentation of Financial Statements* lists the required contents of a company's financial statements. It also gives guidance on how items should be presented in the financial statements.

IAS 1 specifies what should be included in a statement of financial position and includes a suggested format. It also provides guidance on the current/non-current distinction.

IAS 1 specifies what should be included in a statement of profit or loss and other comprehensive income and includes a suggested format. Some items must be disclosed on the face of the statement.

IAS 1 requires an entity to provide a statement of changes in equity. The statement of changes in equity shows the movements in the entity's equity for the period.

2. Financial statements

A complete set of financial statements includes a statement of financial position, a statement of profit or loss and other comprehensive income, a statement of changes in equity, a statement of cash flows and disclosures notes.

3. Statement of profit or loss and other comprehensive income

This statement shows all of the realised gains and losses from the statement of profit or loss and the unrealised gains and losses from the statement of financial position in one statement of performance.

The statement can be presented in one of two ways:

- As one single statement
- As two separate statements

4. Disclosures

You must be comfortable with drafting disclosure notes for tangible and intangible non-current assets, inventory, provisions and events after the reporting period.

5. Proforma financial statements

In the multi-task accounts preparation question, you might be required to produce an entire statement of profit or loss and other comprehensive income, statement of financial position or statement of changes in equity or an extract thereof.

The statement of changes in equity shows the movements on each of the accounts in the equity section of the statement of financial position in a separate statement.

Further study guidance

Question practice

Now try the following from the Further question practice bank (available in the digital edition of the Workbook):

Questions 77 to 80

Activity answers

Activity 1: Statement of changes in equity

	Share capital $'000	Share premium account $'000	Retained earnings $'000	Revaluation surplus $'000	Total equity $'000
Balance at 30 September 20X5	1,500	200	1,250	800	3,750
Issue of share capital	250	385			635
Dividends			(300)		(300)
Total comprehensive income			923	600	1,523
Balance at 30 September 20X6	1,750	585	1,873	1,400	5,608

Working

Rights issue

Issue is on a 1 for 6 basis, therefore issue 3,000,000 ÷ 6 = 500,000 shares at $1.27 each.

Dr Bank (500,000 × $1.27)	$635,000	
Cr Share capital (500,000 × 50c)		$250,000
Cr Share premium (500,000 × 77c)		$385,000

21

Events after the reporting period

Learning objectives

On competition of this chapter, you should be able to:

	Syllabus reference no.
Define an event after the reporting period in accordance with International Financial Reporting Standards.	F4(a)
Classify events as adjusting or non-adjusting.	F4(b)
Distinguish between how adjusting and non-adjusting events are reported in the financial statements.	F4(c)

Exam context

Questions on this topic are likely to require you to identify adjusting and non-adjusting events from a list of options and the appropriate accounting treatment of each event.

Chapter overview

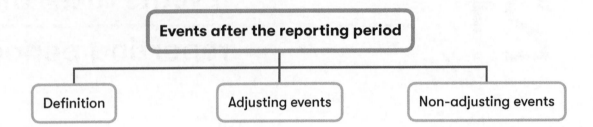

1 Definition

Events after the reporting period: Events, both favourable and unfavourable, that occur between the end of the reporting period and the date when the financial statements are authorised for issue.

There are two types of event after the statement of financial position (period end) date.

2 Adjusting and non-adjusting events

Adjusting events	Non-adjusting events
Events which provide evidence of conditions which **existed** at the end of the reporting period	Events that relate to conditions which **arose** **after** the end of the reporting period
Examples:	Examples:
(1) Resolution of a court case	(1) Destruction of major asset, eg by flood or fire
(2) Bankruptcy of a major customer	(2) Major share transactions
(3) Evidence of NRV of inventories	(3) Announcement of a plan to close part of a business
(4) Discovery of fraud or errors that show the financial statements were incorrect	
Accounting treatment:	Accounting treatment:
Change the amounts in the financial statements.	**Disclose** non-adjusting event in a note to the financial statements.

Dividends proposed or declared after the end of reporting period but before the financial statements are approved should be disclosed in a note to the financial statements.

A non-adjusting event that affects going concern becomes an adjusting event.

Activity 1: Non-adjusting events

Which of the following events after the reporting period would normally qualify as a non-adjusting event?

(1) A fall in the market price of shares held by the entity as investments.

(2) Insolvency of a trade receivable with a balance of $200,000 outstanding at the end of the reporting period.

(3) Declaration of the year-end dividend by the directors.

(4) Confirmation of the amount of damages awarded to an employee who sued for unfair dismissal after being sacked two months before the year end.

O 2 only

O 1 and 3 only

O 1, 3 and 4 only

O 2 and 4 only

Chapter summary

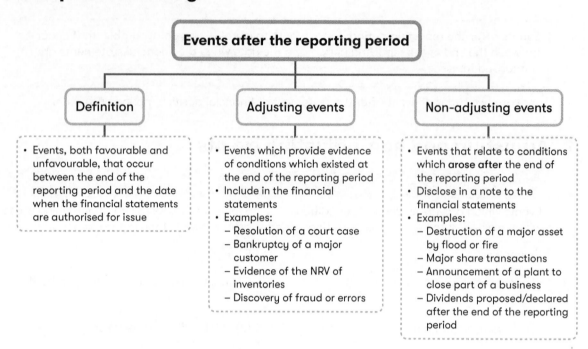

Events after the reporting period

Definition
- Events, both favourable and unfavourable, that occur between the end of the reporting period and the date when the financial statements are authorised for issue

Adjusting events
- Events which provide evidence of conditions which existed at the end of the reporting period
- Include in the financial statements
- Examples:
  - Resolution of a court case
  - Bankruptcy of a major customer
  - Evidence of the NRV of inventories
  - Discovery of fraud or errors

Non-adjusting events
- Events that relate to conditions which **arose after** the end of the reporting period
- Disclose in a note to the financial statements
- Examples:
  - Destruction of a major asset by flood or fire
  - Major share transactions
  - Announcement of a plant to close part of a business
  - Dividends proposed/declared after the end of the reporting period

Knowledge diagnostic

1. Definition

Events after the end of the reporting period are events which occur between the end of the reporting period and the date the financial statements are approved for issue.

2. Adjusting events

Adjusting events provide evidence of conditions that existed at the end of the reporting period. The financial statements should be changed to include this information.

3. Non-adjusting events

Non-adjusting events relate to conditions which arose after the end of the reporting period. These should be disclosed as a note to the financial statements.

Further study guidance

Question practice

Now try the following from the Further question practice bank (available in the digital edition of the Workbook):

Questions 81 to 83

Activity answers

Activity 1: Non-adjusting events

The correct answer is: 1 and 3 only

(1) and (3) are non-adjusting events as the condition did not exist at the end of the reporting period.

22

Statements of cash flows

Learning objectives

On competition of this chapter, you should be able to:

	Syllabus reference no.
Differentiate between profit and cash flows.	F5(a)
Understand the need for management to control cash flow.	F5(b)
Recognise the benefits and drawbacks to users of the financial statements of a statement of cash flows.	F5(c)
Classify the effect of transactions on cash flows.	F5(d)
Calculate the figures needed for the statement of cash flows including cash flows from operating, investing and financing activities.	F5(e)
Calculate the cash flow from operating activities using the direct and indirect method.	F5(f)
Prepare statements of cash flows and extracts from statements of cash flows from given information.	F5(g)

Exam context

Questions on this chapter are likely to focus on whether you can identify which items should and should not go into the statement of cash flows and also on performing basic calculations. For example, in an objective test question, you may be asked to calculate a figure such as the cash generated from operations from given information or the cash paid to acquire property, plant and equipment. The multi-task accounts preparation question could also require preparation of a full statement of cash flows.

Chapter overview

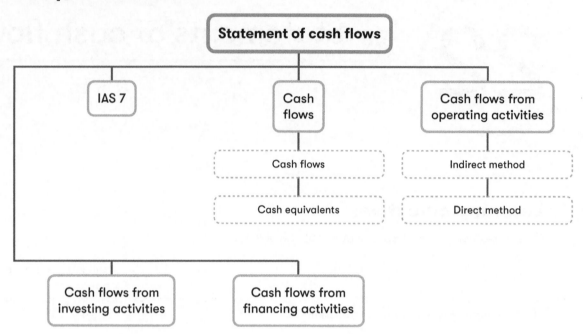

1 Purpose

The purpose of the cash flow statement is to show the effect of a company's commercial transactions on its cash balance.

It is thought that users of accounts can readily understand cash flows, as opposed to statements of profit or loss and statements of financial position which are subject to manipulation by the use of different accounting policies.

Cash flows are used as an investment appraisal method such as net present value and hence a statement of cash flows gives potential investors a method with which to evaluate a business.

It has been argued that 'profit' does not always give a useful or meaningful picture of a company's operations. Readers of a company's financial statements might even be **misled by a reported profit figure**.

(a) Shareholders might believe that if a company makes a profit after tax of, say, $100,000 then this is the amount that it could afford to **pay as a dividend**. Unless the company has **sufficient cash** available to stay in business and also to pay a dividend, the shareholders' expectations would be wrong.

(b) Employees might believe that if a company makes profits, it can afford to **pay higher wages** next year. This opinion may not be correct: the ability to pay wages depends on the **availability of cash**.

(c) Survival of a business entity depends not so much on profits as on its **ability to pay its debts when they fall due**. Such payments might include 'profit and loss' items, such as material purchases, wages, interest and taxation, but also capital payments for new non-current assets and the repayment of loan capital when this falls due (for example on the redemption of loan stock).

It is crucial that management control cash flow in order to maintain the operating ability of the company. For example, imagine a furniture company that makes and sells its own furniture. Now imagine that the company is financed largely by debt and this debt is secured on the furniture making assets of the business. If management do not control cash flow and end up in a situation where they cannot make their loan repayments, then the bank could repossess the assets. Without these assets the company would not be able to make the products that it sells and would therefore have to shut down.

2 IAS 7 Statement of Cash Flows

Before we look at the detail of a statement of cash flows, it is important to remind ourselves of the difference between the accruals basis and the cash basis. Remember that when we account according to the accruals basis, we add in items that we have not yet paid for and we exclude items that we have paid for but which relate to the next year. We also include sales revenue which we have not received any money for.

Under the cash basis, we only show items that have been physically received or paid for in the year.

That is the key to understanding the difference between the financial statements and a statement of cash flows. In a statement of cash flows we are looking ONLY at cash and therefore any transactions in the financial statements that are not cash have to be removed. A good example of this is depreciation. Depreciation is simply an accounting adjustment, it is never cash.

IAS 7 splits cash flows into the following headings:

(a) Cash flows from operating activities

(b) Cash flows from investing activities

(c) Cash flows from financing activities

2.1 Definitions

Cash: Comprises cash on hand and demand deposits.

Cash equivalents: Short-term, highly liquid investments that are readily convertible to known amounts of cash and which are subject to an insignificant risk of changes in value.

Cash flows: Inflows and outflows of cash and cash equivalents.

(IAS 7 para. 6)

2.2 Proforma

Indirect method:

XYZ Co Statement of cash flows for the year ended 31 December 20X7

	$'000	$'000
Cash flows from operating activities		
Profit before taxation	3,390	
Adjustment for:		
Depreciation	450	
Investment income	(500)	
Interest expense	400	
	3,740	
Increase in trade and other receivables	(500)	
Decrease in inventories	1,050	
Decrease in trade payables	(1,740)	
Cash generated from operations	2,550	
Interest paid	(270)	
Income taxes paid	(900)	
Net cash from operating activities		1,380
Cash flows from investing activities		
Purchase of property, plant and equipment	(900)	
Proceeds from sale of equipment	20	
Interest received	200	
Dividends received	200	
Net cash used in investing activities		(480)
Cash flows from financing activities		
Proceeds from issue of share capital	250	
Proceeds from long-term borrowings	250	

	$'000	$'000
Dividends paid*	(1,290)	
Net cash used in financing activities		(790)
Net increase in cash and cash equivalents		110
Cash and cash equivalents at beginning of period		120
Cash and cash equivalents at end of period		230

* This could be shown as an operating cash flow.

3 Cash flows from operating activities

These represent cash flows derived from operating or trading activities.

An entity should report cash flows from operating activities using either:

(a) The **direct method**, whereby major classes of gross cash receipts and payments are disclosed (preferred method per IAS 7 – see Section 6.1); or

(b) The **indirect method** (as above), whereby reported profit or loss is adjusted for the effects of transactions of a non-cash nature, any accruals or prepayments of operating expenses, and items relating to investing or financing cash flows.

3.1 Income taxes paid

Income taxes paid may need to be calculated from other data given to you. This is best achieved by putting the relevant figures into a T-account working.

Activity 1: Tax

The income tax payable balances at 31 December 20X9 and 31 December 20X8 for Tacks Co were as follows:

	20X9	20X8
	$	$
Income tax payable	156,000	168,000

The tax expense in the statement of profit or loss tax for 20X9 was $104,000.

Required

What is the amount of income taxes paid during the year?

Solution

INCOME TAXES PAID

	$'000		$'000
	———		———
	═══		═══

4 Cash flows from investing activities

The cash flows included in this section are those related to the acquisition or disposal of any non-current assets or investments together with returns received in cash from investments, ie dividends and interest. This section shows the extent to which expenditures have been made for resources intended to generate future income and cash flows.

Activity 2: Property, plant and equipment

On 31 December 20X8, the value of plant and equipment in the books of Erosion Co was as follows:

	$
Plant and equipment at cost	200,000
Accumulated depreciation	80,000
Plant and equipment at net book value	120,000

On 1 January 20X9, an item of plant was sold for $8,000 which had originally cost $20,000 when new, but had a net book value of $11,000 at the time of sale. (The statement of financial position values shown above do not show that this sale has taken place.)

On 31 December 20X9, the value of plant and equipment in the statement of financial position was:

	$
Plant and equipment at cost	280,000
Accumulated depreciation	111,000
Plant and equipment at net book value	169,000

Required

Show the relevant entries for property, plant and equipment which would appear in a statement of cash flows (under the indirect method) for Erosion Co in 20X9.

Solution

Cash flows from operating activities (extract)

	$
Adjustments for	
Depreciation	
Loss on sale of plant	_____
	_____

Cash flows from investing activities (extract)

	$
Purchase of property, plant and equipment	
Proceeds from sale of plant	_____

Workings

1 *Plant and equipment – cost (SOFP)*

PLANT AND EQUIPMENT

	$'000		$'000
	___		___
	═══		═══

2 *Accumulated depreciation*

DEPRECIATON

	$'000		$'000
	___		___
	═══		═══

3 *Disposal (SPL)*

DISPOSAL

	$'000		$'000
	─		___
	═══		═══

5 Cash flows from financing activities

Financing cash flows comprise receipts from, or repayments to, external providers of finance in respect of principal amounts of finance. Examples of financing cash flows are:

(a) Cash proceeds from issuing shares

(b) Cash proceeds from issuing debentures, loans notes, bonds, mortgages and other short- or long-term borrowings

(c) Cash repayments of amounts borrowed

(d) Dividends paid to shareholders

In order to calculate such figures, the closing statement of financial position figure for debt or share capital and share premium is compared with the opening position for the same items.

5.1 Dividends paid

The cash outflows included in dividends paid are dividends paid on the reporting company's equity shares.

Activity 3: Dividends

Distribution Co Statement of financial position extract for the year ended 31 December 20X9

	20X9	20X8
	$'000	$'000
Dividends payable	45	35

Dividends charged to retained earnings were $60,000.

Required

What are the dividends paid during the year ended 31 December 20X9?

Solution

DIVIDENDS PAYABLE

	$'000		$'000
	‾‾‾		‾‾‾
	══		══

Activity 4: Statement of cash flows – preparation

The summarised accounts of the Emma Co for the year ended 31 December 20X8 are as follows:

Statement of financial position as at 31 December

	20X8	20X7
	$'000	$'000
Non-current assets		
Property, plant and equipment	628	514
Current assets		
Inventories	214	210
Trade receivables	168	147
Cash	7	–
	389	357
	1,017	871
Equity		
Share capital ($1 ordinary shares)	250	200
Share premium account	70	60
Retained earnings	314	282

	20X8	20X7
	$'000	$'000
Revaluation surplus	110	100
	744	642
Non-current liabilities		
10% debentures	80	50
Current liabilities		
Trade payables	136	121
Income tax payable	39	28
Dividends payable	18	16
Overdraft	–	14
	193	179
	1,017	871

Statement of profit or loss for the year ended 31 December 20X8

	$'000
Revenue	600
Cost of sales	319
Gross profit	281
Other expenses (including depreciation of $42,000)	186
Finance costs (interest paid)	8
Profit before tax	87
Income tax expense	31
Profit for the year	56

Movement of retained earnings

	$'000
Balance at 31 December 20X7	282
Profit for the year	56
Dividends	(24)
Balance at 31 December 20X8	314

You are additionally informed that there have been no disposals of property, plant and equipment during the year. The new debentures were issued on 1 January 20X8.

Required

Produce a statement of cash flows for Emma Co for the year ended 31 December 20X8.

Solution

Emma Co Statement of cash flows for the year ended 31 December 20X8

	$'000	$'000
Cash flows from operating activities		
Profit before taxation		
Adjustments for:		
Depreciation		
Interest expense	_____	
Increase in trade receivables ⬚		
Increase in inventories ⬚		
Increase in trade payables ⬚	_____	
Cash generated from operations		
Interest paid		
Income taxes paid ⬚	_____	
Net cash from operating activities		
Cash flows from investing activities		
Purchase of property, plant and equipment		
⬚		
Net cash used in investing activities	_____	
Cash flows from financing activities		
Proceeds from issue of shares ⬚		
Proceeds from issue of debentures		
Dividends paid ⬚	_____	
Net cash from financing activities		_____
Net increase in cash and cash equivalents		
Cash and cash equivalents at beginning of year		_____
Cash and cash equivalents at end of year		_____

Workings

1 **Property, plant and equipment**

PROPERTY, PLANT AND EQUIPMENT

	$'000		$'000
	_____		_____
	══════		══════

2 **Income tax payable**

INCOME TAX PAYABLE

	$'000		$'000
		SPL expense	
	_____		_____
	══════		══════

3 **Dividends payable**

DIVIDENDS PAYABLE

	$'000		$'000
	_____		_____
	══════		══════

6 Cash flows from operating activities using the direct method

The direct method derives the 'cash generated from operations' figure in a different way. The operating element of the statement of cash flows should be shown as follows:

	$'000	$'000
Cash flows from operating activities		
Cash receipts from customers	30,150	
Cash payments to suppliers and employees	(27,600)	
Cash generated from operations	2,550	
Interest paid	(270)	
Income taxes paid	(900)	
Net cash from operating activities		1,380

6.1 Cash received from customers

This represents cash flows received during the accounting period in respect of sales.

6.2 Cash payments to suppliers and employees

This represents cash flows made during the accounting period in respect of goods and services and amounts paid to employees.

 Activity 5: Cash flows from operating activities – direct method

Using the information in Activity 4, produce the 'cash flows from operating activities' section of the cash flow statement using the direct method

Solution

	$'000	$'000
Cash flow from operating activities		
Cash receipts from customers [_____]		
Cash payments to suppliers and employees		
[_____]		_____
Cash generated from operations		
Interest paid		
Income taxes paid		_____
Net cash from operating activities		

Workings

1 **Trade receivables**

TRADE RECEIVABLES

	$'000		$'000
	___		_____
	_____		_____

2 **Trade payables**

TRADE PAYABLES

	$'000		$'000
	_____		_____
	_____		_____

7 Advantages and disadvantages of cash flow accounting

7.1 Advantages

The advantages of cash flow accounting are as follows:

(a) Survival in business depends on the ability to generate cash. Cash flow accounting directs attention towards this critical issue.

(b) Cash flow is more comprehensive than 'profit' which is dependent on accounting conventions and concepts.

(c) Creditors of the business (both long and short term) are more interested in an enterprise's ability to repay them than in its profitability. While 'profits' might indicate that cash is likely to be available, cash flow accounting gives clearer information.

(d) Cash flow reporting provides a better means of comparing the results of different companies than traditional profit reporting.

(e) Cash flow reporting satisfies the needs of all users better.

    (i) For management, it provides the sort of information on which decisions should be taken (in management accounting, 'relevant costs' to a decision are future cash flows). Traditional profit accounting does not help with decision making.

    (ii) For shareholders and auditors, cash flow accounting can provide a satisfactory basis for stewardship accounting.

    (iii) As described previously, the information needs of creditors and employees will be better served by cash flow accounting.

(f) Cash flow forecasts are easier to prepare, as well as more useful, than profit forecasts.

(g) They can, in some respects, be audited more easily than accounts based on the accruals concept.

(h) The accruals concept is confusing, and cash flows are more easily understood.

    (i) Cash flow information can be retrospective and can also include a forecast for the future. This is of great information value to all users of accounting information.

    (ii) Forecasts can subsequently be monitored by the publication.

7.2 Disadvantages of cash flow accounting

The main disadvantage of cash flow accounting is that there is no matching of items that relate to one another. For example, purchases of stock could be made this year but the cash from the sale will not be included until next year.

Another disadvantage is that they are backward looking. All the information in a statement of cash flows is historic, just like the information in the other financial statements.

BPP
LEARNING
MEDIA

Chapter summary

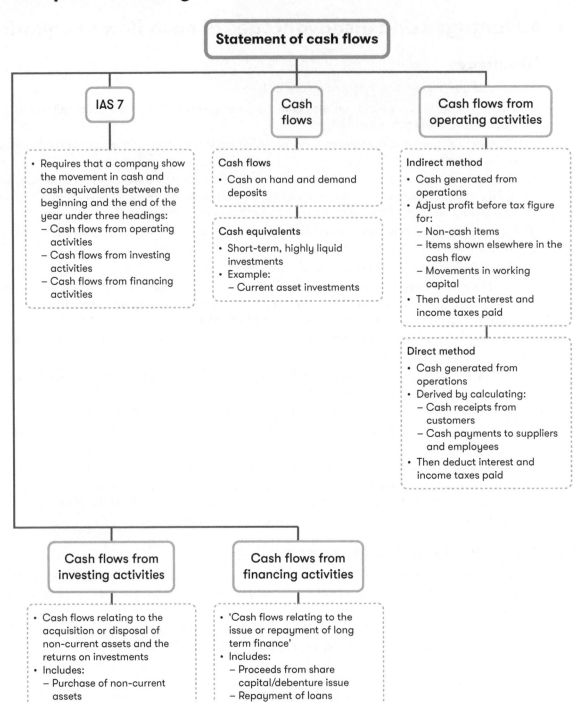

Statement of cash flows

IAS 7

- Requires that a company show the movement in cash and cash equivalents between the beginning and the end of the year under three headings:
  - Cash flows from operating activities
  - Cash flows from investing activities
  - Cash flows from financing activities

Cash flows

Cash flows
- Cash on hand and demand deposits

Cash equivalents
- Short-term, highly liquid investments
- Example:
  - Current asset investments

Cash flows from operating activities

Indirect method
- Cash generated from operations
- Adjust profit before tax figure for:
  - Non-cash items
  - Items shown elsewhere in the cash flow
  - Movements in working capital
- Then deduct interest and income taxes paid

Direct method
- Cash generated from operations
- Derived by calculating:
  - Cash receipts from customers
  - Cash payments to suppliers and employees
- Then deduct interest and income taxes paid

Cash flows from investing activities

- Cash flows relating to the acquisition or disposal of non-current assets and the returns on investments
- Includes:
  - Purchase of non-current assets
  - Proceeds from sale of non-current assets
  - Interest/dividends received

Cash flows from financing activities

- 'Cash flows relating to the issue or repayment of long term finance'
- Includes:
  - Proceeds from share capital/debenture issue
  - Repayment of loans
  - Ordinary dividends paid

BPP
LEARNING
MEDIA

Knowledge diagnostic

1. Purpose

The statement of cash flows shows the movement between a company's cash and cash equivalents at the beginning and the end of the year.

2. Statements of cash flows (IAS 7)

Cash comprises cash on hand and on demand deposits, less bank overdrafts.

Cash equivalents are short-term, highly liquid investments such as current asset investments (shares) which can be converted in to known amounts of cash relatively quickly without having a major impact on the entity's activities.

3. Cash flows from operating activities

This section of the statement of cash flows shows the cash and cash equivalents generated by and used in the entity's main trading activities.

4. Cash flows from investing activities

This section shows the cash flows related to the acquisition and disposal of non-current assets and returns on investments such as interest and dividends received.

5. Cash flows from financing activities

Cash flows from financing activities include the monies raised from issuing shares and loans and the cash used in the repayment of loans and the payment of dividends.

6. Cash flow from operating activities using the direct method

The statement of cash flows can be produced using one of two methods: the **indirect** or the **direct** method.

The direct method provides exactly the same cash flow information but calculates the cash flow from operating activities using a slightly different calculation from the indirect method.

Further study guidance

Question practice

Now try the following from the Further question practice bank (available in the digital edition of the Workbook):

Questions 84 to 86

Activity answers

Activity 1: Tax

INCOME TAXES PAID

	$'000		$'000
Income tax paid (balancing figure)	116	Bal b/d	168
Bal c/d	156	SPL	104
	272		272

Activity 2: Property, plant and equipment

Cash flows from operating activities (extract)

	$
Adjustments for	
Depreciation	40,000
Loss on sale of plant	3,000
	43,000

Cash flows from investing activities (extract)

	$
Purchase of property, plant and equipment	(100,000)
Proceeds from sale of plant	8,000
	(92,000)

Workings

1 **Plant and equipment – cost (SOFP)**

PLANT AND EQUIPMENT

	$'000		$'000
Bal b/d	200	Disposal	20
Addition (balancing figure)	100	Bal c/d	280
	300		300

2 **Accumulated depreciation**

DEPRECIATON

	$'000		$'000
Disposal	9	Bal b/d	80
Bal c/d	111	Charge (balancing figure)	40
	120		120

3 *Disposal (SPL)*

DISPOSAL

	$'000		$'000
PPE cost	20	PPE Accumulated depreciation	9
		Proceeds	8
		Transfer loss on disposal to SPL	3
	20		20

Activity 3: Dividends

DIVIDENDS PAYABLE

	$'000		$'000
Dividends paid	50	Bal b/d	35
Bal c/d	45	Retained earnings	60
	95		95

Activity 4: Statement of cash flows – preparation

Emma Co Statement of cash flows for the year ended 31 December 20X8

	$'000	$'000
Cash flows from operating activities		
Profit before taxation	87	
Adjustments for:		
Depreciation	42	
Interest expense	8	
	137	
Increase in trade receivables (168 – 147)	(21)	
Increase in inventories (214 – 210)	(4)	

	$'000	$'000
Increase in trade payables (136 – 121)	15	
Cash generated from operations	127	
Interest paid	(8)	
Income taxes paid (W2)	(20)	
Net cash from operating activities		99
Cash flows from investing activities		
Purchase of property, plant and equipment (W1)	(146)	
Net cash used in investing activities		(146)
Cash flows from financing activities		
Proceeds from issue of shares ($250 + $70 – $200 – $60)	60	
Proceeds from issue of debentures	30	
Dividends paid (W3)	(22)	
Net cash from financing activities		68
Net increase in cash and cash equivalents		21
Cash and cash equivalents at beginning of year		(14)
Cash and cash equivalents at end of year		7

Workings

1 **Property, plant and equipment**

PROPERTY, PLANT AND EQUIPMENT

	$'000		$'000
Bal b/d	514	Depreciation	42
Revaluation during the year ($110 – $100)	10		
Additions	146	Bal c/d	628
	670		670

2 **Income tax payable**

INCOME TAX PAYABLE

	$'000		$'000
Income tax paid	20	Bal b/d	28
Bal c/d	39	SPL expense	31

	$'000		$'000
	59		59

3   **Dividends payable**

DIVIDENDS PAYABLE

	$'000		$'000
Dividends paid	22	Bal b/d	16
Bal c/d	18	Dividend for the year	24
	40		40

Activity 5: Cash flows from operating activities – direct method

	$'000	$'000
Cash flow from operating activities		
Cash receipts from customers (W1)	579	
Cash payments to suppliers and employees (W2)	(452)	
Cash generated from operations	127	
Interest paid	(8)	
Income taxes paid	(20)	
Net cash from operating activities		99

Workings

1   **Trade receivables**

TRADE RECEIVABLES

	$'000		$'000
Bal b/d	147	∴ cash received	579
Revenue (SPL)	600		
		Bal c/d	168
	747		747

2   **Trade payables**

TRADE PAYABLES

	$'000		$'000
		Bal b/d	121
Cash paid	452	Expenses (W3)	467
Bal c/d	136		
	588		588

Workings

1 **Expenses**

	$'000	$'000
Cost of sales	319	
Add: closing inventories	214	
Less: opening inventories	(210)	
Purchases		323
Other expenses	186	
Less: depreciation	(42)	
		144
		467

Skills checkpoint 5

Correction of errors

Overview

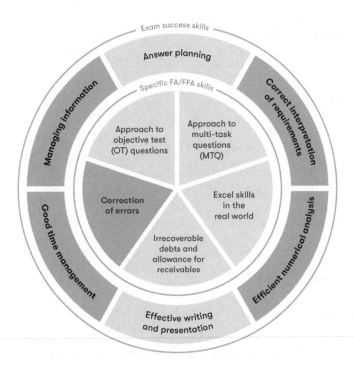

Introduction

The correction of errors area of the examination often causes difficulties for candidates as they are required to think around the subject rather than just rote learning.

Correction of errors

There are many types of errors that can occur when items are posted to the ledger accounts. Here is a reminder of the key errors:

Type of error	Example
Error of omission	When both sides of a transactions are omitted
Error of commission	The entry is to the correct account but it is for the wrong amount.
Error of principle	When a transaction goes against the laws of double entry, eg a capital expense recorded as a revenue expense

Type of error	Example
Compensating error	When two unrelated errors compensate for each other, eg a debit error of $9 and a credit error of $9
Transposition error	When there is a difference between the debit value as a result of two of the numbers being switched, eg Dr 29 and Cr 92. The resulting error is divisible by nine. This error will stop the trial balance from balancing and will require an entry into a suspense account.

Key steps

Often with these questions, the easiest thing to do is think:

Step 1: What was posted?

Step 2: What should have been posted?

Step 3: What needs to be posted to correct the error?

Illustration

A trainee accountant posted a non-current assets purchase as follows:

Dr Motor vehicle expense account $10,000

Cr Cash at bank account $10,000

STEP 1   What was posted?

Dr Motor vehicle expense account $10,000

Cr Cash at bank account $10,000

STEP 2   What should have been posted?

Dr Motor vehicle non-current asset cost account $10,000

Cr Cash at bank account $10,000

At this point, we can see that the cash account posting was correct but the debit entry was incorrect.

STEP 3   What needs to be posted to correct the entry?

Dr Motor vehicle non-current asset cost account $10,000

Cr Motor vehicle expense account $10,000

One important thing to notice about this error is that it would have affected the profit figure.

It was originally posted to the expense account on the statement of profit and loss when it should have been posted to the non-current asset account on the statement of financial position.

The result of this error would have been a decrease in profit of $10,000.

Skills activity

The following is taken from the examiner's report for the September 2018 to August 2019 exam sittings.

A business prepared draft financial statements for the year ended 31 December 20X7, which showed a profit for the year of $240,000. Subsequent investigation of the underlying records found the following errors and omissions:

(a) An annual insurance premium of $12,000 payable in advance and due on 1 January 20X7 had been paid on that date but the transaction had been completely omitted from the books

(b) Rent receivable of $50,000, which is receivable annually in advance and due on 1 July 20X7, had been received on that date and had been credited in full to the current year's statement of profit or loss.

What would be the revised figure for profit following the corrections of the above errors and omissions? (Insert the figure below.)

$_____

This question required candidates to use the information provided to arrive at an adjusted profit figure. The most common reason for an incorrect answer in this question was due to the adjustment being incorrectly added. For adjustments to profit style questions, it is worth remembering that debit entries reduce profit in the profit or loss whereas credit entries increase profit.

To answer this question, candidates needed to review the information carefully and consider the impact on profit. This is explained below.

Note (1) indicates that an error of omission has occurred. The transaction has not been recorded and will therefore require adjustment in the financial statements, for example:

Dr Insurance expense (SOPL) $12,000

Cr Cash (SOFP) $12,000

In terms of thinking about Steps 1 to 3:

STEP 1 What was posted?

Nothing was posted.

STEP 2 What should have been posted?

Dr Insurance expense (SOPL) $12,000

Cr Cash (SOFP) $12,000

STEP 3 What is required to correct the error?

Post the journal in Step 2.

Accruals and prepayments do not need to be considered for this adjustment as the insurance premium is in line with the financial year. Therefore, an expense of $12,000 should be recorded. This will result in a reduction in profit.

Note (2) required candidates to use their knowledge of prepaid income (sometimes known as deferred income). On 1 July 20X7, the cash received would have been recorded as follows:

Dr Bank $50,000

Cr Other income (SOPL) $50,000

Six months of the rental income received relates to the next accounting period and therefore needs to be removed from the current year's profit or loss as follows:

Dr Other income (SOPL) $25,000

Cr Prepaid income (SFP) $25,000

Again, this adjustment will result in a reduction in profit.

The closing profit should therefore be:

Draft profit	$240,000
Insurance receipt	$(12,000)
Prepaid rental income	$(25,000)
	$203,000

Skills activity

Now, let's have a look at a question that involves the suspense account.

The trial balance of Z failed to agree, the totals being:

Debit $836,200

Credit $819,700

A suspense account was opened for the amount of the difference; the following errors were found and corrected:

(a) The total of the cash discount received column in the cash book had not been posted to the discount received account. The figure for discounts received was $5,100.

(b) A cheque for $19,000 received from a customer was correctly entered in the cash book but was posted to the control account as $9,100.

What will the remaining balance be on the suspense after the correction of these errors?

$_____ credit

The difference on the trial balance is currently $16,500 credit.

For the two errors, we shall look at the step again. Once you get familiar with these questions, you may be able to answer them without the steps but, for now, we shall use them.

Error 1

STEP 1   **What was posted?**

Dr Payables $5,100

Cr Discounts received   0

This will have resulted in a suspense account of $5,100 credit.

STEP 2   **What should have been posted?**

Dr Payables $5,100

Cr Discounts received $5,100

STEP 3   **What correction is required?**

Dr Suspense $5,100

Cr Discounts received $5,100

Error 2

STEP 1   **What was posted?**

Dr cash at bank $19,000

Cr receivables $9,100

This will give rise to a suspense account entry of Cr Suspense account $9,900.

STEP 2   **What should have been posted?**

Dr Cash at bank $19,000

Cr Receivables control account $19,000

STEP 3   **What correction is required?**

Dr Suspense account $9,900

Cr Receivables control account $9,900

Opening suspense balance	$16,500 credit
Error 1	$(5,100) debit
Error 2	$(9,900) debit
Closing suspense balance	**$1,500 credit**

Skills activity

Now, let's look at a question where the steps cannot really be used.

The suspense account shows a debit balance of $100. What could this balance be due to?

(a) Entering $50 received from A Turner on the debit side of A Turner's account

(b) Entering $50 received from A Turner on the credit side of A Turner's account

(c) Undercasting the sales day book by $100

(d) Undercasting the purchases account by $100

Firstly, let's think about what is meant by the phrase 'the suspense account shows a debit balance of $100'.

This would imply that there were too many credits and not enough debits and so the $100 debit had to be posted to suspense to make the trial balance balance.

Now let's go through the multiple-choice options:

Option 1 and 2 both talk about personal accounts. This means that they are talking about receivables or payables ledgers, which are not part of the double entry system and so we can immediately rule out the first two options.

Option 3. Undercasting the sales day book by $100 means that the sales day book total is wrong by $100. The sales day book total is used to post both sides of the double entry, eg to sales and receivables control account and, as such, this cannot be the correct answer as this would not create an imbalance. The sales and receivables control accounts would both be wrong by $100.

Option 4. Now we have ruled out the first three options, let's hope this one works!

When totalling up all of the ledger accounts and transferring their balances to the trial balance, the purchases account has been added up incorrectly. The purchases account is a debit balance and therefore, if it has been undercast, we would be missing $100 debit.

So, Option 4 is the correct answer.

Exam success skills diagnostic

Every time you complete a few questions, use the diagnostic below to assess how effectively you demonstrated the exam success skills in answering the questions. The table has been completed below for the above activities to give you an idea of how to complete the diagnostic.

Exam success skills	Your reflections/observations
Managing information	Did you take your time to read the question carefully to ensure you were answering the question set?
Correct interpretation of requirements	These questions are quite tricky and reading the information and requirement carefully is crucial.?
Efficient numerical analysis	Be careful to ensure you are adding things that need to be added and deducting things that need to be deducted. Using the last activity, if the purchases account is undercast by $100, you would need to add $100 onto the purchases balance and remove $100 from the suspense account.
Good time management	Did you complete the question in the allotted time? 2 mark questions should take 2.4 minutes.

Most important action points to apply to your next question. (Complete this for any learning from this checkpoint that you want to carry forward to your revision.)

Summary

Error and suspense account questions are very tricky and the questions need to be read carefully and often a few times over. Where possible, practice the questions using the three steps and, with time, you will get much quicker at working through the steps and eventually be able to resolve errors without going through the three-step process. Remember: take your time and read the question!

23

Introduction to consolidated financial statements

Learning objectives

On competition of this chapter, you should be able to:

	Syllabus reference no.
Define and describe the following terms in the context of group accounting: i) Parent ii) Subsidiary iii) Control iv) Consolidated or group financial statements v) Non-controlling interest vi) Trade/simple investment	G1(a)
Identify subsidiaries within a group structure.	G1(b)
Define and identify an associate and significant influence and identify situations where significant influence or participating interest exists.	G2(a)
Describe the key features of a parent-associate relationship and be able to identify an associate within a group structure.	G2(b)
Describe the principle of the equity method of accounting for associate entities.	G2(c)

Exam context

This chapter introduces the concept of group accounting. Questions on this area will most likely focus on:

- Identifying whether an entity is a subsidiary, associate or trade investment
- The accounting treatment for a subsidiary or associate in the consolidated financial statements

Chapter overview

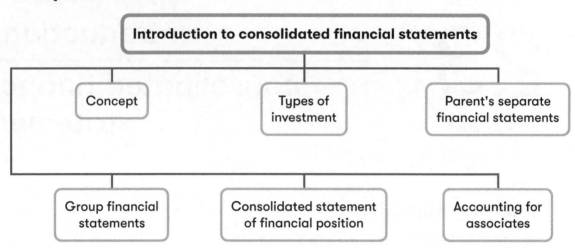

1 Concept

Exam focus point

This is an important area so make sure you read carefully this and the following two chapters and attempt all the examples and questions. You should also make sure that you attempt the questions on this topic, including the long questions, in the Practice & Revision Kit for FFA/FA.

There are two articles – 'Preparing a group statement of financial position' and 'Preparing simple consolidated financial statements' on the ACCA website. You are advised to read these articles as part of the preparation for your exam.

Companies may expand organically by building up their business from their own trading, or by acquisitive growth (ie by acquiring shares in other entities).

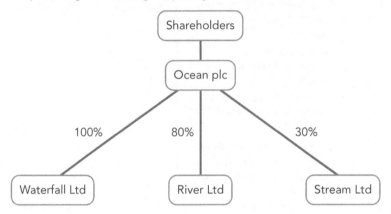

Ocean plc is known as the parent or holding company.

Parent: An entity that controls one or more entities (IFRS 10, Appendix A).

Control: An investor controls an investee when the investor is exposed, or has rights, to variable returns from its involvement with the investee and has the ability to affect those returns through its power over the investee (IFRS 10, Appendix A).

2 Types of investment

2.1 Subsidiary

Subsidiary: A subsidiary is an entity that is controlled by another entity.

An investor controls an investee if and only if the investor has all the following:

(a) Power over the investee to direct the relevant activities;

(b) Exposure, or rights, to variable returns from its involvement with the investee; and

(c) The ability to use its power over the investee to affect the amount of the investor's returns.

(IFRS 10, para. 7)

Application

```
                            ┌─────────────┐
                            │   Control   │
                            └──────┬──────┘
        ┌──────────────────────────┼──────────────────────────┐
┌───────┴────────┐        ┌────────┴────────┐         ┌────────┴────────┐
│  Power to direct│        │ Exposure or     │         │ Ability to use  │
│relevant activities│      │ rights to       │         │ power to affect │
│                │        │ variable returns │         │the amount of returns│
└────────────────┘        └─────────────────┘         └─────────────────┘
```

Power to direct **relevant activities**

Examples of power:
- Voting rights
- Rights to appoint, reassign or remove key management personnel
- Rights to appoint or remove another entity that directs relevant activities
- Management contract

Examples of relevant activities:
- Selling and purchasing goods/services
- Selecting, acquiring, disposing of assets
- Researching & developing new products/processes
- Determining funding structure/obtaining funding

Exposure or rights to **variable returns**

Examples of variable returns:
- Dividends
- Interest from debt
- Changes in value of investment
- Remuneration for servicing investee's assets or liabilities
- Fees/exposure to loss from providing credit/liquidity support
- Residual interest in assets and liabilities on liquidation
- Tax benefits
- Access to future liquidity
- Returns not available to other interest holders, eg cost savings

Ability to use power to affect the amount of returns

An investor can have the current **ability** to direct the activities of an investee even **if it does not actively direct the activities** of the investee

2.2 Associate

> **Associate:** An associate is an entity over which the investor has significant influence.

Significant influence is the power to participate in the financial and operating policy decisions of the investee but is not control or joint control over those policies. This could be shown by:

(a) Representation on the board of directors

(b) Participation in policy-making processes

(c) Material transactions between the entity and investee

(d) Interchange of managerial personnel

(e) Provision of essential technical information

(IAS 28, para. 3 and 6)

Presumptions

If an investor holds, directly or indirectly:

(a) 20% or more of voting power

    (i) Presumption of significant influence unless demonstrated otherwise

(b) < 20% of voting power

    (i) Presumption of no significant influence unless demonstrated otherwise

2.3 Trade investment

> **Trade investment:** A trade investment is a simple investment in the shares of another entity that is not an associate or a subsidiary.

This means that the investor does not have significant influence or control. In absence of information to the contrary, if an investor holds less than 20% of the voting power, the entity is considered to be a trade investment.

Trade investments are simply shown as investments under non-current assets in the statement of financial position. Dividends received from trade investments are recorded as investment income in the statement of profit or loss and other comprehensive income.

2.4 Summary

The solution to the information gap depends on the type of investment held by an investor.

The accounting treatment depends on the extent of influence achieved.

Degree of influence	Presumed if size of investment is	Type of investment	Accounting treatment
Control	> 50%	Subsidiary	Consolidate
Significant influence	20% to 50%	Associate	Equity account
No influence	0% to < 20%	Trade investment	Investment in SOFP and investment income in SPLOCI

Activity 1: Subsidiaries

J has a 40% shareholding in each of the following three companies:

- K: J has a management agreement with K stating that J is responsible for all key operating and financial decisions in K.
- L: J has significant influence over the affairs of L.
- M: J has the right to appoint or remove a majority of the directors of M.

Required

Which of these companies are subsidiaries of J for financial reporting purposes?

O   None of them

O   K, L and M only

O   K and L only

O   K and M only

3 Parent's separate financial statements

Statement of financial position

When the parent company acquires shares in a subsidiary, associate or trade investment, in the parent's statement of financial position, an **investment** is recorded at cost (for exam purposes) within non-current assets.

Statement of comprehensive income

Any dividends received from the subsidiary, associate or trade investment are recorded as **investment income** in the parent company's statement of profit or loss and other comprehensive income.

4 Group financial statements

The parent company's shareholders will only have access to the parent's separate financial statements (not the subsidiary's financial statements). Therefore, they will only be able to see the investment at cost in the statement of financial position and dividend income in the statement of profit or loss and other comprehensive income. They will not be able to see the impact of the parent's control over the net assets and profit of the subsidiary.

The purpose of group financial statements is to bridge the information gap. Provided the parent has a controlling influence, it is required to produce an additional set of financial statements which aim to record the **substance** of its relationship with its subsidiaries (single economic entity) rather than its strict **legal form** (separate legal entities).

This additional set of accounts is referred to as group, or consolidated financial statements which:

(a) Present the results and financial position of a group of companies as if it was a **single business entity**;

(b) Are issued to the shareholders of the parent;

(c) Are issued in **addition** to and not **instead** of the parent's own financial statements; and

(d) Provide information on all companies controlled by the parent.

5 Consolidated statement of financial position

5.1 Consolidation method for statement of financial position (SOFP)

Part of SOFP	Action required	Reason
Assets and liabilities (excluding the investment in subsidiary)	**Add** parent and subsidiary's assets and liabilities **line by line**	To show **control**
Investment in subsidiary	Cancel with share capital and pre-acquisition reserves of subsidiary	From a group perspective, the shares are held internally so need to be eliminated. The pre-acquisition reserves of the subsidiary were not generated under the parent's control and should be eliminated.
Share capital and share premium	Show the **parent's** only	To show **ownership** Group accounts are prepared for the parent's shareholders and the subsidiary's share capital/premium is eliminated as described above.
Reserves	Show the parent's plus the group share of post-acquisition reserves of subsidiary.	To show ownership Only want to include subsidiary's reserves generated under parent's control

Activity 2: Consolidated statement of financial position (1)

Pegasus acquired 100% of the share capital of Sylvester on 1 January 20X1 for $1,300,000 in cash.

The statements of financial position of Pegasus and Sylvester as at 1 January 20X1 are set out below:

	Pegasus	Sylvester
	$'000	$'000
Assets		
Non-current assets		
Property, plant and equipment	20,000	900
Investment in Sylvester	1,300	
	21,300	
Current assets		
Inventories	3,200	400
Trade receivables	2,500	175
Cash	500	125
	6,200	700
	27,500	1,600
Equity and liabilities		
Equity		
Share capital	5,000	100
Retained earnings	19,450	1,200
	24,450	1,300
Current liabilities		
Trade payables	2,500	260
Income tax payable	550	40
	3,050	300
	27,500	1,600

Required

Prepare the consolidated statement of financial position of the Pegasus Group as at 1 January 20X1.

Solution

Pegasus Group Statement of financial position at 1 January 20X1

	$'000
Assets	
Non-current assets	
Property, plant and equipment	[ ]
	_____
	_____
Current assets	
Inventories	[ ]
Trade receivables	[ ]

$'000

Cash [   ]

_____
_____
===============

Equity and liabilities

Equity

  Share capital

  Retained earnings
_____
_____

Current liabilities

  Trade payables [   ]

  Income tax payable [   ]

_____
_____
===============

Workings

1 **Group structure**

2 **Cancellation**

	$'000	$'000
Consideration (investment)		
Share capital		
Retained earnings (W1)	____	
		____
		==

5.2 Pre- and post-acquisition reserves

In the previous lecture example, Sylvester's net assets were represented not just by share capital but also reserves. We call those reserves 'pre-acquisition reserves' since they were controlled by someone else prior to Pegasus' investment in Sylvester on 1 January 20X1. They are not consolidated as they are cancelled with the cost of the investment.

Any profits made after acquisition – post-acquisition reserves – must be consolidated in the group financial statements.

Activity 3: Consolidated statement of financial position (2)

Three years later, 31 December 20X3, the summarised statement of financial position of Pegasus and Sylvester is as follows:

	Pegasus	Sylvester
	$'000	$'000
Assets		
Non-current assets		
Property, plant and equipment	24,000	4,200
Investment in Sylvester	1,300	
	25,300	4,200
Current assets	8,500	2,100
	33,800	6,300
Equity and liabilities		
Equity		
Share capital	5,000	100
Retained earnings	26,800	5,200
	31,800	5,300
Current liabilities	2,000	1,000
	33,800	6,300

Required

Prepare the consolidated statement of financial position of the Pegasus Group as at 31 December 20X3.

Solution

Pegasus Group Statement of financial position at 31 December 20X3

$'000

Assets

Non-current assets

Property, plant and equipment ☐

Current assets ☐

Equity and liabilities

Equity

Share capital

Retained earnings ☐

$'000

Current liabilities [   ]   _____

                                                            _____

Workings

1 **Group structure**

2 **Cancellation**

	$'000	$'000
Consideration (investment)		
Share capital		
Retained earnings [ ]	_____	
		_____
		=

3 **Retained earnings**

	Pegasus	*Sylvester*
	$'000	$'000
Per question		
Pre-acquisition retained earnings		_____
		_____
Sylvester – share of post acq'n earnings		
[ ]	_____	
	_____	

6 Accounting treatment for an associate

> ### Exam focus point
>
> In your exam, you may be asked to define significant influence or to determine whether an entity is an associate. The ACCA examining team has commented that students need to be able to describe the principle of equity accounting.
>
> Furthermore, in the January to June 2015 exam report, the ACCA examining team re-iterated that candidates need to have an understanding of IAS 28 *Investments in Associates and Joint Ventures*, in particular, the application of equity accounting.

Definition

Remember that an associate is an entity in which the parent has **significant** influence. In absence of other information, this is presumed when the parent holds 20% to 50% of the voting rights.

Consolidated financial statements

An investment in an associate is accounted for in consolidated financial statements using the **equity method**.

As the parent does not have control, 100% of the associate's assets, liabilities, income and expenses cannot be added to the parent's line by line. Instead, significant influence is reflected by bringing in the **group share** of the associate in two lines in each of the consolidated statement of financial position and statement of profit or loss and other comprehensive income.

Equity method

Statement of financial position

Non-current assets

Investment in associates *(Working)*	X

Working

Cost of associate	X
Share of post-acquisition retained reserves	A
Less: impairment losses on associate to date	(B)
	X

Retained earnings

	Parent	Subsidiary	**Associate**
Per question	X	X	**X**
Less: pre-acquisition retained earnings		(X)	**(X)**
		X	**X**
Subsidiary – group share of post-acquisition retained earnings	X		
Associate – group share of post-acquisition retained earnings	**A**		
Less: impairment of associate	**(B)**		
	X		

Statement of profit or loss and other comprehensive

Profit or loss

Associate's profit for the year × Group % (less impairment loss for year)	X

This is shown before group profit before tax.

Other comprehensive income

Associate's other comprehensive income for the year × Group %	X

Exam focus point

The FFA/FA syllabus requires you to understand the principle of equity accounting, but you will not be expected to perform calculations using equity accounting techniques in your exam.

Illustration 1: Investment in associate

P owns several subsidiaries. On 1 January 20X5, P purchased 30% of the ordinary shares of A for $100,000. At that date, A's retained earnings were $40,000.

As at 31 December 20X7, A's retained earnings had risen to $90,000. A's profit and other comprehensive income for the year ended 31 December 20X7 were $24,000 and $6,000 respectively. A has not paid any dividends since the acquisition date.

Up to 31 December 20X6, there was no impairment of the investment in the associate but, during the year ended 31 December 20X7, the investment in the associate suffered an impairment loss of $3,000.

Required

Prepare the extracts of the accounts showing how A should be accounted for.

Solution

Consolidated statement of financial position as at 31 December 20X7 (extract)

	$
Non-current assets	
Investment in associate (Working)	112,000

Working

Investment in associate

	$
Cost of associate	100,000
Share of post-acquisition retained reserves [($90,000 – $40,000) × 30%]	15,000
Less: impairment losses on associate to date	(3,000)
	112,000

Retained earnings

	Parent	Subsidiary	Associate
Per question	X	X	90,000
Pre-acquisition retained earnings		(X)	(40,000)
		X	50,000
Subsidiary – group share of post-acquisition retained earnings	X		
Associate – group share of post-acquisition retained earnings ($50,000 × 30%)	15,000		
Less: impairment of associate	(3,000)		
	X		

Consolidated statement of profit or loss and other comprehensive income for the year ended 31 December 20X7 (extract)

Profit or loss	$
Share of associate's profit for year [($24,000 × 30%) – 3,000 impairment]	4,200

This is shown before group profit before tax.

Other comprehensive income

Share of associate's other comprehensive income ($6,000 × 30%)	1,800

Activity 4: Associates – true or false

Which **TWO** of the following statements regarding associates is true?

(1) Associates are consolidated in the group financial statements.

(2) An associate is an entity over which the parent has control.

(3) Associates are incorporated in group financial statements using the equity accounting method.

(4) An associate is an entity in which the parent has significant influence.

○ 1 and 4

○ 1 and 2

○ 3 and 4

○ 2 and 3

PER alert

One of the competences you require to fulfil Performance Objective 7 (PO7) of the PER is the ability to "contribute to drafting or reviewing primary financial statements according to accounting standards and legislation". You can apply the knowledge you obtain from this chapter and the following two chapters on consolidated financial statements to help demonstrate this competence.

Chapter summary

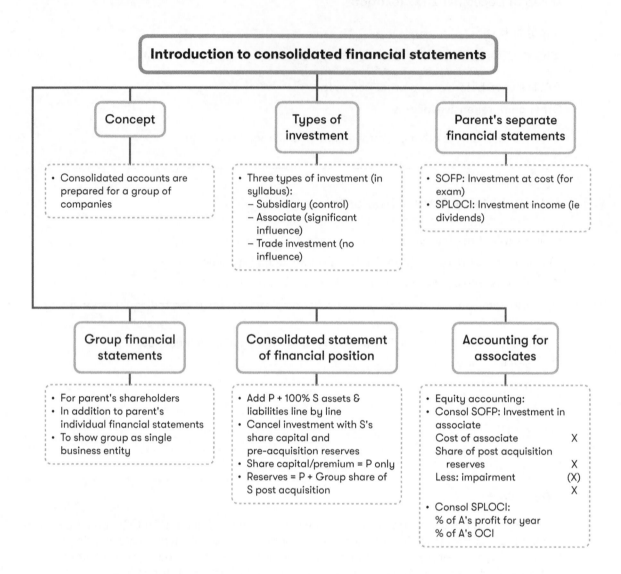

Introduction to consolidated financial statements

Concept
- Consolidated accounts are prepared for a group of companies

Types of investment
- Three types of investment (in syllabus):
  - Subsidiary (control)
  - Associate (significant influence)
  - Trade investment (no influence)

Parent's separate financial statements
- SOFP: Investment at cost (for exam)
- SPLOCI: Investment income (ie dividends)

Group financial statements
- For parent's shareholders
- In addition to parent's individual financial statements
- To show group as single business entity

Consolidated statement of financial position
- Add P + 100% S assets & liabilities line by line
- Cancel investment with S's share capital and pre-acquisition reserves
- Share capital/premium = P only
- Reserves = P + Group share of S post acquisition

Accounting for associates
- Equity accounting:
- Consol SOFP: Investment in associate

Cost of associate	X
Share of post acquisition reserves	X
Less: impairment	(X)
	X

- Consol SPLOCI:
  % of A's profit for year
  % of A's OCI

Knowledge diagnostic

1. Concept

Consolidated accounts are prepared for a group of inter-related companies.

2. Types of investment

There are three types of investment in the syllabus:

- Subsidiaries (where there is control)
- Associates (where there is significant influence)
- Trade investments (no influence)

3. Parent's separate financial statements

An investment in a subsidiary, associate or financial asset is shown in the parent's statement of financial position at cost (for exam purposes). Dividends are show as investment income in the statement of profit or loss and other comprehensive income.

4. Group financial statements

Group financial statements are issued to the shareholders of the parent only, in addition to the parent's own financial statements. They show the group as a single business entity.

5. Consolidated statement of financial position

Add parent and subsidiary's **assets and liabilities** line by line. Show **parent's share capital and share premium** only.

The investment cancels with the share capital and pre-acquisition reserves of the subsidiary.

Consolidated reserves comprise the parent's reserves plus the **group share** of the subsidiary's post acquisition reserves.

6. Accounting for associates

Associates should be **equity accounted** in the consolidated financial statements.

Consolidated statement of financial position:

Investment in associate (cost + share of post-acquisition reserves – impairment)

Consolidated reserves (include group share of associate's post-acquisition reserves and deduct impairment in associate)

Consolidated statement of profit or loss and other comprehensive income:

Share of associate's profit for the year

Share of associate's other comprehensive income

Further study guidance

Question practice

Now try the following from the Further question practice bank (available in the digital edition of the Workbook):

Questions 87 to 89

Further reading

There are two articles – 'Preparing a group statement of financial position' and 'Preparing simple consolidated financial statements' on the ACCA website. You are advised to read these articles as part of the preparation for your exam.

Activity answers

Activity 1: Subsidiaries

The correct answer is: K and M only

Both K and M are subsidiaries even though J owns less than 50% of the ordinary shares. IAS 27 defines a subsidiary as an entity controlled by another entity. J has control over K because of the management agreement giving J responsibility for all key operating and management decisions, ie the power to direct the relevant activities of K. J has control over M because it can appoint or remove the majority of the directors.

J only has significant influence over L so L is an associate of J, not a subsidiary.

Activity 2: Consolidated statement of financial position (1)

Pegasus Group Statement of financial position at 1 January 20X1

	$'000
Assets	
Non-current assets	
Property, plant and equipment ($20,000 + $900)	20,900
	20,900
Current assets	
Inventories ($3,200 + $400)	3,600
Trade receivables ($2,500 + $175)	2,675
Cash ($500 + $125)	625
	6,900
	27,800
Equity and liabilities	
Equity	
Share capital	5,000
Retained earnings	19,450
	24,450
Current liabilities	
Trade payables ($2,500 + $260)	2,760
Income tax payable ($550 + $40)	590
	3,350
	27,800

BPP
LEARNING
MEDIA

Workings

1 **Group structure**

Pegasus

1.1.X1 | 100%
| Pre-acquisition ret'd earnings $1,200k

Sylvester

2 **Cancellation**

	$'000	$'000
Consideration (investment)		1,300
Share capital	100	
Retained earnings (W1)	1,200	
		(1,300)
		=

Activity 3: Consolidated statement of financial position (2)

Pegasus Group Statement of financial position at 31 December 20X3

	$'000
Assets	
Non-current assets	
Property, plant and equipment ($24,000 + $4,200)	28,200
	28,200
Current assets ($8,500 + $2,100)	10,600
	38,800
Equity and liabilities	
Equity	
Share capital	5,000
Retained earnings (W3)	30,800
	35,800
Current liabilities ($2,000 + $1,000)	3,000
	38,800

Workings

1 **Group structure**

Pegasus

1.1.X1 | 100%
Pre-acquisition ret'd earnings $1,200k

Sylvester

2 **Cancellation**

	$'000	$'000
Consideration (investment)		1,300
Share capital	100	
Retained earnings (W1)	1,200	
		(1,300)
		=

3 **Retained earnings**

	Pegasus	Sylvester
	$'000	$'000
Per question	26,800	5,200
Pre-acquisition retained earnings		(1,200)
		4,000
Sylvester – share of post acq'n earnings ($4,000 × 100%)	4,000	
	30,800	

Activity 4: Associates – true or false

The correct answer is: 3 and 4

Statements (3) and (4) are correct as an associate is an entity in which the parent has significant influence. The equity method of accounting is used to include an associate in the consolidated financial statements. Statement (1) is incorrect because subsidiaries (not associates) are consolidated. Statement (2) is incorrect because if the parent has control, the entity is a subsidiary not an associate.

BPP
LEARNING
MEDIA

24

The consolidated statement of financial position

Learning objectives

On competition of this chapter, you should be able to:

	Syllabus reference no.
Define and describe the term 'non-controlling interest' in the context of group accounting.	G1(a)(v)
Describe the components of and prepare a consolidated statement of financial position or extracts thereof, including: i) Fair value adjustments at acquisition on land and buildings (excluding depreciation adjustments); ii) Fair value of consideration transferred from cash and shares (excluding deferred and contingent consideration); iii) Elimination of inter-company trading balances (excluding cash and goods in transit); iv) Removal of unrealised profit arising on inter-company trading; and v) Acquisition of subsidiaries partway through the financial year.	G1(c)
Calculate goodwill (excluding impairment of goodwill) using the full goodwill method only.	G1(d)

Exam context

This chapter focuses on the skills required to prepare a consolidated statement of financial position. This topic is most likely to be tested in the group's multi-task question. Questions on this area will most likely focus on:

- Preparing one or more of the consolidated statements of financial position workings (eg goodwill, consolidated retained earnings, non-controlling interest);
- Consolidation adjustments (eg fair value adjustment or elimination of unrealised profit); and
- Preparation of a consolidated statement of financial position or extracts thereof.

Chapter overview

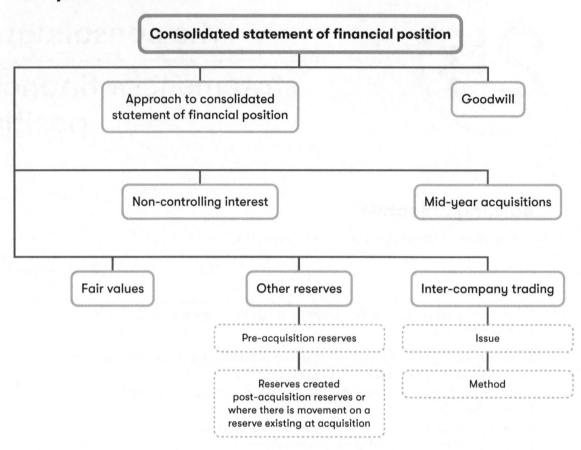

1 Approach to the consolidated statement of financial position

Step 1 Read the question (requirement first) and draw up the group structure (W1), highlighting useful information:

- The % owned
- Acquisition date
- Pre-acquisition reserves

Step 2 Draw up a proforma consolidated statement of financial position taking into account the group structure identified:

- Leave out cost of investment
- Put in lines for goodwill and non-controlling interest (will see in Sections 2 and 3)

Step 3 Work methodically down the statement of financial position, transferring figures to proforma or workings:

- Add P and 100% of S's assets/liabilities line by line in brackets on face of proforma, ready for adjustments
- Investment in subsidiary to goodwill working
- Reserves to consolidated reserves working(s)
- Share capital and share premium (parent only) to face of answer
- Open up a (blank) working for non-controlling interest (will see in Section 3)

Step 4 Read through the additional notes and attempt the adjustments showing workings for all calculations (will see in Sections 4 and 5).

Do the double entry for the adjustments onto your proforma answer and onto your group workings (where the group workings are affected by one side of the double entry).

Examples:

- Cancel any intragroup items, eg current a/c balances, loans
- Adjust for unrealised profits:

Unrealised profit on intragroup sales	X		
% held @ y/e	%		
= Provision for unrealised profit (PUP)	X̲	Dr	Retained earnings
(adjust in company **selling** goods)		Cr	Group inventories

- Make fair value adjustments

Fair value of land and buildings	X	
Book value of land and buildings	(X)	
Fair value adjustment	X	Post to goodwill working and add to PPE

Step 5 Complete goodwill calculation:

Fair value of consideration		X
Fair value of non-controlling interest		X
Less: Fair value of net assets at acquisition		
Share capital	X	
Share premium	X	
Retained earnings at acquisition	X	
Other reserves at acquisition	X	
Fair value adjustments at acquisition	X̲	

		(X)
Goodwill at acquisition		X

Step 6 Complete the consolidated retained earnings calculation:

	Parent	Subsidiary
Per question	X	X
Provision for unrealised profit (seller's column)	(X)	(X)
Pre-acquisition retained earnings		(X)
		A
Group share of post acq'n ret'd earnings:		
Subsidiary (A × %)	X	
	X	

Note. Other reserves are treated in a similar way.

Step 7 Complete the non-controlling interest calculation.

NCI at acquisition (from goodwill working)	X
NCI share of post acq'n reserves (from reserves working × NCI %)	X
	X

Exam focus point

There is a technical article on the ACCA website on the preparation of consolidated financial statements, written by a member of the ACCA examining team. We recommend that you read this article – called 'Preparing simple consolidated financial statements' – as part of your studies for the FFA/FA exam.

There is also an article specifically on the consolidated statement of financial position – called 'Preparing a group statement of financial position' – and we recommend you read this article as well.

Furthermore, it is advisable to note the following common errors in preparing consolidated financial statements, highlighted by the ACCA examining team:

(a) In valuing goodwill, deducting the fair value of the NCI from the consideration instead of adding it on.

(b) Not adjusting for intra-group balances. Amounts owed between the parent and subsidiary should be eliminated from receivables and payables in the consolidated statement of financial position.

(c) Not adjusting for intra-group transactions. Intra-group sales should be eliminated from revenue and cost of sales in the consolidated statement of profit or loss.

(d) Incorrectly adding together the equity share capital of the parent and subsidiary. The share capital in the consolidated statement of financial position should be only that of the parent.

---

2 Goodwill

Position to date

In the previous chapter, the cost of the investment equalled the value of the identifiable net assets acquired and accordingly, no surplus or deficit remained on cancellation.

Goodwill

Where the value of a business as a whole (cost of the investment + any non-controlling share not purchased) is greater than the net assets acquired, the investor controls (and has paid for) something more than the net assets of the acquired business.

The difference is called goodwill and is measured at the acquisition date (under IFRS 3 *Business Combinations*) as:

	$
Goodwill	
Fair value of consideration (investment)	X
Fair value of non-controlling interest	X
Less: Fair value of net assets at acquisition	(X)
Goodwill at acquisition	X

2.1 Accounting treatment

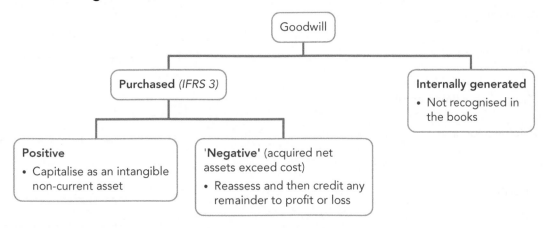

Exam focus point

You are highly likely to get a question requiring the calculation of goodwill in your exam so make sure you go through this section carefully, working through all the examples and the question. The ACCA examining team has highlighted the calculation of goodwill as a topic which is poorly answered in the exams.

Activity 1: Consolidated statement of financial position (1)

Pogo acquired the entire share capital of Stick for $8 million on 1 February 20X0 when the statements of financial position of the two companies were as follows:

	Pogo	Stick
	$'000	$'000
Investment in Stick	8,000	–
Other assets	9,500	6,500
	17,500	6,500
Share capital	9,000	3,000
Retained earnings	6,000	2,000

	Pogo	Stick
	$'000	$'000
	15,000	5,000
Liabilities	2,500	1,500
	17,500	6,500

Required

Prepare the consolidated statement of financial position of the Pogo group as at 1 February 20X0.

Solution

Pogo Group Consolidated statement of financial position as at 1 February 20X0

$'000

Goodwill ☐

Other assets ☐

_____

Share capital [Pogo only]

Retained earnings ☐

_____

Liabilities ☐

_____

_____

Workings

1 **Group structure**

2 **Goodwill**

	$'000	£'000
Consideration		
Non-controlling interest		
Net assets at acquisition represented by:		
Share capital		
Retained earnings	_____	
		_____
Goodwill arising on acquisition		_____

3 *Retained earnings*

	Pogo	Stick
	$'000	$'000
Per question		
Pre-acquisition retained earnings		_____
		_____
Group share of post-acquisition earnings:		
Stick [ ]	_____	
	_____	

3 Non-controlling interest

3.1 What is the non-controlling interest?

P
|
80%
|
S

The parent *controls* a subsidiary because it has >50% of the voting power

The parent does not *own* all of the subsidiary

The non-controlling interest is the "equity in a subsidiary not attributable, directly or indirectly, to a parent", ie the non-group shareholders' interest in the net assets of the subsidiary (IFRS 10, App. A).

Points to note:

(a) Add P and 100% of S's net assets line by line to show control.

(b) In the equity section, include a new heading for 'non-controlling interest' to show the extent to which the assets and liabilities are controlled by the parent, but are owned by other parties, namely the non-controlling interest.

3.2 Measurement of non-controlling interest at acquisition

For the purposes of the exam, non-controlling interest at the acquisition date should be measured at fair value (ie how much it would cost of the acquirer to acquire the remaining shares).

If not given in a question, the fair value of non-controlling interest (NCI) can be calculated as the number of shares belonging to NCI multiplied by the share price.

The fair value of non-controlling interest (NCI) at acquisition is effectively the NCI share of the subsidiary's net assets and goodwill at the acquisition date.

3.3 Measurement of non-controlling interest at the year end

The subsidiary's net assets (or equity) will increase as the subsidiary's reserves increase. Therefore, to update NCI to its year-end value, the NCI share of post-acquisition reserves needs to be added to the NCI at acquisition.

NCI at acquisition (at **fair value**) (from goodwill working)	X
NCI share of post-acquisition reserves (year-end reserves – pre-acquisition reserves* × NCI %)	X
NCI at year end (ie NCI share of year-end net assets and goodwill)	X

* from reserves working

Activity 2: Consolidated statement of financial position (2)

Pop acquired 75% of the issued share capital of Snap on 1 January 20X8 when Snap had a retained earnings balance of $1 million. The fair value of the non-controlling interest at that date was $1.5 million. One year later, the two companies had the following statements of financial position:

	Pop	Snap
	$'000	$'000
Investment in Snap	6,000	–
Other assets	10,500	9,200
	16,500	9,200
Share capital	10,000	4,000
Retained earnings	1,500	2,200
	11,500	6,200
Liabilities	5,000	3,000
	16,500	9,200

Required

Produce the consolidated statement of financial position of Pop and its subsidiary as at 31 December 20X8.

Solution

Pop Group Consolidated statement of financial position as at 31 December 20X8

	$'000
Goodwill (W2)	
Other assets ☐	
	_____
	_____
Share capital [P only]	
Retained earnings ☐	
	_____
Non-controlling interest ☐	
	_____
Liabilities ☐	
	_____
	_____

Workings

1 **Group structure**

2 **Goodwill**

	$'000	$'000
Consideration		
Non-controlling interest		
Net assets at acquisition represented by:		
Share capital		
Retained earnings	_____	
		_____
Goodwill arising on acquisition		

3 **Retained earnings**

	Pop	Snap
	$'000	$'000
Per question		
Pre-acquisition retained earnings		_____
		_____
Group share of post-acquisition earnings:		
Snap ⬚	_____	
	_____	

4 **Non-controlling interest**

	$'000
NCI at acquisition (W2)	
NCI share of post-acquisition earnings ⬚	_____
	_____

Points to note

(a) The assets and liabilities sections of the statement of financial position show what the group controls.

(b) The equity section of the statement of financial position shows who actually owns the consolidated net assets of the group.

4 Other reserves

Exam questions may give other reserves (such as a revaluation surplus) as well as retained earnings. These reserves should be treated in exactly the same way as retained earnings, which we have already seen.

Any part of the reserve which existed pre-acquisition will form part of the calculation of net assets at the date of acquisition and is therefore used in the goodwill calculation.

5 Fair values

We calculate goodwill as:

	$
Goodwill	
Fair value of consideration (investment)	X
Fair value of non-controlling interest	X
Less: Fair value of net assets at acquisition	(X)
Goodwill at acquisition	X

5.1 Fair value of net assets acquired

Assets and liabilities in an entity's own financial statements are often not stated at their fair value, eg where the entity's accounting policy is to use the cost model for assets. If the subsidiary's financial statements are not adjusted to their fair values, where, for example, an asset's value has risen since purchase, goodwill would be overstated (as it would include the increase in value of the asset).

Under IFRS 3 *Business Combinations*, the net assets acquired are therefore required to be brought into the consolidated financial statements at their fair value rather than their book value.

The difference between fair values and book values is a consolidation adjustment made only for the purposes of the consolidated financial statements.

> ### Exam focus point
>
> If there is a difference between the carrying amount and the fair value of a subsidiary's land and buildings in an exam question, you will be given the fair value.
>
> The ACCA examining team commented that in the December 2013 exam, the question on the calculation of goodwill had a low pass rate. In calculating goodwill, some students incorrectly used the net assets at the year-end date instead of at the acquisition date. Students were required to derive the net assets at the acquisition date by deducting post-acquisition retained earnings from net assets at the year end.

5.2 Fair value of consideration

The consideration transferred (which is the same as the figure recorded as the cost of the investment in the parent's separate financial statements) is also measured at fair value. For the purposes of the exam, the consideration could consist of cash or shares. The fair value of cash is simply the amount of cash paid. The fair value of shares is the quoted share price at the acquisition date.

5.3 Fair value of non-controlling interest

For the purposes of the exam, non-controlling interest at the acquisition date is to be measured at fair value (ie how much it would cost of the acquirer to acquire the remaining shares).

Activity 3: Goodwill

X acquired 300,000 of Y's 400,000 $1 ordinary shares on 1 January 20X5 when Y's retained earnings were $500,000. The fair value of the non-controlling interest in Y at that date was $280,000.

The purchase consideration comprised:

* $250,000 in cash payable at acquisition
*   New shares issued in X on a 1 for 3 basis

The quoted price of X's shares on the acquisition date was $7.35.

The fair value of Y's land and buildings at 1 January 20X5 was $160,000 but the book value was only $100,000. All other net assets had a fair value equivalent to their book value.

Required

Calculate the goodwill arising on acquisition of Y.

Solution
Goodwill

	$	$
Fair value of consideration:		
Cash		
Shares [_____]		_____
Fair value of non-controlling interest		
Less: Fair value of net assets at acquisition		
Share capital		
Retained earnings		
Fair value adjustment [_____]	_____	
		_____
Goodwill at acquisition		

Working

Group structure

6 Inter-company trading

Issue

IFRS 10 *Consolidated Financial Statements* requires inter-company balances, transactions, income and expenses to be eliminated in full.

The purpose of consolidation is to present the parent and its subsidiaries as if they are trading as one entity.

Therefore, only amounts owing to or from outside the group should be included in the statement of financial position, and any assets should be stated at cost to the group.

6.1 Inter-company balances

Trading transactions will normally be recorded via a current account between the trading companies, which would also keep a track of amounts received and/or paid.

The current account receivable in one company's books should equal the current account payable in the other. These two balances should be cancelled on consolidation as inter-company receivables and payables should not be shown.

The double entry required is:

*   Dr (↓) Inter-company payable
*   Cr (↓) Inter-company receivable

6.2 Unrealised profit

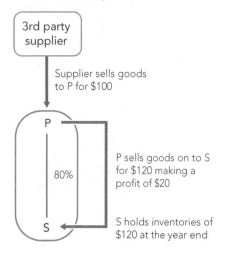

3rd party supplier

Supplier sells goods to P for $100

P

80%

S

P sells goods on to S for $120 making a profit of $20

S holds inventories of $120 at the year end

There are two issues here:

(a) In the consolidated accounts, we treat the group as a single entity. In substance, P has made profit from selling goods to itself (as the goods are still in inventory at the year end). This unrealised profit must be eliminated.

(b) Inventories should be valued at the lower of cost and NRV to the group. Inventories are currently in S's books at $120 but they cost the group (to buy from the third party supplier) $100. So inventories are overvalued by $20.

6.3 Adjustment for unrealised profit

The double entry for closing inventories is:

Dr Inventories (SOFP)

Cr Cost of sales (SPLOCI)

Therefore, as closing inventories have been overvalued, the double entry to remove the unrealised profit is simply the opposite:

Dr Cost of sales (SPLOCI) (increasing expenses and reducing profit, eliminating the unrealised profit)

Cr Inventories (SOFP)

When preparing a consolidated SOFP, the debit to cost of sales must feed through to retained earnings. Therefore, the adjustment required to eliminate the unrealised profit in the consolidated SOFP is:

Dr (↓) Retained earnings of the seller

Cr (↓) Consolidated inventories

Note that this adjustment only applies to goods from inter-company trading still left in inventories at the year end.

6.4 Method for unrealised profit

Calculate the unrealised profit included in inventories and mark the adjustments by reducing inventories on your proforma answer and by reducing the seller's retained earnings in the retained earnings working.

Activity 4: Consolidated statement of financial position (3)

Poach acquired 60% of the share capital of Steal on its incorporation. The statements of financial position of the two companies as at 31 December 20X8 are as follows:

	Poach	Steal
	$'000	$'000
Non-current assets		
Property, plant and equipment	200	50
Investment in Steal	6	
	206	50
Current assets		
Inventories	22	18
Receivables – from Poach	–	30
– other	96	29
Cash	4	15
	122	92
	328	142
Equity		
Share capital	100	10
Retained earnings	147	73
	247	83
Current liabilities		
Trade payables – to Steal	30	–
– other	51	59
	81	59
	328	142

Notes.

1 The fair value of the non-controlling interest in Steal at acquisition was $4,000.

2 Steal sells goods to Poach at a profit margin of 25% on selling price. At the year end, $12,000 of the goods that Poach had purchased from Steal remained in inventories.

Required

Prepare a consolidated statement of financial position as at 31 December 20X8.

Solution

Poach Group Consolidated statement of financial position as at 31 December 20X8

$'000

Non-current assets

Property, plant and equipment [＿＿＿＿＿]

Current assets

Inventories [＿＿＿＿＿]

Receivables – from Poach [＿＿＿＿＿]

　　　　　　　 – other [＿＿＿＿＿]

Cash [＿＿＿＿＿]

　　　　　　　　　　　　　　　　　　　　　　　　　　　　　　＿＿＿＿＿＿

　　　　　　　　　　　　　　　　　　　　　　　　　　　　　　＿＿＿＿＿＿

　　　　　　　　　　　　　　　　　　　　　　　　　　　　　　＿＿＿＿＿＿

Equity attributable to the owners of the parent

Share capital

Retained earnings (W2)

　　　　　　　　　　　　　　　　　　　　　　　　　　　　　　＿＿＿＿＿＿

Non-controlling interest (W3)

　　　　　　　　　　　　　　　　　　　　　　　　　　　　　　＿＿＿＿＿＿

　　　　　　　　　　　　　　　　　　　　　　　　　　　　　　＿＿＿＿＿＿

Current liabilities

Trade payables – to Steal [＿＿＿＿＿]

　　　　　　　　– other [＿＿＿＿＿]

　　　　　　　　　　　　　　　　　　　　　　　　　　　　　　＿＿＿＿＿＿

　　　　　　　　　　　　　　　　　　　　　　　　　　　　　　＿＿＿＿＿＿

Workings

1 ***Group structure***

2 Consolidate retained earnings

	Poach $'000	Steal $'000
Per question		
Provision for unrealised profit (PUP)	[ ]	
Pre-acquisition retained earnings		_____
Group share of post-acquisition retained earnings:		
Steal [ ]		_____
		_____

3 Non-controlling interest

	$'000
NCI at acquisition	
NCI share of post-acquisition retained earnings [ ]	_____
	_____

4 Provision for unrealised profit

---

7 Mid-year acquisitions

So far, we have considered acquisitions only at the end of the reporting period. Thus, since companies produce statements of financial position at that date anyway, there has been no special need to establish the net assets of the acquired company at that date.

With a mid year acquisition, a statement of financial position is unlikely to exist at the date of acquisition as required. Accordingly, we have to estimate the net assets at the date of acquisition using various assumptions.

Rule for mid-year acquisitions

Assume that profits accrue evenly throughout the year unless specifically told otherwise.

Activity 5: Goodwill at acquisition (1)

Pat acquired 80% of the issued share capital of Slap on 30 September 20X7. The share price for each of the non-controlling interest shares in Slap was $4.50 at the acquisition date.

At the year end of 31 December 20X7 the two companies have the following statements of financial position:

	Pat		Slap	
	$'000	$'000	$'000	$'000
Investment in Slap		4,000		–
Other assets		10,500		6,000
		14,500		6,000
Share capital ($1 shares)		6,000		1,000
Share premium		–		500
Retained earnings				
1 Jan 20X7	4,000		1,500	
Profit for 20X7	2,000		1,000	
		6,000		2,500
		12,000		4,000
Liabilities		2,500		2,000
		14,500		6,000

Required

Calculate the goodwill at the date of acquisition.

Solution

Goodwill

	$'000	$'000
Fair value of consideration transferred		
Fair value of non-controlling interests	[ ]	
Fair value of net assets at acquisition:		
Share capital		
Share premium		
Retained earnings (W2)		_____
		_____
Goodwill		_____

Workings

1 *Group structure*

2 *Slap – retained earnings 30.9.X7*

		$'000
Retained earnings at 1.1.X7		
For the nine months to 30.9.X7	_____	_____
Retained earnings at 30.9.X7		_____

8 Exam standard multi-task example

Activity 6: Goodwill on acquisition (2)

On 1 January 20X1, Reprise Co purchased 80% of Encore Co for $2.4 million. The retained earnings at that date were $1.7 million.

The following draft statements of financial position for the two companies have been prepared as at 31 December 20X7 and are as follows:

	Reprise	Encore
	$'000	$'000
Investment in Encore	2,400	0
Other assets	6,820	3,470
Total assets	9,220	3,470
Equity		
Share capital – $1 ordinary shares	1,000	500
Retained earnings	6,720	2,600
	7,720	3,100
Liabilities	1,500	370
	9,220	3,470

The non-controlling interest (NCI) was valued at $600,000 as at 1 January 20X1.

Required

1 Complete the following to determine the goodwill arising on acquisition.

	$'000
Value of investment at acquisition	
Investment in Encore Co held by Reprise Co	(1)
(2)	(1)
Total value of investment at acquisition **(A)**	3,000
Fair value of Encore Co's net assets at acquisition	

	$'000
Equity share capital	(3)
(4)	(3)
Total fair value of Encore's net asset at acquisition **(B)**	2,200
Goodwill at acquisition expressed as a formula	(5)

Pull down list 1

- 1,044
- 2,400
- 2,600
- 500
- 600

Pull down list 2

- Equity share capital
- Investment in Encore held by Reprise
- NCI at acquisition
- Other assets
- Retained earnings

Pull down list 3

- 1,700
- 2,600
- 3,470
- 370
- 500

Pull down list 4

- Equity share capital
- Liabilities
- Other assets
- Retained earnings

Pull down list 5

- A + 100% of B
- A + 75% of B
- A – 100% B
- A – 75% of B

2   Are each of the following statements regarding consolidation correct? (Write 'yes' or 'no' beside each statement.)

	Yes/No
Consolidation shows legal form rather than substance.	
The parent's and the group share of the subsidiary's assets and liabilities	

	Yes/No
should be aggregated.	
Goodwill is calculated using the acquisition date fair values.	

3   Select the formula which correctly calculates NCI at 31 December 20X7, in accordance with IFRS 10 *Consolidated Financial Statements*.

   O   Fair value of NCI at acquisition + 20% of retained earnings at 31 December 20X7

   O   Fair value of NCI at acquisition + 20% of post-acquisition retained earnings

   O   25% of net assets at 31 December 20X7

4   Calculate the following figures which will be reported in Reprise's consolidated statement of financial position at 31 December 20X7.

Solution

4

$'000

   Investment

   Other assets ▭

   Share capital

   Retained earnings ▭

   Liabilities ▭

Exam focus point

Your FFA exam is a CBE, so you will not have to set out a full proforma as you would in a paper-based exam.

You will be given the financial statements and additional information as above and you will then complete the consolidated statements by way of separate tasks.

For each of these tasks, such as goodwill on acquisition or NCI, you will be given a proforma to complete.

You will not be required to show workings.

However, learning to complete a full statement as above with correct workings is very good practice both for your exam and for later papers.

Chapter summary

Consolidated statement of financial position

Approach to consolidated statement of financial position

1. Group structure
2. Proforma
3. Add P + 100% S's assets & liabilities line by line, post P's share capital/premium & 1st line of workings
4. Adjustments
5. Goodwill working
6. Retained earnings working
7. NCI working

Goodwill

- FV of consideration   X
  FV of NCI   X
  FV of net assets acquired:
     Share capital   X
     Retained earnings   X
     FV adjustment   <u>X</u>
                       <u>(X)</u>
  Goodwill   X
- Positive goodwill – capitalise as intangible non-current asset
- Negative goodwill – to SPL

Non-controlling interest

- 3rd party shareholders in subsidiary
- NCI working for consol SOFP:
  NCI at acquisition (goodwill working)   X
  NCI share of post acquisition reserves   X
                                             X

Mid-year acquisitions

- Estimate pre-acquisition retained earnings (if not given):
  B/f retained earnings   X
  Profit for year
  (pro-rated up to acq'n date)   X
  Pre-acq'n retained earnings   X

Fair values

- Assets and liabilities in an entity's own financial statements are often not stated at their fair value
- The net assets acquired are therefore required to be brought into the consolidated financial statements at their fair value rather than their book value

Other reserves

Pre-acquisition reserves
- Included in net assets at the date of acquisition (and included in the goodwill calculation)

Reserves created post-acquisition reserves or where there is movement on a reserve existing at acquisition
- Show in the parent's reserves plus its share of movement on the subsidiary's reserve

Inter-company trading

Issue
- Treat group as if it were a single entity
- Eliminate intragroup trading and unrealised profit

Method
- Eliminate intragroup revenue and cost of sales
  - Debit Group (↓) Revenue
  - Credit Group (↓) Cost of sales for all intragroup trading in the year
- Eliminate unrealised profit on goods still in inventory at the year end
  - Debit (↑) Cost of sales
  - Credit (↓) Inventories
- Eliminate inter-company balances at the year end
  - Debit (↓) Inter-company payable
  - Credit (↓) Inter-company receivable

Knowledge diagnostic

1. Approach to consolidated financial position

In the exam, a methodical approach to consolidation is key

2. Goodwill

Positive goodwill is capitalised as an intangible non-current asset. 'Negative' goodwill (once reassessed to ensure it is accurate) is recognised as a bargain purchase in the profit or loss.

3. Non-controlling interest

Non-controlling interest shows the amount of the assets and liabilities under the control of the parent, but which are not owned by the parent's shareholders.

4. Other reserves

Other reserves, ie a revaluation surplus, are calculated using the same process as retained earnings, ie only post-acquisition reserve movements are consolidated.

5. Fair values

In order for the goodwill figure to be accurately measured, both the consideration transferred and the fair value of the assets acquired and liabilities assumed must be recognised at fair value at the date of acquisition.

6. Inter-company trading

At the year end, inter-company payables and receivables must be eliminated.

Unrealised profit in year-end inventories from inter-company trading must be eliminated by reducing inventories and the seller's retained earnings.

7. Mid-year acquisitions

Only post-acquisition profits are consolidated. Therefore, if the acquisition is mid-year, a retained earnings figure must be estimated for the goodwill and retained earnings calculations.

Further study guidance

Question practice

Now try the following from the Further question practice bank (available in the digital edition of the Workbook):

Questions 90 to 93

Further reading

There is a technical article on the ACCA website on the preparation of consolidated financial statements, written by a member of the examining team. We recommend that you read this article – called 'Preparing simple consolidated financial statements' – as part of your studies for the FFA/FA exam.

There is also an article specifically on the consolidated statement of financial position – called 'Preparing a group statement of financial position' – and we recommend you read this article as well.

Activity answers

Activity 1: Consolidated statement of financial position (1)

Pogo Group Consolidated statement of financial position as at 1 February 20X0

	$'000
Goodwill (W2)	3,000
Other assets ($9,500 + $6,500)	16,000
	19,000
Share capital [Pogo only]	9,000
Retained earnings (W3)	6,000
	15,000
Liabilities ($2,500 + $1,500)	4,000
	19,000

Workings

1 Group structure

Pogo

1.2.X0   100%

           Pre-acquisition ret'd earnings $2m

Stick

2 Goodwill

	$'000	£'000
Consideration		8,000
Non-controlling interest		0
Net assets at acquisition represented by:		
Share capital	3,000	
Retained earnings	2,000	
		(5,000)
Goodwill arising on acquisition		3,000

3 Retained earnings

	Pogo	Stick
	$'000	$'000
Per question	6,000	2,000
Pre-acquisition retained earnings		(2,000)

	Pogo	Stick
	$'000	$'000
		0

Group share of post-acquisition earnings:

Stick (0 × 100%)	0	
	6,000	

Activity 2: Consolidated statement of financial position (2)

Pop Group Consolidated statement of financial position as at 31 December 20X8

	$'000
Goodwill (W2)	2,500
Other assets ($10,500 + $9,200)	19,700
	22,200
Share capital [P only]	10,000
Retained earnings (W3)	2,400
	12,400
Non-controlling interest (W4)	1,800
	14,200
Liabilities ($5,000 + $3,000)	8,000
	22,200

Workings

1 **Group structure**

Pop

1.1.X8   75%

Pre-acquisition ret'd earnings $1m

Snap

2 **Goodwill**

	$'000	$'000
Consideration		6,000
Non-controlling interest		1,500
Net assets at acquisition represented by:		

	$'000	$'000
Share capital	4,000	
Retained earnings	1,000	
		(5,000)
Goodwill arising on acquisition		2,500

3 Retained earnings

	Pop	Snap
	$'000	$'000
Per question	1,500	2,200
Pre-acquisition retained earnings		(1,000)
		1,200
Group share of post-acquisition earnings:		
Snap ($1,200 × 75%)	900	
	2,400	

4 Non-controlling interest

	$'000
NCI at acquisition (W2)	1,500
NCI share of post-acquisition earnings ($1,200 (W3) × 25%)	300
	1,800

Activity 3: Goodwill

Goodwill

	$	$
Fair value of consideration:		
Cash		250,000
Shares [(1/3 × 300,000) × $7.35]		735,000
		985,000
Fair value of non-controlling interest		280,000
Less: Fair value of net assets at acquisition		
Share capital	400,000	
Retained earnings	500,000	

	$	$
Fair value adjustment ($160,000 – $100,000)	60,000	
		(960,000)
Goodwill at acquisition		305,000

Working

Group structure

X

1.1.X5   300/400 = 75%
Pre-acquisition ret'd earnings $500,000

Y

Activity 4: Consolidated statement of financial position (3)

Poach Group Consolidated statement of financial position as at 31 December 20X8

	$'000
Non-current assets	
Property, plant and equipment ($200 + $50)	250
Current assets	
Inventories ($22 + $18 – 3 (W4))	37
Receivables – from Poach ($30 – $30)	–
– other ($96 + $29)	125
Cash ($4 + $15)	19
	181
	431
Equity attributable to the owners of the parent	
Share capital	100
Retained earnings (W2)	189
	289
Non-controlling interest (W3)	32
	321
Current liabilities	
Trade payables – to Steal ($30 – $30)	–
– other ($51 + $59)	110
	431

Workings

1 Group structure

Poach

On incorporation | 60% ∴ non-controlling interest 40%
(∴ no goodwill) | Pre-acquisition ret'd earnings $0

Steal

2 Consolidate retained earnings

	Poach	Steal
	$'000	$'000
Per question	147	73
Provision for unrealised profit (PUP) (W4)		(3)
Pre-acquisition retained earnings		(0)
		70
Group share of post-acquisition retained earnings:		
Steal ($70 × 60%)	42	
	189	

3 Non-controlling interest

	$'000
NCI at acquisition	4
NCI share of post-acquisition retained earnings ($70 (W2) × 40%)	28
	32

4 Provision for unrealised profit

On consolidation:

Profit element in inventories:

$12,000 × 25% = $3,000

DR Steal's retained earnings $3,000

CR Group inventories $3,000

Activity 5: Goodwill at acquisition (1)

Goodwill

	$'000	$'000
Fair value of consideration transferred		4,000
Fair value of non-controlling interests (1,000 × 20% × $4.50)		900

	$'000	$'000
Fair value of net assets at acquisition:		
Share capital	1,000	
Share premium	500	
Retained earnings (W2)	2,250	
		(3,750)
Goodwill		1,150

Workings

1 Group structure

Pat

30.9.X7   80%

      Pre-acquisition ret'd earnings – see W2

Slap

2 Slap – retained earnings 30.9.X7

	$'000
Retained earnings at 1.1.X7	1,500
For the nine months to 30.9.X7 ($1,000 × 9/12)	750
Retained earnings at 30.9.X7	2,250

Activity 6: Goodwill on acquisition (2)

1

	$'000
Value of investment at acquisition	
Investment in Encore Co held by Reprise Co	2,400
NCI at acquisition	600
Total value of investment at acquisition **(A)**	3,000
Fair value of Encore Co's net assets at acquisition	
Equity share capital	500
Retained earnings	1,700
Total fair value of Encore's net asset at acquisition **(B)**	2,200
Goodwill at acquisition expressed as a formula	A – 100% B

2

	Yes/No
Consolidation shows legal form rather than substance.	No
The parent's and the group share of the subsidiary's assets and liabilities should be aggregated.	No
Goodwill is calculated using the acquisition date fair values.	Yes

3   The correct answer is: Fair value of NCI at acquisition + 20% of post-acquisition retained earnings

4

	$'000
Investment	0
Other assets ($6,820 + $3,470)	10,290
Share capital	1,000
Retained earnings ($6,720 + [80% × ($2,600 – $1,700)])	7,440
Liabilities ($1,500 + $370)	1,870

25

The consolidated statement of profit or loss

Learning objectives

On competition of this chapter, you should be able to:

	Syllabus reference no.
Describe the components of and prepare a consolidated statement of profit or loss or extracts thereof including: i) Elimination of intra-group trading balances ii) Removal of unrealised profit arising on intra-group trading iii) Acquisition of subsidiaries part way through the financial year	G1(e)

Exam context

The multi-task groups question could ask you to prepare a full consolidated statement of profit or loss, figures from a consolidated SPL and/or consolidation adjustments (such as intra-group trading and unrealised profit).

Chapter overview

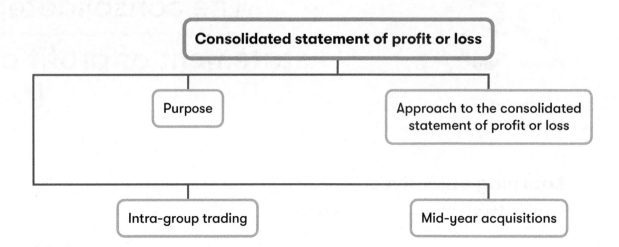

1 Purpose of the consolidated statement of profit or loss

The aim of the consolidated statement of profit or loss and other comprehensive income is to show the results of the group for an accounting period as if it were a single entity. The 'other comprehensive income' element of this statement is beyond the scope of the FFA/FA syllabus.

Exactly the same philosophy is adopted as for the consolidated statement of financial position, ie control in the first instance. Accordingly, we are then able to show the profits resulting from the control exercised by the parent.

> ## Exam focus point
>
> In the July to December 2014 ACCA examining team's report, the ACCA examining team provided the following comments which may help students to improve their performance:
>
> Know the format for a consolidated statement of profit or loss and understand consolidation techniques. Some questions may require you to calculate key figures such as a profit figure when given a mark-up percentage, before you can calculate unrealised profit.
>
> Some of the common errors when preparing the consolidated statement of profit or loss include not:
>
> - Adjusting the revenue figure and cost of sales figure for the intra-group transactions
> - Adjusting the cost of sales for the goods remaining unsold at the year end
> - Clearly showing the profit attributable to the parent company and the non-controlling interest
> - Adjusting the subsidiary profit for unrealised profit
> - Showing workings for the calculation of the non-controlling interest

1.1 Method

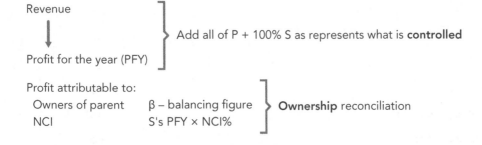

2 Approach to the consolidated statement of profit or loss

Step 1 Read the question (requirement first) and draw up the group structure and where subsidiaries are acquired in the year identify the proportion to consolidate. A timeline may be useful.

Step 2 Draw up a proforma. Remember the ownership reconciliation at the foot of the statement.

Step 3 Work methodically down the statement of profit or loss, transferring figures to proforma or workings:

- Add 100% of all income and expenses (time-apportioned $\times \, ^x/_{12}$ if appropriate) in brackets on face of proforma, ready for adjustments
- Exclude dividends receivable from subsidiary
- Subsidiary's PFY (for NCI) to face of proforma in brackets (or to a working if many adjustments)

Step 4 For any intra-group trading, cancel intra-group revenue and cost of sales in brackets, directly on the face of your proforma. For any inventories remaining at the year end from intra-group trading, cancel the unrealised profit by increasing the seller's cost of sales and adjusting non-controlling interest where the subsidiary is the seller.

Step 5 Complete non-controlling interest in subsidiary's PFY calculation:

	PFY
PFY per question (time-apportioned × $^x/_{12}$ if appropriate)	X
PUP on sales made by S	(X)
	X
× NCI%	X

Then post to the ownership reconciliation at the foot of the consolidated statement of profit or loss.

Step 6 Complete the ownership reconciliation:
- Copy down consolidated PFY.
- Find profit attributable to the owners of the parent as a balancing figure (ie total – NCI).

Activity 1: Consolidated statement of profit or loss (1)

On 1 July 20X4, Patois acquired 90% of Slang at a cost of $55,000. The balance on Slang's reserves was $15,000 at that date. Patois has ordinary share capital of $100,000 and Slang $20,000 ($1 ordinary shares).

Statements of profit or loss for both companies for the year ended 30 June 20X9:

	Patois	Slang
	$'000	$'000
Revenue	100	90
Cost of sales	(75)	(55)
Gross profit	25	35
Distribution costs	(5)	(6)
Administrative expenses	(8)	(10)
Dividend from subsidiary	4.5	–
Profit before tax	16.5	19
Income tax expense	(4)	(6)
Profit for the year	12.5	13

Required

Prepare the consolidated statement of profit or loss for the Patois group for the year ended 30 June 20X9.

Solution

Patois Group Consolidated statement of profit or loss for the year ended 30 June 20X9

	$'000
Revenue	
Cost of sales	

Gross profit

Distribution costs [   ]

Administrative expenses [   ]   _____

Profit before tax

Income tax expense [   ]   _____

Profit for the year   _____

Profit attributable to:

Owners of the parent [   ]

Non-controlling interest [   ]   _____

                                                       _____

Working

Group structure

---

3 Intra-group trading

Issue

When considering the group as if it were a single entity, intra-group trading represents transactions, which the group undertakes with itself. Clearly, these have to be stripped out of the results. The value of inventories in the consolidated statement of profit or loss needs to be checked to make sure it represents the cost to the group.

Method

There are two potential adjustments needed when group companies trade with each other:

(a) Eliminate intra-group transactions from the revenue and cost of sales figures:

Dr (↓) Group revenue   X

Cr (↓) Group cost of sales   X

with the total amount of the intra-group sales between the companies. This adjustment is needed regardless of whether any of the goods are still in inventories at the year end or not.

(b) Eliminate unrealised profit on goods still in inventories at the year end:

Dr (↑) Cost of sales (P/L) × (PUP) (and Dr (↓) Seller's retained earnings (SOFP))

Cr (↓) Inventories (SOFP) × (PUP)

in the books of the company making the sale. If the subsidiary is the seller, there is a need to adjust non-controlling interest in PFY.

Activity 2: Consolidated statement of profit or loss (2)

Pouch acquired 75% of the issued share capital of Sack on 1 January 20X2.

Sack had sold goods to Pouch during the year for $8 million at a mark up of 25%. At the year end, three quarters of these goods had been sold on to third parties.

Statements of profit or loss for the year ended 31 December 20X2

	Pouch	Sack
	$'000	$'000
Revenue	24,500	15,600
Cost of sales and expenses	(14,000)	(10,000)
Dividend from subsidiary	1,500	–
Profit before tax	12,000	5,600
Income tax expense	(5,000)	(1,600)
Profit for the year	7,000	4,000

Required

Prepare the consolidated statement of profit or loss for the Pouch group for the year ended 31 December 20X2.

Solution

Pouch Group Consolidated statement of profit or loss for the year ended 31 December 20X2

	$'000
Revenue	
Cost of sales and expenses	
Profit before tax	
Income tax expense	
Profit for the year	
Profit attributable to:	
Owners of the parent	
Non-controlling interest	

Workings

1 **Group structure**

2 Non-controlling interest

	PFY
	$'000
Per question	
PUP on sales made by Sack (W3)	_____
	_____
	_____

3 Unrealised profit

Points to note

The provision for unrealised profit on inventories reduces the closing inventories figure. It is therefore added to cost of sales in the working, thereby reducing gross profit.

When it is the subsidiary that sells goods to other group companies which remain unsold at the year end, any provision for unrealised profit must be shared between the group and the non-controlling interest.

4 Mid-year acquisitions

Rule for mid-year acquisitions

Simply include results in the normal way but only from the date of acquisition, ie time apportion them as appropriate. Assume revenue and expenses accrue evenly unless told otherwise.

Activity 3: Consolidated statement of profit or loss (3)

Perilous acquired 80% of the issued share capital of Safe on 1 January 20X5. The statements of profit or loss for the two companies for the year ended 30 September 20X5 are as follows:

Statements of profit or loss

	Perilous	Safe
	$'000	$'000
Revenue	10,000	1,000
Cost of sales and expenses	(6,000)	(700)
Profit before tax	4,000	300
Income tax expense	(1,400)	(120)
Profit for the year	2,600	180

On 14 September 20X5, Perilous sold inventories to Safe at a transfer price of $200,000, which included a profit on transfer of $30,000. Half of these inventories had been sold by Safe by the year end.

Required

Prepare the consolidated statement of profit or loss for Perilous Group for the year ended 30 September 20X5.

Solution

Perilous Group Consolidated statement of profit or loss for the year ended 30 September 20X5

	$'000
Revenue	
Cost of sales and expenses	_____
Profit before tax	
Income tax expense	_____
Profit for the year	_____
Attributable to:	
Owners of the parent	
Non-controlling interest	_____
	_____

Workings

1 **Group structure and timeline**

2 **Non-controlling interest**

	PFY
	$'000
Per question (pro-rated) [ ]	
	_____

3 **Unrealised profit**

5 Exam standard multi-task example

Activity 4: Consolidated statement of profit or loss (extract)

On 1 July 20X4, Panther paid $2 million to acquire a 60% interest in Sabre.

The statements of profit or loss of Panther and Sabre for the year ended 31 December 20X4 are as follows:

	Panther	Sabre
	$'000	$'000
Revenue	22,800	4,300
Cost of sales	13,600	2,600
Gross profit	9,200	1,700
Less: Operating expenses	4,700	800
Profit before tax	4,500	900
Less: Tax	1,300	220
Profit for the year	3,050	680

Since acquisition, Panther sold goods costing $280,000 to Sabre for $320,000. At 31 December 20X4, 25% of these goods remained in Sabre's inventory.

Required

1 Use the information above to complete the extract from the consolidated statement of profit or loss below.

2 Calculate the profit for the year ended 31 December 20X4 attributable to the non-controlling interest of Sabre.

State whether the formula below are the correct or incorrect ways to calculate profit attributable to the owners of the parent.

Profit attributable to NCI of Sabre: $ [   ]

Working = [   ]

	Correct/Incorrect
Group profit before tax	[ ]
Group profit before tax + non-controlling interest	[ ]
Group profit after tax – non-controlling interest	[ ]
Group profit after tax + non-controlling interest	[ ]

3 State whether each of the following factors indicate the existence of a parent-subsidiary relationship or not?

	Yes/No
Power over the investee to direct relevant activities	[ ]

	Yes/No
Owning greater than 50% of the preference shares	
Owning 90% of the equity shares	
Significant influence	
Right to appoint the majority of the directors on the board	
Exposure to variable returns (change in share price, dividends)	
Inability to direct the activities of the investee	
Control	

Solution

1

$'000

Revenue [　　　　　]

Cost of sales [　　　　　]   _____

Gross profit [　　　　　]

Less: Operating expenses   _____

Profit before tax

Less: Tax [　　　　　]   _____

Profit for the year   _____

Chapter summary

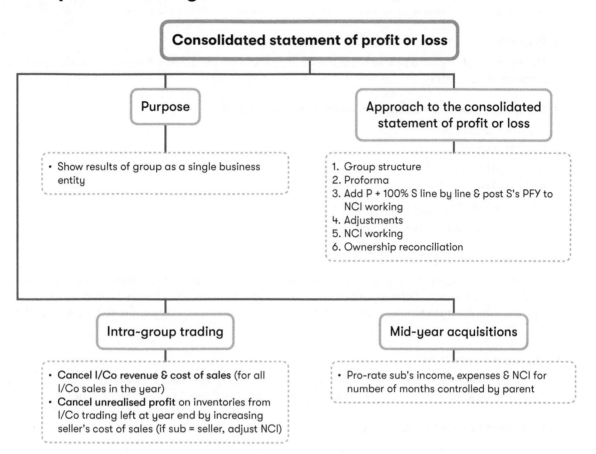

Knowledge diagnostic

1. Purpose

The purpose of the consolidated statement of profit or loss is to show the results of the group as a single business entity.

2. Approach to the consolidated statement of profit or loss

(a) Group structure

(b) Proforma

(c) Add P + 100% S's income/expenses line by line and post S's PFY to NCI working

(d) Adjustments

(e) Complete NCI working

(f) Complete ownership reconciliation

3. Intra-group trading

In order not to overstate group revenue and costs, revenue and cost of sales from intra-group trading are cancelled. Similarly, unrealised profits on year-end inventories from intragroup trading are eliminated by increasing cost of sales (NCI working is also adjusted if the subsidiary is the seller).

4. Mid-year acquisitions

Where an acquisition occurs part way through an accounting period, income and expenses are only consolidated for the number of months that the subsidiary is controlled by the parent.

5. Exam standard multi-task example

Exam standard question practice is key to success.

Further study guidance

Question practice

Now try the following from the Further question practice bank (available in the digital edition of the Workbook):

Questions 94 to 97

Activity answers

Activity 1: Consolidated statement of profit or loss (1)

Patois Group Consolidated statement of profit or loss for the year ended 30 June 20X9

	$'000
Revenue ($100 + $90)	190
Cost of sales ($75 + $55)	(130)
Gross profit	60
Distribution costs ($5 + $6)	(11)
Administrative expenses ($8 + $10)	(18)
Profit before tax	31
Income tax expense ($4 + $6)	(10)
Profit for the year	21
Profit attributable to:	
Owners of the parent (balancing figure: $21 – $1.3)	19.7
Non-controlling interest ($13 × 10%)	1.3
	21.0

Working

Group structure

Patois

1.7.X4   90% ∴ non-controlling interest 10%
Pre-acquisition ret'd earnings $15,000

Slang

Activity 2: Consolidated statement of profit or loss (2)

Pouch Group Consolidated statement of profit or loss for the year ended 31 December 20X2

	$'000
Revenue ($24,500 + $15,600 – $8,000)	32,100
Cost of sales and expenses ($14,000 + $10,000 – $8,000 + $400 (W3))	(16,400)
Profit before tax	15,700
Income tax expense ($5,000 + $1,600)	(6,600)
Profit for the year	9,100

	$'000
Profit attributable to:	
Owners of the parent ($9,100 – $900)	8,200
Non-controlling interest (W2)	900
	9,100

Workings

1 **Group structure**

Pouch

1.1.X2 | 75% ∴ non-controlling interest 25%

Sack

2 **Non-controlling interest**

	PFY
	$'000
Per question	4,000
PUP on sales made by Sack (W3)	(400)
	3,600
× 25%	900

3 **Unrealised profit**

Sack → Pouch

PUP = $8m × 25/125 × ¼ in inventories = $400,000

Add $400,000 to cost of sales and as the subsidiary is the seller, adjust NCI

Activity 3: Consolidated statement of profit or loss (3)

Perilous Group Consolidated statement of profit or loss for the year ended 30 September 20X5

	$'000
Revenue ($10,000 + ($1,000 × 9/12) – $200)	10,550
Cost of sales and expenses ($6,000 + ($700 × 9/12) – $200 + $15 (W3))	(6,340)
Profit before tax	4,210
Income tax expense ($1,400 + ($120 × 9/12))	(1,490)
Profit for the year	2,720

Attributable to:

	$'000
Owners of the parent	2,693
Non-controlling interest (W2)	27
	2,720

Workings

1 **Group structure and timeline**

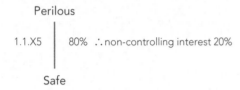

Perilous

1.1.X5 | 80% ∴ non-controlling interest 20%

Safe

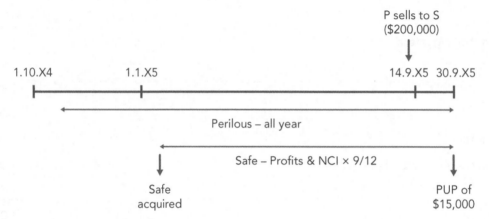

P sells to S
($200,000)

1.10.X4   1.1.X5   14.9.X5   30.9.X5

Perilous – all year

Safe – Profits & NCI × 9/12

Safe
acquired

PUP of
$15,000

2 **Non-controlling interest**

	PFY
	$'000
Per question (pro-rated) ($180 × 9/12)	135
× 20%	27

3 **Unrealised profit**

Perilous → Safe

PUP = $30,000 × 1/2 in inventories = $15,000

Add $15,000 to cost of sales.

Activity 4: Consolidated statement of profit or loss (extract)

1

	$'000
Revenue ($22,800 + ($4,300 × 6/12) – $320)	24,630
Cost of sales ($13,600 + ($2,600 × 6/12) – $320 + (25% × $40))	(14,590)
Gross profit ($4,700 + ($800 × 6/12))	10,040

	$'000
Less: Operating expenses	(5,100)
Profit before tax	4,940
Less: Tax ($1,300 + ($220 × 6/12))	(1,410)
Profit for the year	3,530

2   Profit attributable to NCI of Sabre: $ 136,000

Working = $680,000 × 6/12 × 40% = $136,000

	Correct/Incorrect
Group profit before tax	Incorrect
Group profit before tax + non-controlling interest	Incorrect
Group profit after tax – non-controlling interest	Correct
Group profit after tax + non-controlling interest	Incorrect

3

	Yes/No
Power over the investee to direct relevant activities	Yes
Owning greater than 50% of the preference shares	No
Owning 90% of the equity shares	Yes
Significant influence	No
Right to appoint the majority of the directors on the board	Yes
Exposure to variable returns (change in share price, dividends)	Yes
Inability to direct the activities of the investee	No
Control	Yes

26 Interpretation of financial statements

Learning objectives

On completion of this chapter, you should be able to:

	Syllabus reference no.
Describe how the interpretation and analysis of financial statements is used in a business environment.	H1(a)
Explain the purpose of interpretation of ratios.	H1(b)
Calculate key accounting ratios: i) Profitability ii) Liquidity iii) Efficiency iv) Position	H2(a)
Explain the interrelationships between ratios.	H2(b)
Calculate and interpret the relationship between the elements of the financial statements with regard to profitability, liquidity and efficient use of resources and financial position.	H3(a)
Draw valid conclusions from the information contained within the financial statements and present these to the appropriate user of the financial statements.	H3(b)

Exam context

The exam is likely to test one or more of the following:

- Calculating specified ratio(s);
- Explaining the difference in ratio(s) between years or different companies; and
- Explaining/identifying the purpose and limitations of interpretation of financial statements.

One or more of these areas could feature in either an objective test question in Section A or as part of the multi-task question in Section B.

Chapter overview

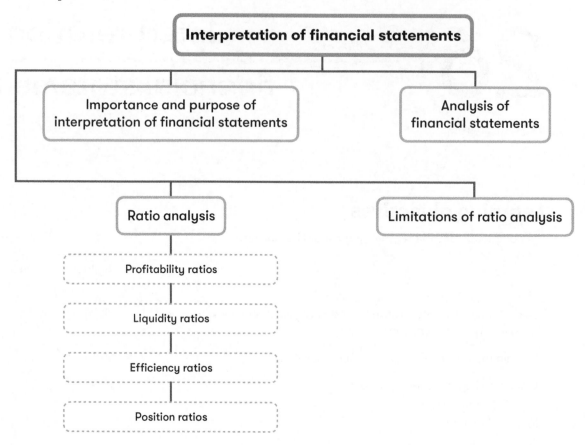

BPP
LEARNING
MEDIA

1 Importance and purpose of interpretation of financial statements

The financial statements of a company are designed to provide users with information about its performance and financial position. The figures by themselves, however, are not particularly useful and it is only through comparisons (usually with ratios) that their significance can be established. This will then enable the end user to make an informed decision.

Comparisons may be made with:

- Previous financial periods
- Similar businesses
- Industry averages

1.1 Users of financial statements

There are a number of users of a company's financial statements. Each user has differing needs. In the exam, you may need to interpret financial statements or ratios for a particular user so it is important to understand the key concerns each type of user will have.

Activity 1: Benefits of ratio analysis

How do the following users of financial statements benefit from ratio analysis?

(1) Shareholders and potential investors

(2) Bank and other capital providers

(3) Employees

(4) Management

(5) Suppliers

(6) Government

Solution

2 Analysis of financial statements

If you are presented with a set of accounts, you should make a note of all the obvious trends or changes in figures before calculating any ratios.

You are likely to be given a set of figures with comparatives either to the previous year, or to a different company, or to the industry averages.

Examples of the above are:

(a) Increase/decrease in revenue

(b) Increase/decrease in cash balance

(c) Issue of shares during the year

(d) Increase/decrease in non-current assets

(e) Increase/decrease in receivables/inventory not justified by increase/decrease in revenue

(f) Increase/repayment of loans during the year

If asked for, wherever possible, give realistic reasons for any trends/changes.

For example, if non-current assets have increased, why was this (purchase or revaluation?) and how were any purchases financed?

If required, you should also try to explain the significance of this change for the future, eg has the purchase of non-current assets increased the productive capacity of the business? Are they now short of cash? Which of the two businesses is more profitable? etc.

Ratio analysis will then assist in a more detailed investigation into why the figures differ between years or companies.

3 Ratio analysis

Accounting ratios help to summarise and present financial information in a more understandable form. Once calculated, they can then be interpreted to give an indication of the company's performance and position. The ratios can be split into the following categories:

(a) Profitability

(b) Liquidity

(c) Efficiency

(d) Position

Ratios do not give us much information when taken in isolation. In order for them to be useful, we need to have something to compare them to such as previous periods, similar businesses or industry averages.

4 Profitability ratios

Purpose

Profitability ratios measure the company's use of its assets and control of its expenses to generate an acceptable rate of return.

4.1 Gross profit margin

$$\text{Gross profit margin} = \frac{\text{Gross profit}}{\text{Revenue}} \times 100\%$$

The gross profit margin measures how well a company is running its core operations. The gross profit percentage should be similar from year to year for the same company.

A significant change may be due to:

(a) A change is sales price

(b) A change in product mix

(c)   An incorrect inventory valuation (will affect two years)

(d)   A change in cost of sales due to efficiency or price movements

4.2 Operating profit margin

$$\text{Operating profit margin} = \frac{\text{Profit before interest and tax}}{\text{Revenue}} \times 100\%$$

Profit before interest and taxation (PBIT) is used because it avoids distortion when comparisons are made between two different companies where one is heavily financed by means of loans, and the other is financed entirely by ordinary share capital.

The extra consideration for the operating margin over the gross margin is how well the company is controlling its overheads.

A significant change (especially a fall) may be due to:

(a)   The reasons for the movement in the gross profit margin as stated above

(b)   Changes in control over administration and distribution costs

(c)   One off expenses, eg advertising

4.3 Return on capital employed (ROCE)

$$\text{Return on capital employed} = \frac{\text{Profit before interest and taxation}}{\text{Total equity} + \text{non-current liabilities}^*} \times 100\%$$

* or total assets less current liabilities (TALCL). This is referred to as 'capital employed' so you may see this equation written as PBIT/Capital employed.

Total equity includes share capital, share premium and reserves. Return on capital employed measures how efficiently a company uses its capital to generate profits. A potential investor or lender should compare the return to a target return or a return on other investments/loans.

Careful consideration of the industry is required as ROCE for a manufacturing company is likely to be lower than that of a services company as a manufacturing company has higher assets (eg factories, plant and machinery, three types of inventories: raw materials, work in progress, finished goods). Reasons why profits may change have been discussed above.

Other reasons for a significant change may include:

(a)   New assets acquired during the year which are not yet running at capacity

(b)   Assets aging

(c)   Revaluations

4.4 Return on equity (ROE)

$$\text{Return on equity} = \frac{\text{Profit after tax and preference dividend}}{\text{Total equity}} \times 100\%$$

Total equity can also be referred to as 'equity shareholders funds'.

Whilst the return on capital employed looks at the overall return on the long-term sources of finance, return on equity focuses on the return for the ordinary shareholders. Reasons for changes in the ROE will be similar to the ROCE with the extra consideration of changes in interest paid and gearing. This is because ROE uses profit after tax whereas ROCE uses PBIT.

5 Liquidity ratios

Purpose

Liquidity measures the availability of a company's cash to pay its short-term debts.

BPP
LEARNING
MEDIA

5.1 Current ratio (working capital ratio)

$$\text{Current ratio (working capital ratio)} = \frac{\text{Current assets}}{\text{Current liabilities}}$$

This ratio measures a company's ability to pay its current liabilities out of its current assets.

Working capital (current assets – current liabilities) is needed by all companies in order to finance day-to-day trading activities. Sufficient working capital enables a company to:

(a) Hold adequate inventories;

(b) Allow a measure of credit to its customers; and

(c) Pay its suppliers on the due date.

A company should not operate at a level that is too low as they will not have sufficient assets to cover their debts as they fall due. However, a company should not operate at a level that is too high as this may suggest that the company has too much inventory, receivables or cash.

The specific industry the company operates in should also be taken into account as, for example, a supermarket holds relatively low levels of inventories as they are perishable, few receivables as customers generally pay in cash and high payables as supermarkets typically have superior bargaining power to their smaller suppliers.

5.2 Quick ratio

$$\text{Quick ratio (liquid capital ratio or acid test)} = \frac{\text{Current assets} - \text{inventories}}{\text{Current liabilities}}$$

This is similar to the current ratio except that it omits the inventories figure from current assets. This is because inventories are the least liquid current asset that a company has, as it has to be sold, turned into receivables and then the cash has to be collected.

A ratio of less than 1:1 could indicate that the company would have difficulty paying its debts as they fall due.

6 Efficiency ratios

Purpose

Efficiency measures how well the company uses its assets to generate profit, revenue and cash.

6.1 Inventory turnover period (days)

$$\text{Inventory turnover period (days)} = \frac{\text{Inventories}}{\text{Cost of sales}} \times 365$$

This ratio measures the number of days inventories are held by a company on average. This figure will depend on the type of goods sold by the company.

A company selling fresh fruit and vegetables should have a low inventory holding periods as these goods will quickly become inedible.

A manufacturer of aged wine will by default have very long inventory holding periods. It is important for a company to keep its inventory days as low as possible, subject of course to being able to meet its customers' demands.

A significant change may be due to:

(a) A change in type of inventory held;

(b) Improved or worsened inventory controls; or

(c) Changes in the popularity of certain inventory items.

6.2 Receivables collection period (days)

$$\text{Receivables collection period (days)} = \frac{\text{Trade receivables}}{\text{Revenue}} \times 365$$

This ratio shows, on average how long it takes for the trade receivables to settle their account with the company. The average credit term granted to customers should be taken into account as well as the efficiency of the credit control function within the company.

A significant change may be due to:

(a) Increased/decreased credit terms offered to customers;

(b) Change in the mix between cash and credit transactions; or

(c) Better/worse credit control.

6.3 Payables payment period (days)

$$\text{Payables payment period (days)} = \frac{\text{Trade payables}}{\text{Cost of sales}} \times 365 \text{ days}$$

Technically this ratio should be trade payables/purchases but it is rare to find purchases disclosed in the published accounts and so cost of sales serves as an approximation.

This ratio is measuring the time it takes the company to settle its trade payable balances. Trade payables provide the company with a valuable source of short-term finance, but delaying payment for too long a period of time can cause operational problems as suppliers may stop providing goods and services until payment is received.

A significant change may be due to:

(a) Increased/decreased credit terms from suppliers;

(b) Increase/decrease in cash; or

(c) Better/worse management of the payables ledger.

6.4 Working capital cycle

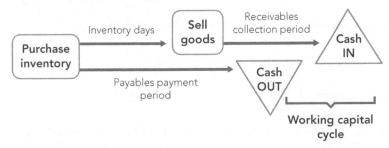

The working capital cycle has to be financed as cash has not yet been received from the sale of goods before the supplier has to be paid. The longer the cycle, the more financing is required and the higher the risk of bankruptcy. This is why it is good to have short inventory days and receivables collection periods, and longer payables payment periods.

However, this must be weighed up with the fact that a company must not run a risk of stock outs (if inventory days are too low) or customer and supplier dissatisfaction by insisting on short and long payment periods respectively.

6.5 Asset turnover ratio

$$\text{Asset turnover ratio} = \frac{\text{Revenue}}{\text{Total assets} - \text{current liabilities}} = \text{X times}$$

This ratio measures the efficiency of the use of net assets in generating revenue. Ideally, the ratio should be increasing, but we need to be careful when making assessments based on this ratio, because the company could have bought lots of assets late in the year and they simply have not had much time to start generating revenue. If this is the case, the ratio will almost certainly fall, but this is not a reflection on the ability of the assets to generate revenue; it is simply a timing issue.

6.6 Link between ratios

We often sub-analyse ROCE, to find out more about why the ROCE is high or low, or better or worse than last year. There are two factors that contribute towards a return on capital employed, both related to sales revenue.

(a) **Profit margin**. A company might make a high or low profit margin on its sales. For example, a company that makes a profit of 25c per $1 of sales is making a bigger return on its revenue than another company making a profit of only 10c per $1 of sales.

(b) **Asset turnover**. Asset turnover is a measure of how well the assets of a business are being used to generate sales. For example, if two companies each have capital employed of $100,000 and Company A makes sales of $400,000 per annum whereas Company B makes sales of only $200,000 per annum, Company A is making a higher revenue from the same amount of assets (twice as much asset turnover as Company B) and this will help A to make a higher return on capital employed than B. Asset turnover is expressed as 'x times' so that assets generate x times their value in annual turnover. Here, Company A's asset turnover is four times and B's is two times.

Profit margin and asset turnover together explain the ROCE and if the ROCE is the primary profitability ratio, these other two are the secondary ratios. The relationship between the three ratios can be shown mathematically:

Operating profit margin × Asset turnover ratio = Return on capital employed

$$\frac{PBIT}{Revenue} \times \frac{Revenue}{TALCL\,*} = \frac{PBIT}{TALCL\,*}$$

* or total equity + non-current liabilities

7 Position ratios

Purpose

Position ratios consider the company's long-term solvency and its capital structure.

7.1 Interest cover

$$\text{Interest cover } = \frac{PBIT}{Finance\ costs} = \text{ X times}$$

The interest cover ratio considers the number of times a company could pay its interest payments using its profit from operations. The main concern is that a company does not have so much debt finance that it risks not being able to settle the debt as it falls due.

7.2 Gearing

$$\text{Gearing } = \frac{Non\text{ - current liabilities}}{Total\ equity\ +\ Non\text{ - current liabilities}}$$

Gearing is concerned with the long-term financial stability of the company. It is looking at how much the company is financed by debt. Debt is cheaper than equity as interest is tax deductible but, the higher the gearing ratio, the less secure the financing of the company will be and possibly the company's future.

Activity 2: Ratio calculations

TJF is a national supermarket chain selling food, clothes and household appliances with a 31 December year end. The finance director would like the management accountant to prepare some financial data and analysis to present to the board. They have provided the management accountant with extracts from the financial statements to assist them in their analysis.

Extracts from statement of profit or loss for the year ended 31 December 20X5 (with comparatives)

	20X5	20X4
	$m	$m
Revenue	20,510	17,835
Cost of sales	18,970	16,835
Gross profit	1,540	1,000
Operating profit	650	530
Finance costs	200	130

Extracts from statement of financial position as at 31 December 20X5 (with comparatives)

	20X5	20X4
	$m	$m
Non-current assets	9,100	8,390
Inventories	850	1,000
Total current assets	1,570	1,610
Trade payables	2,100	2,280
Total current liabilities	2,920	2,650
Non-current liabilities	3,250	2,530
Equity	5,050	4,935

	20X4
Gross profit margin	5.6%
Operating profit margin	3.0%
ROCE	7.1%
Current ratio	0.61
Inventory holding period	22 days
Payables payment period	49 days
Interest cover	4.08

The finance director has also supplied the following information regarding events in the year ended 31 December 20X5:

- Online food home delivery increased by 25%.

- The number of stores grew by 10% in the year. This was financed by long-term borrowings.

In the year ended 31 December 20X5, 40% of customers purchased at least one clothing item during the year whereas in the year ended 31 December 20X4, only 20% of customers did.

A strong marketing campaign took place during the year.

The new strengthened Grocery Supplier Code of Practice came into force to improve grocery retailers' treatment of suppliers.

BPP
LEARNING
MEDIA

Required

1   Calculate the ratios below for the year ended 31 December 20X5. State whether it has improved or deteriorated and provide one possible reason for the movement in each ratio:

- Gross profit margin
- Operating profit margin
- Return on capital employed
- Current ratio
- Inventory holding period
- Payables payment period
- Interest cover

2   Explain why it would not be relevant to calculate receivables collection period in this example.

Solution

8 Limitations of ratio analysis

The usefulness of ratio analysis is limited by distorting factors. For example:

- **Inflation** when comparing to previous years
- Different **accounting policies**/classifications when comparing to different companies, eg ROCE higher if use cost models for assets
- **Lack of information**/breakdown of information
- Trading may be **seasonal** within a period (or over different accounting periods)
- **Year end** figures are **not representative** because they include year-end accounting adjustments and may be subject to 'window dressing' (the intentional manipulation of year-end figures)
- **Related party transactions** make the ratios incomparable with other companies (ie selling to your friend at a discount will have an adverse effect of your overall margin vs a competitor)
- Different **ratio definitions/formula** used by different companies
- Different companies in the same business may have **different risk profiles** or specific factors affecting them, making industry comparisons less meaningful
- Where financial statements are **manipulated**, this is often done to improve key ratios
- A new company will have **no comparatives** to compare with

9 Exam standard questions

Activity 3: Working capital ratio

Priestly has the following working capital ratios:

	20X2	20X1
Quick ratio	1.1	0.9
Receivables days	65 days	75 days
Payables days	50 days	45 days
Inventory turnover	36 days	41 days

Required

Which of the following statements is correct?

- O Priestly's credit control has worsened in 20X2.
- O Priestly's inventory is at greater risk of obsolescence in 20X2 than 20X1
- O Priestly is paying its suppliers more quickly in 20X2 than in 20X1.
- O Priestly's working capital management and liquidity have improved in 20X2.

Activity 4: Return on capital employed

The following extracts are from Mya's financial statements:

	$
Profit before interest and tax	21,230
Interest on loan notes	(2,000)
Tax	(5,200)
Profit after tax	14,030
Share capital	40,000
Share premium	10,000
Reserves	26,500
	76,500
10% loan notes	20,000
	96,500

Required

What is Mya's ROCE?

- O 15%
- O 22%
- O 20%
- O 18%

Chapter summary

```
                    ┌─────────────────────────────────────────┐
                    │  Interpretation of financial statements  │
                    └─────────────────────────────────────────┘
```

Importance and purpose of interpretation of financial statements	Analysis of financial statements
• To provide users with information about financial performance and position and to enable them to make decisions	• Make a note of all obvious changes or trends before calculating any ratios • Give reasons for change and significance for the future

Ratio analysis

Profitability ratios

- Gross profit margin = $\dfrac{\text{Gross profit}}{\text{Revenue}} \times 100\%$

- Operating profit margin = $\dfrac{\text{Profit before interest and tax}}{\text{Revenue}} \times 100\%$

- Return on capital employed = $\dfrac{\text{Profit before interest and tax}}{\text{Total equity + non-current liabilities}} \times 100\%$

- Return on equity = $\dfrac{\text{Profit after tax and preference dividends}}{\text{Total equity}} \times 100\%$

Liquidity ratios

- Current ratios = $\dfrac{\text{Current assets}}{\text{Current liabilities}} = X:1$

- Quick ratio or acid ratio = $\dfrac{\text{Current assets - Inventories}}{\text{Current liabilities}} = X:1$

Efficiency ratios

- Inventory turnover period = $\dfrac{\text{Inventories}}{\text{Cost of sales}} \times 365 \text{ days}$

- Receivables collection period = $\dfrac{\text{Trade receivables}}{\text{Revenue}} \times 365 \text{ days}$

- Payables payment period = $\dfrac{\text{Trade payables}}{\text{Cost of sales}} \times 365 \text{ days}$

- Working capital cycle = Inventory days + Receivable days − Payable days

- Asset turnover = $\dfrac{\text{Revenue}}{\text{Total assets - Current liabilities}} = X \text{ times}$

Position ratios

- Interest cover = $\dfrac{\text{Profit before interest and tax}}{\text{Finance costs}} = X \text{ times}$

- Gearing = $\dfrac{\text{Non-current liabilities}}{\text{Total equity + non-current liabilities}} = X \text{ times}$

Limitations of ratio analysis

- Inflation
- Different accounting policies
- Lack of information
- Seasonal trading
- Year end figures not representative
- Related party transactions
- Different ratio definitions
- Financial statements manipulated
- New company – no comparatives

Knowledge diagnostic

1. Importance and purpose of interpretation of financial statements

To provide users with information about financial performance and position to enable them to make a decision.

2. Analysis of financial statements

Make a note of all obvious changes or trends before calculating any ratios.

If required, give reasons for the change and significance in the future.

3. Ratio analysis

Split into categories:

- Profitability
- Liquidity
- Efficiency
- Position

Only useful if compared with:

- Previous financial periods
- Similar businesses
- Industry averages

4. Profitability ratios

- Gross profit margin
- Operating profit margin
- Return on capital employed
- Return on equity

5. Liquidity ratios

- Current ratio
- Quick ratio

6. Efficiency ratios

- Inventory turnover period (days)
- Receivables collection period (days)
- Payables payment period (days)
- Asset turnover

7. Position ratios

- Interest cover
- Gearing

8. Limitations of ratio analysis

Inflation, different accounting policies, lack of information, trading may be seasonal, year-end figures not representative, related party transactions, different ratio definitions, different risk profiles, financial statements manipulated to improve key ratios and a new company has no comparatives.

Further study guidance

Question practice

Now try the following from the Further question practice bank (available in the digital edition of the Workbook):

Questions 98 to 100

Activity answers

Activity 1: Benefits of ratio analysis

(1) Shareholders and potential investors will use ratios to help them come to a decision on buying or selling the shares of the company.

(2) Banks and other providers of loan capital will assess whether further loans should be made to the company.

(3) Employees may use them as a basis for wage negotiation.

(4) Management will use ratios to highlight weak performing areas in order to focus their attention on these areas.

(5) Suppliers may use ratios to assess creditworthiness.

(6) Governments may use them for statistics or for assessing the worthiness of a government grant.

Activity 2: Ratio calculations

1

	20X5	20X4 (given)
Gross profit margin = $\dfrac{\text{Gross profit}}{\text{Revenue}} \times 100\%$	$\dfrac{1,540}{20,510} = 7.5\%$	5.6%
Gross profit margin has improved. This appears to be because: • Online food home delivery increased by 25% in the year and it attracts a higher margin than sales from supermarket visits due to the delivery charge. • There has been a change in sales mix with higher clothes sales in the current year, probably attracting a higher margin than food sales.		
Operating profit margin = $\dfrac{\text{Profit before interest and tax}}{\text{Revenue}} \times 100\%$	$\dfrac{650}{20,510} = 3.2\%$	3.0%
Operating profit margin has improved but not as much as the gross margin. This appears to be due to: • New, one-off marketing costs incurred in the year • Start-up costs associated with the opening of the new stores		
Return on capital employed = $\dfrac{\text{PBIT}}{\text{Total equity + Non - current liabilities}} \times 100\%$	$\dfrac{650}{5.050 + 3,250} = 7.8\%$	7.1%
There has only been a small improvement in ROCE despite a significant improvement in gross margin.		

	20X5	20X4 (given)

This appears to be because:

- The improvements in gross margin due to the higher margin on home delivery and clothes sales have been largely offset by one off operating costs from marketing and new store start-up costs.
- Non-current liabilities have increased due to new borrowings to open new stores. This has largely offset the improvement in profitability.
- Any stores opened near the year end, will not yet have had a chance to create profits.

Current ratio = $\dfrac{\text{Current assets}}{\text{Current liabilities}}$	$\dfrac{1,570}{2,920} = 0.54$	0.61

The current ratio has deteriorated, meaning that TJF is finding it harder to pay its current liabilities as they fall due.

This appears to be because:

- TJF is holding lower levels of inventories and higher current liabilities

Note. The current ratio is typically low for a supermarket as the receivables are low due to cash sales, inventories are relatively low as they majority are perishable and payables tend to be high due to the strong bargaining power of supermarkets over their smaller suppliers.

Inventory holding period = $\dfrac{\text{Inventories}}{\text{Cost of sales}} \times 365 \text{ days}$	$\dfrac{850}{18,970} \times 365 = 16 \text{ days}$	22 days

Inventory days have decreased meaning that TJF is selling inventories more quickly and holding lower levels of inventories. This is good for cash flow providing TJF is holding sufficient inventories to meet customer demand.

The decrease appears to be due to an increase in sales volume as a result of the marketing campaign, the growth in online food home delivery and increased clothing sales and the new stores. This increase in demand has resulted in inventory levels being depleted more quickly.

Payables payment period = $\dfrac{\text{Trade payables}}{\text{Cost of sales}} \times 365 \text{ days}$	$\dfrac{2,100}{18,970} \times 365 \text{ days} = 40 \text{ days}$	49 days

TJF are paying their suppliers more quickly. This is bad for cash flow as TJF is not taking advantage of the free credit but is good for supplier relationships.

The decrease appears to be due to:

- The new strengthened Grocery Supplier Code of Practice coming into force and, presumably, TJF is paying suppliers more quickly to meet their credit terms and to treat suppliers more fairly in the spirit of the code.

Interest cover = $\dfrac{\text{PBIT}}{\text{Finance costs}}$	$\dfrac{650}{200} = 3.25$	4.08

	20X5	20X4 (given)

Interest cover has deteriorated. However, TJF is still easily able to pay its finance costs out of profit.

The deterioration in interest cover appears to be due to:

- Increased borrowings to cover the financing of the new stores opened in the year

2   In a supermarket, customers have to pay for their purchases immediately. The supermarket will not offer credit to their customers. Therefore, the sales are cash sales rather than credit sales resulting in few if any receivables.

Activity 3: Working capital ratio

The correct answer is: Priestly's working capital management and liquidity have improved in 20X2.

1 is incorrect because Priestly's credit control has improved in 20X2 (they are collecting debts from customers more quickly. 2 is incorrect because Priestly is selling inventory more quickly in 20X2, making it at lower risk of obsolescence. 3 is incorrect because Priestly is taking longer to pay its suppliers in 20X2. 4 is correct because the quick ratio has improved from 0.9 to 1.1 and because the working capital cycle has decreased from 71 to 51 days.

Activity 4: Return on capital employed

The correct answer is: 22%

ROCE =

$$\frac{21,230}{96,500} = 22\%$$

Index

Nominal ledger, 65

Non-controlling interest, 429

Non-current assets, 126

O

Opening inventory, 110

Output tax, 225

P

Parent, 405

Partnership, 9

Petty cash, 54

Petty cash book, 54

Prepayments, 180

Profit or loss ledger account, 94

Property, plant and equipment, 126

Provision, 195

Prudence, 34, 111

Purchase (payables) ledger, 57

Purchase day book, 49

Purchase order, 46

Purchase returns day book, 50

Q

Quotation, 45

R

Receipt, 46

Relevance, 33

Remittance advice, 46

Research, 155

Reserves, 334

Residual value, 131

Revaluations, 137

Revenue, 3

S

Sales (receivables) ledger, 57

Sales day book, 48

Sales order, 46

Sales returns day book, 50

Sales tax, 225

Separate entity, 11

Shares, 330

Sole trader, 4, 9

Statement, 46

Statement of financial position, 5, 95

Statement of profit or loss, 3

Subsidiary, 405

T

Timeliness, 35

Trade investment, 406

Trading account, 109

Trial balance, 93

U

Understandability, 35

Useful life, 131, 155

V

Verifiability, 35

Bibliography

Companies Act 2006. (2006) [Online]. Available from: www.legislation.gov.uk/ [Accessed October 2020].

www.nationalarchives.gov.uk/doc/open-government-licence/version/3/ Contains Parliamentary information licensed under the Open Parliament Licence v3.0.

International Accounting Standards Board (2018) *Conceptual Framework for Financial Reporting*. [Online]. Available from: http://eifrs.ifrs.org [Accessed October 2020].

IFRS Foundation (2016) *IFRS* [Online]. Available at: http://eifrs.ifrs.org [Accessed October 2020].

Tell us what you think

Got comments or feedback on this book? Let us know.
Use your QR code reader:

Or, visit:
https://bppgroup.fra1.qualtrics.com/jfe/form/SV_9TrxTtw8jSvO7Pv